Autobiography and the
Existential Self

Autobiography and the Existential Self

Studies in Modern French Writing

edited by
TERRY KEEFE, *Lancaster University*
and EDMUND SMYTH, *University of Liverpool*

ST. MARTIN'S PRESS
New York

Copyright © 1995 Liverpool University Press

All rights reserved. For information, write:
Scholarly and Reference Division,
St. Martin's Press, 175 Fifth Avenue,
New York, NY 10010

First published in the United States of America in 1995

Printed in the United Kingdom

ISBN 0-312-12593-3

Library of Congress Cataloging in Publication Data
Autobiography and the existential self: studies in modern
French writing / edited by Terry Keefe and Edmund Smyth.
     p.   cm.
    Includes bibliographical references and index.
    ISBN 0-312-12593-3
    1. French literature—20th century—History and criticism.
    2. Autobiography in literature. 3. Self in literature.
    4. Existentialism in literature. I. Keefe, Terry.
    II. Smyth, Edmund J.
    PQ307.A65A93   1995   94-46864
    840.9'492—dc20   CIP

Table of Contents

Introduction

EDMUND SMYTH

Autobiography has become the subject of intense academic interest in recent years, extending beyond literary theory and criticism and comparative literature, into other disciplines including philosophy, psychology, feminist and cultural studies, social history and sociology. In France, the pioneering work of critics such as Philippe Lejeune and Michel Beaujour has been crucial in shaping the evolving agenda. Philippe Lejeune's *Le Pacte autobiographique* (1975) has become in many respects the standard point of reference in the debate surrounding the theory of the genre of autobiography: in its attempt to construct a poetics of autobiography, it is as central to contemporary literary theory and criticism as Gérard Genette's *Discours du récit* in the domain of narratology. In *Le Pacte autobiographique* and other works (including *Je est un autre* and *Moi aussi*), Lejeune has sought to bring to bear upon autobiography the full weight and analytical rigour characteristic of structuralist and poststructuralist thinking. Lejeune has not only provided specific definitions of what constitutes an autobiography (thereby defying Paul De Man's strictures concerning its generic indeterminacy), but has most valuably concentrated on the textuality of such works and the role of the reader in the production of meaning. Drawing upon several authors (in particular Rousseau, André Gide, Michel Leiris, and Jean-Paul Sartre), he has examined modern 'literary' autobiography, in addition to memoirs, diaries, letters, and 'informal' modes, such as the interview and 'récits de vie'. Michel Beaujour in *Miroirs d'encre* (1980) focuses on the rhetorical techniques of autoportraiture and self-expression in a variety of texts from the Renaissance to the present day. The work of these critics has been instrumental in forcing a reconsideration of the value of autobiography, which seemed to have accrued to itself the status of a secondary genre, of little significance other than as an unproblematic adjunct to the study of 'proper' literary texts. This view had perhaps been most apparent in the Anglo-American

1

New Critics' dismissal of autobiographical writing, which was based upon suspicion of the naiveties of the intentional fallacy. Similarly, in French structuralism, the emphasis on the 'death of the author' (originally a Barthesian polemical provocation) was to remain an article of faith.

The publication of both Lejeune and Beaujour in the Editions du Seuil series 'Poétique' was vital in the revaluation which would henceforth occur, as this series has in many ways been the home of contemporary literary theory. The revival of interest in autobiography, therefore, initially seemed to be incongruous with the axiomatic proposition that the author was no longer the source and origin of his discourse. For theorists such as Roland Barthes, Michel Foucault and Jacques Derrida, the self is situated within the texture of discourse; rather than being, in humanist terms, the origin of meaning, it is deeply implicated in language. The sustained analysis by Roland Barthes in *S/Z*, for example, of the codes operating in the reading of a single work, confirmed the view that the text should be seen as a web of intertextual voices: it was especially redundant as a critical strategy to look to the author as an explanation. Just as the text was no longer to be considered as univocal and coherent, so the subject had to be seen as fractured, disconnected and unstable. The emphasis on the decentred self would mean that autobiographical writing could no longer be regarded as a privileged and unproblematic site of self-expression: the unity of the text had been contested in parallel with the unity of the subject. Deconstructive and psychoanalytic criticism in particular seemed to have forced a reappraisal of the relationship between writing and the self.

It is in this respect that an examination of autobiography is especially pertinent, in the sense that it is in the study of such works that the questions of writing and selfhood require to be directly addressed. Removed from the shackles of being considered a referent, the autobiographical subject can be considered in a different light. It becomes urgent that the status of autobiography as a discourse be stressed. Indeed, the study of autobiography emerges as affording the possibility of analysing the processes by which selfhood is constructed; uniquely, it becomes the site of the formation of subjectivity through writing. From this point of view, an autobiography is the locus of the confrontation between a fragmentary self and a multivocal text. As Paul Ricoeur has demonstrated, the narrativity of human experience has to be appreciated.

The fruitful reconsideration of the relationship between writing and selfhood was given added impetus by the appearance of Roland Barthes's own autobiography (*Roland Barthes par Roland Barthes*), and by the development of the 'nouveau roman' during the 1980s. The preoccupation with a poetics of pure textual autonomy (reflexivity as distinct from mimesis), embodied by the 'nouveau roman' and the journal *Tel Quel*, effectively marginalised literary criticism which was in any way author-centred. However, the publication of Nathalie Sarraute's *Enfance* and Alain Robbe-Grillet's *Romanesques* trilogy (although transgressive in generic terms) ensured that many of the previous shibboleths would have to be revised. Although these works were not in any way characteristic of traditional literary autobiography, their appearance forced critics not only to concede the 'respectability' of autobiography as a genre, but, more importantly, to see it as a potentially fertile area of analysis, as a consequence of the very tangible connection between the representation and the textualisation of the self in writing. By focusing on autobiography as a discourse, it therefore becomes possible to apply a wide range of critiques, without resurrecting the reactionary 'naturalising' view of autobiography as unmediated self-portraiture. The way would now be clear to discuss how such texts function, concentrating on the status of the autobiographical narrator's textual voice, and the role of the reader as a 'desired' figure in the discourse set in train. Criticism was therefore liberated from its previous exclusive concern with such topics as 'truth-value', techniques of disclosure and revelation, and the validity of claims to sincerity. Increasingly, autobiography would be considered as 'écriture', governed by certain codes and conventions, and the circumstances of production and reception. Lacanian psychoanalysis and feminist criticism have drawn attention to the construction of self and identity as a condition of writing.

Existentialist writing (in the broadest sense) has played a central role in this revaluation of autobiography for two principal reasons. Firstly, the enduring interest in Jean-Paul Sartre's and Simone de Beauvoir's autobiographical writings, especially *Les Mots* and *Mémoires d'une jeune fille rangée*, widely regarded as classics of twentieth-century French autobiography in their own right, has ensured that existential autobiographical writing in its various forms has itself constituted the object of intense scrutiny by many of the leading critics (notably Lejeune). The very diversity of autobiographical modes used by these writers is itself important: formal literary autobiography, in addition to memoirs (e.g. Simone de Beauvoir's *La Force de l'âge*, *La Force des choses*, *Tout compte fait*); the numerous interviews which constitute Sartre's 'autobiographie parlée'; letters (*Lettres au Castor*, *Lettres à Sartre*); notebooks and diaries (Sartre's *Carnets de la drôle de guerre*, Beauvoir's *Journal de guerre*). Secondly, the specifically theoretical issues associated with Sartrean existentialist thought, are directly related to the critical debate in autobiographical theory and criticism surrounding, for example, selfhood and subjectivity; identity and authenticity; choice, freedom, determinism and predestination. In addition, Sartre's *biographical* project, in the form of his studies of Baudelaire, Genet, and Flaubert, has used conceptual methodologies which have as their aim the attempt to assess the significance of these individuals' lives in the light of certain categories, which theoretically encompass existentialism, psychoanalysis, and Marxism. These volumes are not in any sense supplementary to Sartre's philosophical and literary enterprise; rather, they continue the exploration of the significance of human action. Also, the autobiographical texts produced by the existentialist 'family' (for example, Jean Genet's *Journal du voleur*; André Gorz's *Le Traître*; Violette Leduc's works, Michel Leiris's volumes and Albert Camus's notebooks, letters and journals) contain obvious evidence of a parallel interest in many of these themes. Existential autobiography and biography have thus been a particularly prolific and fecund source of writing in which fundamental questions concerning the nature of autobiographical discourse are explicitly or implicitly addressed.

Initially, to posit an existential selfhood would seem paradoxical in the light of Sartre's rejection of the concept of a 'vie intérieure': in *La Nausée*, this is considered as an extreme form of 'mauvaise foi'. Roquentin's biography of the Marquis de Rollebon has to be abandoned precisely because such an endeavour involves containing a contingent self within a biographical discourse whose very form implies an attempt to impose coherence. The central proposition of Sartrean existentialism is of course that 'existence precedes essence': there is no 'recuperable' inner core of being which resists the ravages of time and change (as suggested, for example, in Proust's *A la recherche du temps perdu*); instead, the individual is in a state of perpetual self-creation, the self is a dynamic entity, the sum of one's acts. Sartre had explicitly condemned the essentialist cargo of connotations in interiority: no *être* can be uncovered by a process of introspection and self-analysis; rather, the self is an existent and not an essence. In political terms, the unified subject is seen as coextensive with bourgeois individualism. For Sartre, the 'significance' of a life can only be measured in terms of the realisation of freedom. Identity can never be fixed as the subject is in a constant state of 'becoming': the self is a construct. It is perhaps in this respect that Sartrean existentialism and poststructuralism converge: the focus on the fragmentation and discontinuity of the self has dominated the post-modern consciousness.

However, in the light of Sartre's intellectual and philosophical itinerary, this position can be said to have been modified. His discovery of historicity (apparent in particular from the *Carnets de la drôle de guerre* and his wartime letters) implies that the subject's freedom may in fact be hampered by historical and socio-cultural factors. The putative determinism of this position was not lost on Sartre, as the existential biographies increasingly illustrate. In *L'Idiot de la famille*, the further complication of a psychoanalytical 'predisposition' towards certain courses of action pushes Sartre further towards a quasi-deterministic and avowedly totalising methodology. His primordial concern with authenticity is also very much at stake in this discussion: if a 'moi' cannot exist, then how specifically can one be 'true to oneself'?

All of these questions and issues still have to be posed, and, informed by the debates in existentialism and the theory of autobiography, the ten chapters in this volume address certain of the recurring themes involved: the relationship between writing and the construction of the self; the validity of the concept of an 'existential self' as a theoretical or philosophical point of reference; the value of conflicting narratives emanating from the various autobiographical modes; the formation of personal identity and the discourses through which this is articulated. In Part I, the autobiographical writings of Sartre and Simone de Beauvoir are examined, including the recent posthumous publications, which have so far received relatively little attention. In Part II, a number of authors belonging to the broad 'family' of existentialist autobiographers are considered (namely Paul Nizan, Albert Camus, Violette Leduc, and Jean Genet), as is Hervé Guibert, whose autobiographical account of his experience of Aids can be viewed in existential terms. In the concluding essay, an attempt is made to draw together some of the various lines of enquiry. The volume therefore furthers both existentialist and autobiographical studies, as well as helping to pursue the wider debates in philosophy, literary theory and comparative literature initiated by the renewed interest in autobiography.

Part I

Sartre and Beauvoir

The War Diary as Autobiography: Sartre 1939-40

MICHAEL SCRIVEN

In the *prière d'insérer* to *L'Age de raison* and *Le Sursis* published in 1945, Sartre underlined the link between a chosen narrative technique and individual and group perceptions of a given historical moment. The passage from pre-Munich individual bourgeois mystification and alienation to a post-Munich demystified historical consciousness is consequently mirrored in the passage from the self-contained narrative technique of *L'Age de raison* to the dispersed narrative form of *Le Sursis*. Sartre describes this movement from the individual to the collective in the following terms:

> Pendant la bonace trompeuse des années 37-38, il y avait des gens qui pouvaient encore garder l'illusion, en certains milieux, d'avoir une histoire individuelle bien cloisonnée, bien étanche. C'est pourquoi j'ai choisi de raconter *L'Age de raison* comme on fait d'ordinaire, en montrant seulement les relations de quelques individus. Mais avec les journées de septembre 1938, les cloisons s'effondrent. L'individu sans cesser d'être une monade, se sent engagé dans une partie qui le dépasse. Il demeure un point de vue sur le monde, mais il se surprend en voie de généralisation et de dissolution: c'est une monade qui fait eau, qui ne cessera plus de faire eau, sans jamais sombrer. Pour rendre compte de l'ambiguïté de cette condition, j'ai dû avoir recours au 'grand écran'. On retrouvera dans *Le Sursis* tous les personnages de *L'Age de raison* mais perdus, circonvenus par une foule d'autres gens.[1]

The overwhelming impact of history on the individual in the aftermath of the events of Munich in September 1938 not only shattered the previous belief in a peaceful future, but also exploded simplistic definitions of the individual as a

9

clearly delineated psychological site. The somewhat conventional narrative order of *L'Age de raison*, itself symbolic of the carefully articulated and coordinated psychological order that it portrays, becomes obsolete in the aftermath of Munich and the accelerating movement to war. The dispersed, wide-ranging and loosely configured narrative order of *Le Sursis* is symptomatic of the manner in which the central characters of the novel have been thrown off course by history, have been forced to reassess the psychological conventions that had previously bestowed an illusory unity upon their lives.[2]

L'Age de raison was completed by Sartre on 9 January 1940.[2] *Les Carnets de la drôle de guerre*,[3] written for the most part between September 1939 and March 1940, therefore constitute an obvious point of comparison with Sartre's fictional enterprise. The dispersed, unstructured narrative order of *Les Carnets* coincides precisely with the disillusioned, self-doubting mood of the French nation on the brink of war. The personal reassessment of the central characters in *Les Chemins de la liberté* is consequently reflected in Sartre's reassessment of his own pre-war persona in *Les Carnets*.

It is worth beginning this analysis by stressing the importance of the historical moment of production of *Les Carnets*. They were not produced in a historical vacuum, and are not historically disembodied texts. They constitute a formal response to a historical provocation. The Second World War was a crucial moment in Sartre's personal and intellectual development. The Phoney War which began in September 1939 and ended in the ignominious French military collapse of June 1940, the subsequent German Occupation of France, the ensuing complex process of resistance and collaboration, together constitute so wide-ranging and momentous a socio-historical context that it is not surprising that Sartre, like so many of his intellectual peers, was driven by force of circumstances to engage in a fundamental reappraisal of his own individual existence. The disruption to the patterns of a previous life-style, the need to face up to the possibility of death as a soldier conscripted to the front-line, the demoralisation of defeat and the physical deprivation of life in a prisoner-of-war camp, the dilemma of living in an occupied French state, all these factors coalesced to create the conditions when history entered into the very marrow of Sartre's being. The abstract, rootless, bourgeois individual of the pre-war period was thrown into the historical process by a social and political maelstrom over which he had absolutely no control. The illusion of bourgeois individualism was shattered initially by the events leading to the Phoney War, later by the social promiscuity of Stalag XIID, finally by the need to choose between resistance and collaboration. 'The breaking-point', Sartre noted in the late 1950s, 'was 1940. We saw that we had been living through an absolutely faked age ... We had been fooled and we knew it. We had experienced a situation of violence, of contradictions and conflicts ... From then on, many who, like myself, are in their early fifties, changed.'[4] In other words, the war transformed Sartre in the same way that it transformed the fictional character Mathieu in *L'Age de raison*, contradicting in the process the concluding remarks of the novel itself: '[Mathieu] ne changerait plus: il était fait'.[5] The terrifying capacity of war to shatter the previously tranquil and predictable course of an individual existence was to be the catalyst for far-reaching change, both for Mathieu and for Sartre himself.

The war represents, therefore, a critical moment of transformation and redefinition of the Sartrean self, a moment of deep and sustained introspection, when Sartre scrutinises and evaluates his own persona. Two preliminary points need to be made regarding this process of introspection and change. Firstly, as Sartre himself notes in *Les Carnets*, self-analysis prior to 1939-40 was an activity that he had repudiated as a pointless exercise:

> Je suis resté plus de quinze ans sans me regarder vivre. Je ne m'intéressais pas du tout. J'étais curieux des idées et du monde et du coeur des autres. La psychologie d'introspection me semblait avoir donné son meilleur avec Proust ... et ... les résultats étaient assez monotones ... il me semblait qu'à mettre le nez sur de minimes bassesses on les grossissait, on leur conférait de la force.[6]

It was consequently the sheer weight of historical pressures that forced him to seek the causes of his own previous blindness to the true nature of his social situation. It needs to be registered, however, that this introspective phase during 1939 and 1940 was not perceived by Sartre as a debilitating process. Unlike his close friend, Paul Nizan, who was struggling with his conscience in the aftermath of the Nazi-Soviet pact of non-aggression and his own resignation from the French communist party,[7] Sartre accepted introspection as a necessary prelude to future action. The pitiless lucidity with which he examines his existential self during the Phoney War is therefore a necessary strategy of deepening self-awareness and self-reorientation, not a self-defeating process.

Not everyone, however, shares Sartre's retrospective gloss that the change was for the better, and this is the second preliminary point. Sartre's official version of events is a form of exemplary narrative in which the abstract, de-politicised writer-hero is transformed by cataclysmic social turbulence and becomes a politically committed intellectual, imbued with a profoundly humanistic sense of social justice and a burning desire to put the world to rights. Michel Tournier refuses to accept the underlying value-judgement of this exemplary transformation thesis that Sartre was at pains to publicise throughout the post-war period. Tournier graphically records the sense of disillusionment that he experienced in 1945 on becoming aware of Sartre's conversion to 'humanism'. In Tournier's eyes, the destructively critical and subversive attitudes of Roquentin in *La Nausée* had been transformed into the platitudinous clichés of the 'Autodidacte' in the same novel:

> Nous avions vécu pendant l'occupation dans l'image d'un métaphysicien
> hautain et qui ne fait aucune concession à rien. Et puis alors arrive la
> libération. Il y a cette malheureuse conférence ... 'L'Existentialisme est
> un humanisme' ... Nous étions atterrés. Ainsi notre maître ramassait dans
> la poubelle où nous l'avions enfouie cette ganache éculée puant la sueur
> et la vie intérieure, l'humanisme; et il accolait comme également sienne
> cette absurde notion d'existentialisme ... Tout était clair. Prisonnier en
> 1940, Sartre nous revenait métamorphosé en autodidacte.[8]

The war, in short, had debilitated Sartre, had devitalised what Tournier
perceived as the dazzling clarity and originality of pre-war texts such as *La
Nausée* and *L'Etre et le néant*,[9] and had left in their place the nauseating
spectacle of the socially committed, humanist self-taught-man, burdened with
social obligations and vaguely formulated moral imperatives.

This post-war transformation of the Sartrean self has, of course, been
accounted for in some quarters by Sartre's sense of guilt at not having been more
active in Resistance activities during the Occupation. The Czech philosopher,
Vladimir Jankélévitch, forcefully made this point in an interview published in
1978: 'L'engagement de Sartre après la guerre a été une espèce de compensation
maladive, un remords, une recherche du danger qu'il n'avait pas voulu courir
pendant la guerre'.[10] More recently, George Steiner has taken up this claim
again, asserting that Sartre's Resistance credentials are highly dubious, and that
overall this archetypal committed intellectual is a 'suspect witness': 'The Sartre-
Beauvoir attitudes during the Nazi Occupation verge on the nauseating'.[11]

It is not the task of this analysis to attempt to assess the truth of such
allegations. The principal objective of these opening remarks is to highlight the
fact that Sartre underwent a fundamental change in 1939-40 and throughout the
war period. Whether one subscribes to Sartre's own thesis that the abrupt move
to social awareness was a beneficial process, or to Michel Tournier's views that
Sartre's transformation was a cause of intellectual debilitation, whether one
accepts or repudiates the assertions of Jankélévitch and Steiner that Sartre's
wartime Resistance activities were at best half-hearted, at worst bordering on
the collaborative, what is indisputable is that 1940 is the key historical date in
Sartre's personal itinerary. There are, of course, other significant dates in
Sartre's intellectual evolution, notably perhaps 1953 and 1968. With hindsight,
however, it can be seen that 1940 is particularly important to the extent that it
divides his life into two halves. It is a point of equilibrium and transition, a
moment when individualism is abandoned and the socio-historical process is
embraced.

Les Carnets de la drôle de guerre, written essentially between September

1939 and March 1940, constitute the textual record of this Sartrean metamorphosis. In assessing *Les Carnets*, our approach will be as much contextual and intertextual as purely textual, since, as will become clear later, the diaries themselves are principally a narrative site traversed by a series of discourses, which, although configured in a specifically discontinuous pattern, nonetheless refer not only to the socio-historical context of the time, but also to the cultural ethos within which the text itself is naturally embedded. Comment will be divided into three parts. The first will clarify the material state of the diaries, and offer one or two preliminary methodological points as a prelude to analysis. The second will focus specifically on the portrayal of the existential self in *Les Carnets*, stressing particularly the link between the dispersal of the self and the dispersed narrative form of the diaries. And the third will attempt to evaluate the significance of *Les Carnets* as a narrative autobiographical site both formally and substantively.

Preliminaries

It is important to establish the material state of *Les Carnets* at the outset. Although written in 1939-40, they were published for the first time in 1983, three years after Sartre's death. Of the fifteen original notebooks, only five have been published, the remainder having been lost. A sixth notebook (carnet 1) has also recently been discovered, but has not yet been published. Sartre wrote the diaries at the age of thirty-four, whilst serving in the meteorological section attached to an Artillery HQ stationed in a series of small towns to the east and north of Strasbourg: Brumath, Morsbronn and Bouxwiller. The other members of Sartre's meteorological unit who figure prominently in *Les Carnets* were called Paul, Pieterkowski and Keller. Notebooks 1-14 were written between 14 September 1939 and 28 March 1940. A fifteenth notebook, which Sartre began in April 1940, remained unfinished.[12] The contents of the diaries can be grouped into four principal areas, reflecting Sartre's major concerns at the time: (i) testimony/commentary on the war; (ii) philosophical notes and analyses that were to serve as a basis for *L'Etre et le néant*; (iii) assessments of other writers, with specific reference to autobiographical discourse; (iv) exploration of the existential self. More simply, all four levels of discourse can be subsumed within the ambit of the two overriding projects visible in *Les Carnets*: on the one hand, the refinement of a theory of 'néantisation'; on the other, self-assessment and re-orientation.

Although the reality of the 1939-40 war situation is present by implication on every page of *Les Carnets*, it is not the predominant discourse throughout. Sartre devotes considerable space to commenting explicitly on intellectual, literary and personal issues. At one level, *Les Carnets* constitute a veritable first draft of Sartre's ideas on nothingness, being, authenticity, freedom, human reality and morality. At another level, they record Sartre's day-to-day responses to whatever he happened to be reading at the time. Assessments of writers such as Romains,[13] Giono,[14] Gide,[15] Saint Exupéry,[16] Flaubert,[17] Renard,[18] Larbaud[19] and Stendhal,[20] for example, display in embryonic form an entire literary theory that Sartre was subsequently to promote in the post-war period. Most significant, perhaps, is Sartre's reference to Michel Leiris's autobiography, *L'Age d'homme*, published for the first time in 1939.[21] Sartre does not analyse *L'Age d'homme* in any detail, although it is clear that this text exercised a particular fascination over him and was instrumental in prompting Sartre to explore his own self: 'Il a fallu la guerre et puis le concours de plusieurs disciplines neuves (phénoménologie, psychanalyse, sociologie), ainsi que la lecture de *L'Age d'homme*, pour m'inciter à dresser un portrait de moi-même en pied'.[22] Leiris's insistence on literature as a dangerous act of self-exposure, akin to the bull-fighter exposing himself to death in the corrida, allied to a genuine attempt to explore the self, rather than conceal it strategically within the formal devices of the autobiographical genre, was doubly instructive for Sartre.[23]

Before assessing the form and content of *Les Carnets* themselves, it is appropriate to reflect on the distinction made recently by Michel Contat between two fundamentally different writing strategies in Sartre's work: on the one hand, what he refers to as 'le factum', on the other, 'le carnet' or 'le cahier'.[24] 'Le factum' is analogous with the project of publication and is the result of careful composition, re-writing and structural control. 'Le carnet', by contrast, represents a more spontaneous writing style, lacking in both formal order and stylistic correction, and consequently destined not for publication, but principally for the self-enlightenment of the author himself. In point of fact, this distinction is not entirely accurate with regard to *Les Carnets*, since Sartre makes it clear in a letter to Simone de Beauvoir in 1939 that he envisaged the diaries as a work written for publication after his death: 'Celui qui le lira après ma mort - car vous ne le publierez que posthume - pensera que j'étais un vilain personnage à moins que vous ne l'accompagniez d'annotations bienveillantes et explicatives'.[25] This is an important point since it is essential to read *Les Carnets* as a text explicitly written by Sartre for posthumous publication, not solely as notes for his own eyes and the eyes of his close friends and associates.

A second relevant issue raised by Contat is Sartre's rejection of the spontaneous and uncorrected writing style of the 'journal intime', implicitly perceived as facile, passive, feminine, onanistic. 'La forme d'écriture qu'induit [le cahier]', notes Contat, 'fait en effet courir le risque au scripteur d'une perte de son identité virile.'[26] There is undoubtedly an analogy to be made here between what Jean Cau has described as Sartre's 'macho' attitude in his relations with women,[27] and the sexual stereotypes that he attributes to impulsive as opposed to carefully stylised writing strategies. What needs to be borne in mind, however, when assessing *Les Carnets* in this light, is the extent to which they themselves constitute not only a parody of the 'journal intime' as a form, but also a systematic deconstruction of the effusive and self-congratulatory writing style traditionally associated with it. It is in this sense that *Les Carnets*, although both spontaneous and unstructured in approach, reach beyond the facile posturing of the traditional 'journal intime'.

Exploring the Existential Self

Régis Debray has described the specific quality of Sartre's writing in the following terms:

> Il y a quelque chose de plus chez Sartre que chez Gide ou que chez Montaigne, disons quelque chose de plus que la rhétorique de la sincérité ou la recherche de la transparence. D'abord il y a une assise philosophique, c'est cette notion du pour-soi, c'est la thématisation qu'il a faite de l'esprit de sérieux et son refus de l'esprit de sérieux, c'est-à-dire au fond un homme qui à mon sens ruinait la coïncidence de soi avec soi-même dans un statut social, au nom de cette conscience interprétée comme néant, néantisation, critique de soi-même ... Et c'est ce qui rend Claudel intolérable ... Quand on a lu Sartre, on ne peut pas admettre Claudel même si Claudel est un grand écrivain.[28]

In Debray's eyes, therefore, what differentiates Sartre's writings from the traditional 'rhetoric of sincerity' exemplified by Gide and Montaigne is a philosophical underpinning that privileges the process of critical negation of the self and the annihilation of the coincidence between the self and the social construction of the self. My contention is that the real originality of *Les Carnets* - and it is this that distinguishes them from *Les Mots* - is the injection of a negating critical consciousness within a dispersed, unstructured narrative form. The formal looseness and spontaneity provide the structural arena within which a nihilating consciousness is given full rein. The process of narration within *Les Carnets* therefore resembles a constant movement from self to others to concepts, with no formal ambition aimed at tying the narrative together as an ordered autonomous unit. The narrative law of *Les Carnets* is therefore dispersal, disintegration, subversion, reassessment. The teleological thrust is the desire simultaneously to shed light on the inner recesses of a past persona and to engage in the elaboration of new philosophical concepts and a new self.

Of the five published notebooks, two (III and V) were written in November and December 1939, two (XI and XII) in January and February 1940, and the last (XIV) in March 1940. In the last of the published notebooks, Sartre refers to

15

a loss of intellectual tension from February 1940 onwards. By March 1940 his daily existence has become a relatively routine affair: 'Les temps héroïques de cette drôle de guerre sont finis pour moi ... je suis devenu quotidien'.[29] At least, it was routine in comparison with the dramatic metamorphosis that he had undergone during the early part of the Phoney War, when the sudden and brutal change in personal circumstances from civilian to soldier had forced him to a fundamental reassessment of his life style; had led him to experience his first premonitions of authenticity; had enabled him to slough off the skin of his past self.[30] In terms of narrative development, therefore, there is a broad movement from an urgency driven by an impending sense of self-discovery in the first notebooks to a more reflective state in the later notebooks. Towards the end of this intellectual itinerary, more emphasis is consequently given to the attempt to categorise a personality (particularly in notebook XII, for example, where the issues of authenticity, his personal crisis with Tania, his attitude to possessions and property, and what he refers to as his 'imperialism' and relations with others are assessed), and the attempt to sketch further lines of self-development.

In order to offer a more specific insight into the narrative construction of *Les Carnets*, we shall briefly examine the textual specificity of notebook XIV, written between 6 and 27 March 1940 in Bouxwiller and Brumath (pages 352-432 of the published text). Two initial points need to be made. First, the metaphysical underpinning of this narrative order would appear to be exactly the opposite of that which Sartre attributes to Faulkner's novels in *Situations I*, where he notes: 'Il semble qu'on puisse comparer la vision du monde de Faulkner à celle d'un homme assis dans une auto découverte et qui regarde en arrière'.[31] In contrast, and in truly existential style, the underlying metaphysical vision of *Les Carnets* is a future perspective on the world. The past self is portrayed solely in order to facilitate the means of future self-development. Sartre's eyes, unlike Faulkner's, are therefore firmly riveted on future possibilities. Hence - and this is the second point - although the narrative form is a process of spontaneous production from day to day, the text is unified throughout by this sense of projection forward, through the process of construction of a new self in the act of narration. The text is consequently discontinuous and unpredictable, but much more than simply a daily inventory of personal reflections.

Substantively, notebook XIV adheres to the following narrative configuration: an initial reflection on the gradual destruction of what Sartre refers to as the military idea, the war having degenerated into a defensive act devoid of heroic aspirations (351-55), followed immediately by a systematic deconstruction of the self in time and space: Sartre, the product of capitalism, parliamentarianism, centralisation and officialdom, concluding with a dismissal of the past self as a rootless, abstract individual and a recognition of the need to construct a committed, substantive self in the future (355-56); then a lengthy assessment of

Ludwig's biography of Guillaume II, a methodological discussion straddling two days, in which the objective is to situate human reality within the historical process, to institute what Sartre refers to as 'une métaphysique de l'historialité' (357-75); then a brief comment on the manner in which the bourgeoisie finally rallied to the war as a means of liquidating communist ideology, the nationalist war propaganda masking underlying civil-war political objectives (375-76); then a continuation of the biographical assessment of Guillaume II, stressing the idea of original choice (377-80); then a brief lament on his inadequacies as a poet (381-82); then a further development of Sartre's biographical reflections focused on Guillaume's relations with England (383-87); then a passing account of Sartre's attraction to beauty, which leads eventually into an assessment of his own frivolity, his lack of grip on reality, his consequent rejection of seriousness and his belief that life is ultimately a game (387-97); subsequent discussions shift rapidly from the history and politics of modern Germany (398-402), to memories of Rouen (402-06), to his attitude to literary prizes, specifically the Prix Populiste (406-09), to his relation to the fictional characters in his novels (409-11), to an account of his return to Brumath (413-14), to the journal of Jules Renard (417-26), and finally to the writing style of André Malraux (429-30).

The exploratory nature of *Les Carnets* is fully revealed in this brief exposition of the contents of notebook XIV. The freely chosen movement from one topic to the next, the willingness to integrate topics of a personal, methodological, political and conjunctural nature, and the general exuberance of the writing style are emblematic of a highly original diary form. Although Sartre speaks of a certain loss of intellectual tension in this notebook compared to earlier notebooks, the dominant aim of the narrative remains the construction of the self in the years to come. Whether it be at the intellectual or methodological level, (the attempt, for example, to devise an existential biographical methodology that was subsequently to lead to extended essays on Baudelaire, Genet, Mallarmé and Flaubert),[32] or at the personal level, (the attempt, for example, to amalgamate a past rejection of seriousness with a newly-discovered need for authenticity), the perspective throughout is the future.

This brief account of the content, structure and writing style of notebook XIV offers a representative picture of the manner in which *Les Carnets* constitute overall an impressive textual site aimed at deconstructing a past self and at regenerating the self in a future perspective. It is this critical deconstruction, predicated principally on the negating qualities of the discourse, the capacity of the text to annihilate any coincidence between an existential self and a socially constructed self, the recurring capacity in other words to deflate 'l'esprit de sérieux', that is at the heart of the narrative success of *Les Carnets*. As Sartre laconically notes, 'Il n'est pas possible de se saisir comme conscience sans penser que la vie est un jeu'.[33]

The success, however, should not be overstated. It is perhaps instructive at this juncture to contrast *Les Carnets* with Leiris's *L'Age d'homme*, published in 1939. Although the philosophical underpinning is absent from Leiris's autobiography, his technique of thematic analogy allied to a willingness to explore the sexual and sub-conscious dimension of his personality is in my view probably more revealing than Sartre's account. Sartre remains relatively silent on his sexual proclivities, for example, and there is little said about his family in *Les Carnets*. Equally, certain parts of *Les Carnets* are shortened in order to avoid discussing specific personalities, Olga and Wanda Kosakiewicz in particular. Sartre's analysis of his relations with others in notebook XIII, for example, was apparently truncated in order to avoid offending Wanda. There is, of course, a direct analogy to be made here with the termination of *Les Mots* prior to Sartre's adolescence in 1916, a decision taken in order to avoid the necessity of speaking publicly of what Sartre perceived as his mother's treacherous decision to marry for a second time and betray her son, Poulou, in the process. Temperamentally, also, Sartre would appear to be taking fewer risks than Leiris. His readiness to discredit a past self was no doubt facilitated by his disarming ability to dissociate himself from a previous self. In this sense, to be critical of his own past self was simply synonymous with criticising an Other, synonymous with criticising, in other words, someone else.

What these omissions and narrative manoeuvres illustrate is what Debray has designated as an underlying cautiousness in Sartre's personality, an unwillingness in the final analysis to go beyond the point of no return, whether it be politically or psychologically:

> Sartre me semble finalement un homme prudent, peut-être plus tacticien qu'il ne l'aurait aimé, qui n'a jamais créé l'irrémédiable autour de lui ou envers lui-même ... il y a un côté gestionnaire chez Sartre, gestionnaire d'une légende, d'une notoriété, d'une position. Même si finalement je continue d'estimer admirable ce refus d'institution, ce refus d'académisme, ce refus du rôle de l'universitaire, je hais tout de même chez lui, je dirais, l'organisateur d'une boutique ... mais c'est vrai qu'au fond il est grand par cette dévotion non pas à soi-même ou à sa légende, mais ... à cette oeuvre à faire; et c'est vrai qu'il y a un côté sacrificiel même dans son acharnement littéraire, dans son travail.[34]

There is perhaps in Leiris's autobiographical quest a certain irremediable quality that sets it apart from *Les Carnets*. Curiously, Sartre himself appears to corroborate Debray's judgement when he notes in the diaries: 'Je pense de plus en plus que, pour atteindre l'authenticité, il faut que quelque chose craque ... Mais je me suis préservé contre les craquements. Je suis ligoté à mon désir d'écrire ... Si je me remets en question, c'est pour écrire les résultats de cet examen.'[35] The writing process is paradoxically perceived as a barrier to existential authenticity. Overall, however, despite these caveats, Sartre's exploration of the existential self in *Les Carnets* exemplifies the effectiveness of a writing strategy aimed at framing a critical negation of a past self and the contemporaneous construction of a future self within the loosely configured pattern of the diary form. Although Debray is doubtless correct to highlight the tactical limitations of Sartre's autobiographical quest, he is nonetheless fulsome in his praise of the self-sacrificial aspect of Sartre's commitment to the act of writing. This sacrificial dimension in which the act of allegiance to writing takes precedence over allegiance to the self or allegiance to one's place in history, is graphically embodied in *Les Carnets*, a dynamic, exuberant text produced at a moment of historical and psychological disintegration by a writer at the peak of his intellectual powers.

Autobiography and the Existential Self

Although unequivocally designating *Les Carnets* as within the boundaries of autobiographical discourse, Philippe Lejeune prefers to employ the term 'autoportrait' rather than 'autobiographie' when referring to the series of texts in which Sartre scrutinises his existential self over a period of fifty years.[36] This would appear to me to be justified to the extent that Sartre's autobiographical writings are the textual site of an on-going transformation of the self. As Lejeune comments, 'ses écrits autobiographiques sont des peaux mortes qu'il laisse derrière lui'.[37] They therefore constitute a portrait of a superseded past self that is in the process of being jettisoned. Sartre's implicit assumption and abiding illusion that the future self will somehow be different from and superior to the self that has been left behind, make it possible to categorise *Les Carnets* as a self-portrait in so far as a critical distance is established between the narrator in the present and the past self that is displayed in the narrative. Sartre notes, for example:

> Il me semble qu'on peut, à l'occasion de quelque grande circonstance, et quand on est en train de changer de vie, comme le serpent qui mue, regarder cette peau morte, cette image cassante de serpent qu'on laisse derrière soi et faire le point. Après la guerre je ne tiendrai plus ce carnet ou bien, si je le tiens, je n'y parlerai plus de moi. Je ne veux pas être hanté par moi-même jusqu'à la fin de mes jours.[38]

What should be highlighted at this juncture is the centrality of the form and style of *Les Carnets* to their undoubted literary success.[39] Reference has already been made to the implicit distinction in Sartre's literary theory between a facile, contingent, spontaneous writing style on the one hand, and a carefully wrought and highly stylised narrative on the other. In 1964, for example, Sartre was at pains to emphasise the stylistic dimension of *Les Mots* as the most crucial aspect of his autobiography: 'le sens du style dans *Les Mots* c'est que le livre est un adieu à la littérature: un objet qui se conteste soi-même doit être écrit le mieux possible'.[40] Such an assertion, however, raises a number of problems. Leaving aside the obvious theoretical contradiction between Sartre's early post-war view that style should be hidden unobtrusively in the literary text so as not to impede the reader's accession to the necessary unveiling of the mystifications of existence,[41] and his contention in 1964 that style should be foregrounded in order to disclose the mystifications of literature, there is nonetheless a major difference between the manner in which the loosely constructed narrative of *Les Carnets* and the tightly constructed discourse of *Les Mots* are received by the reading public.

The essential difference between the two narratives is located precisely in their historical moment of production. Whereas *Les Mots* is a carefully ordered account of a past self viewed from the omniscient vantage point and relative stability of old age, *Les Carnets* are an act of spontaneous literary production, in which Sartre struggles from day to day to invent a new philosophy and a new self in the context of impending war in 1939-40 and at the age of thirty four. In *Les Mots*, the future life-style of the central protagonist is already inscribed in the personal itinerary of the narrator, the celebrated adult writer. In *Les Carnets*, in contrast, both narrator and central protagonist are in the dark. Their future destiny can only be guessed at. The originality and immediacy of the diaries arise from the sense of exhilaration experienced by the narrator personally engaged in a unique voyage of self-discovery. As Lejeune remarks, *Les Carnets* constitute a more authentic text than *Les Mots*, to the degree that they portray a free consciousness in the act of spontaneous self-exploration, self-definition and self-expression.[42]

The significance of this comparison is both formal and historical. It is not simply a matter of comparing two texts in order to indicate a personal preference for one or the other. Rather, these two texts illustrate the importance of the connections to be made between historical context and writing practices. *Les Carnets* are the product of a war situation, when society and the individual were subject to a process of rapid disintegration. The historical situation was itself the necessary prelude to a far-reaching and uncompromising critical dislocation of the existential self. The events of Munich and the slide to war called for radical and rapid responses. *Les Carnets*, in both form and substance, record this transformation in a truly existential and authentic manner, with no clear idea of what the future holds. It is a narrative that maps out an individual existence from day to day. *Les Mots*, in contrast, predicated not only on the desire to foreground stylistic and technical brilliance but also on a retrospective, totalising view of the self, is necessarily ensnared within the conventions of a polite literary ceremony. The process of deconstruction is still present, but in a greatly attenuated form, the stylistic accomplishment of *Les Mots* functioning almost as a brake upon the substantive project of critical nihilation of the self. Geneviève Idt pinpoints the difficulty of attempting to subvert literature through stylistic means, when she notes: 'Loin d'aboutir au degré zéro de l'écriture, la critique de la littérature semble l'exalter ... on oublie que l'objet se conteste pour retenir seulement qu'il est écrit "le mieux possible"; cet adieu à la littérature ressemble à une déclaration d'amour passionnée'.[43]

Paradoxically, it would appear, therefore, that the form of *Les Carnets* rather than the style of *Les Mots* is more representative of the existential quality of Sartre's writing project, and hence of Sartre's existential self. What distinguishes *Les Carnets* from *Les Mots* is the prominence of an authentic strategy of critical negativity, neither formally encumbered by the obligation to foreground stylistic brilliance, nor substantively debilitated by the retrospective totalising vantage-point of old age. The truly Sartrean self is located in *Les Carnets*, above all in the process of critical negation itself rather than in the displayed contents of a discarded past persona. The self, in other words, is most effectively embodied in the ruthless deconstruction of its own being, in the freely chosen act of self-annihilation in the writing process.

NOTES

1   J.-P. Sartre, *Oeuvres romanesques*, édition établie par M. Contat et M. Rybalka, Paris, Gallimard ('Bibliothèque de la Pléiade'), 1981, pp. 1911-12.

2   Ibid., p. 1901: 'Je viens de finir *L'Age de raison*, aujourd'hui (9 janvier 1940)'.

3   J.-P. Sartre, *Les Carnets de la drôle de guerre. Novembre 1939 - Mars 1940* (CG), Paris, Gallimard, 1983. Published in English as J.-P. Sartre, *War Diaries: Notebooks from a Phoney War November 1939 - March 1940*, trans. Quintin Hoare, London, Verso, 1984.

4   'J.-P. Sartre on his Autobiography', interview with O. Todd, *The Listener*, 6 June 1957, p. 915.

5   J.-P. Sartre, *L'Age de raison*, in *Oeuvres romanesques*, p. 729.

6   CG, pp. 174-75.

7   See P. Nizan, 'Correspondence de guerre: septembre 1939 - avril 1940', in J.-J. Brochier (ed.), *Paul Nizan intellectuel communiste 1926-1940*, Paris, Gallimard, 1967, pp. 251-84. For a detailed account of Nizan's writing project, see M. Scriven, *Paul Nizan Communist Novelist*, London, Macmillan, 1988.

8   M. Tournier, in M. Contat and J. Lecarme, 'Les Années Sartre', radio programme broadcast on France Culture, 24 and 25 August 1990.

9   Although written during the early part of the war and published in 1943, *L'Etre et le Néant* encapsulates the philosophical enquiries that Sartre conducted during the 1930s.

10   V. Jankélévitch, *Libération*, 10 June 1985; *Le Monde*, 11 June 1985.

11   G. Steiner, 'Sartre: The Suspect Witness', *The Times Literary Supplement*, 3 May 1991, p. 4. Steiner's negative comments need to be compared with the more balanced view of B.-H. Lévy, 'Retour de captivité (Nouvelles réflexions sur la question Sartre)', in *Les Aventures de la liberté*, Paris, Grasset, 1991, pp. 213-20.

12   For a detailed account of the circumstances surrounding the production of *Les Carnets*, see (i) the translator's introduction to the English edition, pp. vii-xviii; (ii) P. Assouline, 'A la recherche des carnets perdus', *Lire*, no. 175, April 1990, pp. 35-44; (iii) 'Simone de Beauvoir raconte à Pierre Bénichou l'histoire des *Carnets de la drôle de guerre*', *Le Nouvel Observateur*, 25 March 1983, pp. 56-58.

13   CG, pp. 13-17, 28, 144-45.

14   CG, pp. 176-78, 201-03.

15   CG, pp. 89-92, 114-20.

16   CG, pp. 74-75, 78-79, 183-85.

17   CG, pp. 128-32.

18   CG, pp. 417-28.

19   CG, pp. 178-84.

20   CG, p. 309.

21   M. Leiris, *L'Age d'homme*, Paris, Gallimard, 1946; first published in 1939.

22   CG, p. 175.

23   *L'Age d'homme*; see especially 'De la littérature considérée comme une tauromachie', pp. 7-22.

24   M. Contat and J. Deguy, '*Les Carnets de la drôle de guerre* de Jean-Paul Sartre, effets d'écriture, effets de lecture', *Littérature*, no. 80 (December 1990), pp. 17-41.

25   J.-P. Sartre, *Lettres au Castor et à quelques autres*, Paris, Gallimard, 1983, vol. 1, p. 300.

26   Contat and Deguy, op. cit., p. 30.

27   '[Sartre] considérait la femme comme un autre à l'égard duquel il fallait manifester une énorme indulgence ... il n'aimait pas, à proprement parler, les femmes parce qu'il était extrêmement macho lui'; in Contat and Lecarme, op. cit.

28   R. Debray, in Contat and Lecarme, op. cit.

29   CG, p. 428.

30   CG, p. 397.

31   J.-P. Sartre, *Situations I*, Paris, Gallimard, 1947, p. 68.

32   For an account of Sartre's biographical project, see M. Scriven, *Sartre's Existential Biographies*, London, Macmillan, 1984.

33   CG, p. 396.

34   R. Debray, in Contat and Lecarme, op. cit.

35   CG, pp. 43-44.

36   P. Lejeune, 'Les enfances de Sartre', in *Moi aussi*, Paris, Seuil, 1986, pp. 117-63. Lejeune lists Sartre's autobiographical writings as follows: (i) 'Autoportrait écrit pour Simone Jolivet', 1926; (ii) *Les Carnets de la drôle de guerre*, 1939-40; (iii) *Jean sans terre*, première version des *Mots*, 1953-56; (iv) *Les Mots*, 1963; (v) 'Le testament politique', 1970; (vi) 'Sartre parle sa vie', 1972-75.

37   Ibid.

38   CG, p. 175.

39   The importance of *Les Carnets* in Sartre's literary output can be gauged from the following statement by Michel Contat: 'Dans la hiérarchie des oeuvres de Sartre, je mets *Les Carnets* juste après *La Nausée* et *Les Mots*'; cited in P. Assouline, op. cit., p. 36.

40   'Sur L'Idiot de la famille', interview with M. Contat and M. Rybalka, *Le Monde*, 14 May 1971; reprinted in *Situations X*, Paris, Gallimard, 1976, pp. 91-115.

41   J.-P. Sartre, *Situations II*, Paris, Gallimard, 1948, p. 75.

42   P. Lejeune, op. cit., pp. 134-35.

43   G. Idt, 'L'Autoparodie dans *Les Mots* de Sartre', *Cahiers du XXème siècle*, no. 6, Klincksieck, 1976, p. 86.

Autobiography, Contingency, Selfhood:
A Reading of *Les Mots*

EDMUND SMYTH

It has been a feature of several interpretations of *Les Mots*[1] to apply the totalising methodology which Sartre himself claimed to be utilising in his various existential biographies. The biographical subject can thus be revealed by enacting a series of manoeuvres - existential, Marxist, psychoanalytical - designed to situate the subject in terms of the confrontation with the contingency of existence. In his studies of Baudelaire, Genet, and Flaubert, Sartre is able to draw upon these different and apparently contradictory approaches in order to explain the significance of the subject's acts in their totality. It is widely recognised that contingency is a privileged site in Sartre's work, and in his autobiography, *Les Mots*, this revelation is central to the narrative and interpretative thrust of the text. Just as the structure of *La Nausée* had been contrived explicitly so as to valorise this state of awareness (thus entailing a departure in strictly formal terms from the prerequisites of the diary form),[2] so in *Les Mots* a similar discovery by Jean-Paul is presented as crucial to the autobiographical narrator's sense of self. The subsequent demonstration of 'imposture' and 'mauvaise foi' (the text can be read as a sustained illustration of such concepts) is expressly motivated as a consequence of this. In the closing pages, Sartre's ultimate renunciation of the supreme value of a literary vocation is presented as a more authentic mode of awareness, principally as a result of the 'climactic' structural position accorded to this (final) episode in the diegesis: 'histoire' and 'discours' seem to have merged in this conclusion. The totalised and seamless nature of the work as a whole is therefore proposed to the reader rather than a textual manifestation of the contingent.

In addressing the relationship between writing and the experience of contingency, the question of representation requires to be explored. To what extent is the narrative form adopted in the work appropriate to the textualisation of contingency? Is the organising telos of a narrative compatible with the proposition that a contingent and discontinuous selfhood is the only defining characteristic of existence?

It is arguable whether the specifically formal dimension of *Les Mots* has been the object of sufficient consideration, in view of the emphasis placed on the political import of the work or the so-called progressive-regressive method that Sartre may be applying to his own autobiography as he had in his existential biographies.[3] In considering this question of the relationship between writing and contingency, it could of course be maintained that a 'formal' autobiography (however subversive) is inevitably less authentic than such apparently spontaneous works as the *Lettres au Castor* or the *Carnets de la drôle de guerre*, let alone the numerous interviews that constitute an 'autobiographie parlée',[4] which may initially seem more in harmony with the immediate apprehension of existential experience. Thus, a letter or a diary entry may appear to give an unmediated and uncontaminated perception of reality and the self's relationship to that reality. Such works may appear more open and plural, especially if not explicitly designed for publication.

However, this would be to accept the proposition both of subjective truth and the possibility of a neutral and unproblematic writing. Crucially, such a line of argument ignores the role of address in such communicative situations - address to the other as well as address to a version or construction of the self uncontaminated by 'mauvaise foi'. It would involve neglecting the fact that letters and notebooks are no less governed by a specific set of codes and conventions of their own than formal autobiography, which also operates on the horizon of expectations generated by publication. As autobiographical forms, these para-autobiographical acts are therefore no more authentic from a formal realist viewpoint than the highly stylised *Les Mots*. Para-autobiographical modes can have no greater claim to mimetic validity than a more 'formal' work. To posit a more authentic mode of autobiographical writing would be to propose that an 'écriture' exists which is unaffected by questions of reception. Above all, it suggests that a form of representation can be found which is in some way 'natural'. Crucially, such an argument would also be deficient in existentialist terms, precisely because it ignores the Sartrean emphasis on the manner in which a self is constructed rather than given. In *La Nausée*, Sartre had adopted a diary format in order to convey Roquentin's discovery of contingency: thus at the level of form there is an attempt to mirror how this perception takes place. Adventures are rejected because they involve a narrativisation of experience using a pre-established patterning of events governed by a telos. Thus, it is suggested that contingency cannot be represented formally in a conventional teleological structure. This is reflected in the defeat of Roquentin's biography of the marquis de Rollebon. However, as several commentators have pointed out,[5] the text of *La Nausée* is not formally chaotic; rather, the discovery of contingency has entailed an aesthetically necessary 'truquage' on Sartre's part in order to function discursively.

When he came to write *Les Mots*, Sartre had of course become interested in a different set of issues. As Annie Cohen-Solal has pointed out, the writing of the autobiography (from *Jean sans terre* in 1953 to the final text of 1963) coincided with the period of 'sa complaisance, sa faiblesse, son idéalisme envers l'URSS'.[6] His discovery of historicity, preoccupation with Marxism, and reading of Freud led him to contemplate the possibilities of a totalising biographical project, which would reconcile existential reality with more or less inevitable pre-ordained choices. As Sartre commented:

> Je voudrais éviter le romanesque, l'anecdote même dans la mesure où il n'aurait pas d'importance. Ce serait plutôt des mémoires où me définir par rapport à la situation historique en utilisant comme système d'investigation aussi bien une certaine psychanalyse que la méthode marxiste.[7]

In *Questions de méthode*,[8] Sartre had attempted to mediate between historical forces and individual choice. And referring to *L'Idiot de la famille*, his most sustained application of the progressive-regressive method, he prefers to speak about predestination rather than crude determinism: 'D'une certaine façon, nous naissons tous prédestinés. Nous sommes voués à un certain type d'action dès l'origine par la situation où se trouvent la famille et la société à un moment donné'.[9] In terms of the broader theoretical context initiated by *Critique de la raison dialectique*, it is possible to consider *Les Mots* as another exercise in such a reconciliation of previously incompatible theoretical positions. It is certain that *Les Mots* would be informed by a wide range of political and philosophical imperatives operating at this stage of Sartre's intellectual development. For Arnold and Piriou, *Les Mots* and *Critique de la raison dialectique* form 'les deux volets d'un diptyque où théorie et pratique se complètent'.[10] It is of course true that Sartre did welcome and endorse this view. As he confirmed to Olivier Todd, *Les Mots* should be seen as another contribution to existential biography:

> J'ai écrit un certain nombre d'ouvrages - sur Baudelaire et Genet ... où j'essayais de déterminer la signification d'une vie et le projet qui la remplit. J'ai été critiqué sous le prétexte que cette reconstruction de l'extérieur perdait un élément de sympathie ... Personne ne peut blâmer un écrivain d'avoir une certaine sympathie pour lui-même et ses projets: en appliquant ma méthode à moi-même, je profiterai d'un minimum de sympathie.[11]

This comment both accepts the validity of the 'méthode' as applied to himself, and also, through the references to 'sympathie', clearly reveals the close preoccupation with reader response that characterises so many of his utterances on the text.

However, it is by no means the case that his concern with contingency is relegated from the evolving agenda. On the contrary, Sartre does not neglect to provide *Les Mots* with a revelation of contingency à la Roquentin as a 'defining' instance. The comment 'Je me sentais de trop'[12] immediately evokes the language employed in *L'Etre et le Néant* and elsewhere. His reference to the origins of his life as 'quelques gouttes de sperme'[13] is intended to emphasise the arbitrary and gratuitous nature of existence. In the text, he wishes to convey that it was his experience as an unnecessary, fatherless child that had been crucial to his sense of the contingent. In common with several other works (his other major narrative of childhood inauthenticity, 'L'Enfance d'un chef',[14] immediately comes to mind), *Les Mots* presents a kind of object-lesson in 'mauvaise foi': Poulou needs to feel necessary in the world, hence the adoption of a literary vocation to legitimise his existence. Throughout the text, the imagery of theatricality is used as a structural metaphor. Poulou is presented by the narrator as acting, posturing, and role-playing in a characteristically inauthentic manner: he is a willing performer whose reading and writing is designed to win familial approval. In terms of the content of the work, an extensive dramatisation of 'mauvaise foi' is sustained, as the narrator indulges in a thoroughly Sartrean reading of his childhood.

If these retrospective reconstructions and interpretations seem in any way jarring to the reader because of the improbability and implausibility of such an over-sophisticated adult perspective, then this can of course be justified as part of Sartre's impetus in seeking to justify the text as an exercise in ideological demystification. Commenting on *Les Mots* in a number of interviews published both contemporaneously and much later, Sartre would always insist upon the politically subversive nature of his autobiographical enterprise:

> Je voulais que ce soit agaçant ... je voulais que ça soit un adieu à la littérature qui se fasse en bel écrit. C'est-à-dire, je voulais que les gens qui lisent [*Les Mots*] se trouvent entraînés dans une espèce de contestation de la littérature par la littérature elle-même.[15]

The word 'entraîné' is important, because it signals the process of ideological demystification in which he wishes to involve the reader. His aim is therefore to recuperate the text in a manner in harmony with the political direction he has been following. These comments indicate an anxiety on the autobiographer's part surrounding the reception his work will receive. It is vital for Sartre to mobilise a reading of *Les Mots* that is consistent with the ideological imperatives he has set himself. The reader's response is therefore very carefully prepared.

Within the text, the Sartrean commentary, either by means of the presence of an existentialist vocabulary or through the patterning imposed on the events themselves, has a totalising impetus: we find in *Les Mots* an application of a telos, whose ultimate effect paradoxically may be to minimise contingency, from a textual point of view. In short, Sartre would seem to operate a degree of closure, preventing a mobility and plurality of meaning. Such a potential restriction of the reader's freedom would of course run counter specifically to the aesthetic programme outlined in Sartre's literary criticism: the 'metaphysic' of the text may as a consequence be impeded if this occurs. In the context of Sartre's aesthetics, therefore, it is vital to consider whether the teleology is in fact maintained. To what extent is the totalising meta-narrative imposed on the work in order to disguise textual contingency? How plausible and consistent is the telos itself?

Perhaps the most striking feature of *Les Mots* is the way in which Sartre uses contrasting tones, redolent with irony and frequently impermeable to immediate comprehension. The language is far from being the transparent prose advocated in *Qu'est-ce que la littérature?*.[16] Throughout the text, numerous rhetorical tricks are deployed in order to disrupt a continuous, linear and unobstructed reading. The chronological disjunctions also contribute to this of course, as Philippe Lejeune has shown.[17] But at the specifically stylistic level, when asked by Simone de Beauvoir to specify what he meant by 'literary', Sartre said that *Les Mots* 'était plein de trucs, d'astuces, d'art d'écrire, presque de jeux de mots';[18] it was 'très travaillé'.[19] Defamiliarisation is used both in terms of the thematic content and the language itself: the reader is made to feel alienated by the very nature of the style. As Sartre himself states: 'On parle dans sa propre langue, on écrit en langue étrangère'.[20] Distanciation is central to Sartre's politically subversive strategy, because it promotes the demystification of bourgeois literature and the ideology that it supports. The reader is systematically prevented from identifying with the narrator and his language - hence the contestation of a bourgeois discourse is maintained. The vocabulary seems to enact a divorce between 'signifiant' and 'signifié'. The tortuous syntax impedes the reader's immediate comprehension, forcing a distrust not only of the character of Poulou (entirely consonant with the demonstration of 'mauvaise foi') but, more importantly, of the status of the narrator and the discourse itelf, raising serious questions in respect of autobiographical poetics in general. Unlike Sartre's fictional works, the prose of *Les Mots* is far from being transparent: we are not made to feel that this is merely the vehicle of a pre-established sense. Instead, the reader is presented with a discourse which is disruptive and problematic at every level. As the title itself may suggest, 'words' are complex entities. The title not only implies the devaluation of literature (in common with the position enunciated in the conclusion), but also signals linguistic and communicative ambiguity. Viewed in this light, *Les Mots* may appear as an example of a non-transparent, unrecuperable, and self-conscious 'écriture' which has more in common with *Tel Quel* and the 'nouveau roman' than the position enunciated in *Qu'est-ce que la littérature?*. In *Les Mots*, Sartre departs spectacularly from his previous emphasis on the accessibility value of prose.

In his own comments on the text, Sartre signalled the disruptive nature of the writing: stating that 'il y a deux tons dans *Les Mots*' [21] and that 'Le sens du style dans *Les Mots*, c'est que le livre est un adieu à la littérature: un objet qui se conteste soi-même doit être écrit le mieux possible'.[22] Like the books in his grandfather's library, the child is 'un bien culturel'.[23] Poulou is seen to be internalising and resisting the ideological forms of bourgeois society. The bourgeois literary style is made to appear elitist, recondite and alienating. This disorientating clash of languages is apparent at the level of the 'discours', but also in the 'histoire'. A conflict is played out between 'high culture' (as embodied by the representation of Charles Schweitzer, who is himself the spokesman of the positivist and liberal ideology of the Third Republic) and the more democratic popular cultural forms with which Poulou is fascinated. A cultural antithesis is established, setting the great figures of nineteenth-century literature against the detective and adventure stories read by the child. The grandfather's appearance is itself reminiscent of Victor Hugo. The child is interested in the works of Michel Zévaco and Jules Verne. His heroic model is based on such figures as Pardaillan, Michel Strogoff, Cyrano and Arsène Lupin. Poulou's own attempts at writing are inspired by what his grandfather describes as 'mauvaises lectures'.[24] As Jacques Lecarme has stated: 'Dans *Les Mots*, c'est toute la bibliothèque de la littérature contemporaine et classique qui est mise en jeu et en cause'.[25] In this way, the political subversion of the bourgeois reader is achieved by the textual subversion of the fabric of bourgeois ideology. The 'language' of bourgeois hegemony, therefore, is systematically sabotaged in the text's foregrounding of the collision of opposing cultural forms. A revealing contrast is drawn between the vivacity of popular cinema and bourgeois theatre: the former is judged more egalitarian.[26]

It is clear that such discursive heterogeneity was central to Sartre's project; as he revealed to Simone de Beauvoir: 'J'ai voulu être littéraire pour montrer l'erreur d'être littéraire ... Je voulais qu'il y ait des sous-entendus dans chaque phrase ... par conséquent que ça frappe les gens à un niveau ou à un autre.'[27] A very tangible illustration of this can be seen in the story his grandfather tells about Verlaine, in which there is the sudden irruption of a 'vocabulaire grossier' into the highly stylised prose.[28] The disruption of linguistic registers and discursive levels is central to the creation of conflicting tones: words and phrases such as 'faire pipi', 'emmerder', 'Nom de Dieu' and 'con', perforate the linguistic restraint which is otherwise the dominant tone. The elevated literary style is undermined by its very pomposity. All of these features contribute to the disorientation of the reader.

Arguably, these aspects of the text have been neglected to a great extent, in favour of the concentration on the progressive-regressive methodology. As we find it being manipulated with ever-increasing sophistication and rigour in his essays on Baudelaire, Genet, Mallarmé, Tintoretto and Flaubert, a strictly chronological patterning is largely rejected, to be replaced by a theoretical discourse whose aim is to assess the 'global significance' of the biographical subject. Sartre attempts a 'total description' in the light of this theoretical model which is an amalgam of existentialism, Marxism, and Freudian psychoanalysis. In their study of the text, Arnold and Piriou refer to 'la totalisation que représentent *Les Mots*'.[29] According to Michael Scriven, the primary task of Sartre's biographical method is to 'capture the dialectical tension between various important moments in the life of the biographical subject in order to display the total significance of a life rather than a purely anecdotal and contingent chronological development'.[30] Although the progessive-regressive method has been dismissed as a hotch-potch of otherwise irreconcilable and inherently contradictory positions, this is to ignore that it is primarily an endeavour to legitimise the *narrative* methodology employed in the existential biographies. The promotion of this method is carried out in order to allow Sartre to reconcile his primordial concern with contingency with the narrative discourse set in train in these works. It can be seen as allowing Sartre to parry the possible accusation that the narrative discourse may involve a falsification of the contingent nature of existence. Thus Sartre is able to claim that he is being faithful to existential reality, while at the same time working out a theoretical position in which the determinisms of Marxism and Freudian psychoanalysis are not made to appear incompatible with basic existentialist propositions.

Although this question of the relationship between writing and representation is not addressed by Sartre in these terms, it may be productive to consider the progressive-regressive method as a textual strategy designed to legitimise a specific set of narrative manoeuvres rather than as an attempt to marry previously irreconcilable intellectual positions. Indeed, as Christina Howells has suggested: 'In contrast to the massive and often ponderous debate with Marx and Freud in *L'Idiot de la famille*, *Les Mots* seems flippant and even trivial'.[31] Textually, it affords Sartre the opportunity of importing a range of analytical categories to 'explain' the choices made by the biographical subject under consideration. It is outside the scope of the present discussion to query the philosophical validity of this methodology. However, it is very relevant to stress the manner in which this should be considered as a textual manoeuvre that has wide repercussions on the nature of the narrative discourse in action. In so far as the progressive-regressive method is used in *Les Mots*, its viability as a *reading* is severely limited. The Sartrean interpretative discourse, with its battery of concepts such as role-playing, 'mauvaise foi', and contingency, does not have a privileged status if viewed in strictly textual terms, because it has to compete with other codes of signification. The psychoanalytic gloss - by means of references to 'névrose', the 'sur-moi', the Oedipus complex - also seems to be parodied to a great extent and undermined as a wholly satisfactory means of psychological interpretation. The psychoanalytical is another 'code de lecture' making claims on the reader's attention, and competes not only with the existentialist and Marxist codes, but also with the complexity of responses set up by the generic expectations of a literary autobiography.

It is evident that in *Les Mots* Sartre does indeed superimpose an interpretation of events and fashions certain patternings with recourse to a number of familiar existential categories. It cannot be argued that this involves a greater falsification than other modes of organisation. The advocates of 'pure autobiography' would probably maintain that the only authentic means of autobiographical representation is one in which the memory and narrative process are deliberately exhibited as arbitrary and discontinuous. This, however, would be to propound that psychological realism is an attainable and unproblematic textual objective. Such a proposition is predicated on the view that an 'écriture' exists which expresses the self in an unproblematic way. Critically, this ignores the constructed nature of all forms of autobiographical discourse, even when they are contrived to appear fragmentary. Even an autobiography which appears to meet these criteria, such as Alain Robbe-Grillet's *Romanesques*,[32] is forced to acknowledge and indeed flaunt its status as writing. This recognition of existential concepts is crucial to the reading of *Les Mots*. Sartrean existentialist theory must be seen as one of the codes which permit the text to be read. Although Sartre has spoken of 'le grand public bourgeois' to which the work is addressed and whose values are being contested (hence the dialectical nature of the writing), it is also the case that he is addressing a certain reading community, or, rather, reading *communities* with differing intellectual and political assumptions.

Writing about Sartre's fiction in her preface to the Pléiade *Oeuvres romanesques* and in her article in the *Obliques* volume, Geneviève Idt has recourse to a Bakhtinian emphasis on the polyphonic nature of his fiction.[33] It can be contended that a similar reading can be applied to *Les Mots*. In many respects, it would be difficult to find a more appropriate example of a text that contains a multiplicity of voices and a collage of quotations. In the text, Sartre quotes widely (both explicitly and implicitly) - from the numerous references to the culture emanating from his grandfather's vast library to the popular fiction of his childhood. *Les Mots* is a text that almost demands a glossary, such are the allusions to 'high' cultural forms and to what may be termed marginal or para-literary forms, such as popular fiction, including children's adventure stories.

The child preferred narratives that were 'pré-fabriqués'.[34] As Jacques Lecarme has said: 'Il faudrait une vingtaine de pages pour rassembler et classer les références explicites'.[35] Lecarme has also detected stylistic and thematic pastiches of Gide, Giraudoux, Julien Benda, and Anotole France. Indeed, the quotation of the para-literary can be seen as a provocative strategy, in that it directs the reader to ideologically unacceptable non-canonical forms and genres, which contrast with the nineteenth-century liberal-humanist cultural ideology represented by the library. There is an allusion at one point to the 'bric-à-brac de contes noirs et d'aventures blanches',[36] which can almost be read as an example of 'mise en abîme', in the sense that we are faced with a bric-à-brac text, rather than another example of the application of the progressive-regressive method. A striking feature of *Les Mots* is the self-consciously 'anthologisable' nature of much of the writing, very much in the manner of passages for explication and commentary in a 'livre scolaire'. The language is not univocal, but rather contains multiple layers of signification. Sartre himself has spoken of the 'agaçant' aspect of the text: the formal prose is frequently punctured by vulgar 'mots crus'. Indeed, there is a reference to the opposition between 'mots crus' and 'mots couverts' within the family itself.[37] The copying of texts is itself thematised within the work at several points. The narrator explicitly links plagiarism with his 'imposture':[38] it is part of the pretence of being a writer. Such compilations of texts (including the regurgitation of passages from *Le Grand Larousse*) are described as 'ces fourre-tout'.[39]

The pseudo-commentary of Sartre's explanatory discourse is therefore only another textual layer. Competing with other modes of discourse, the totalising and teleological impetus of the text breaks down. It is the fragment which comes to predominate. Sartre's totalising intention is in short contradicted by the textual practice itself. The theoretical framework disintegrates; the 'totalisation complète' fails to materialise. It becomes important, therefore, to consider *Les Mots* in terms of the discontinuities we have been identifying: it is a text in which the 'discours' comes to attract as much attention as the autobiographical 'histoire'.

In Philippe Lejeune's masterly analysis of the narrative structure of *Les Mots*, he dismisses the *Lire/Ecrire* division in favour of five *actes* and the dialectical nature of the structure as a whole. It is his contention that the text is not chronological, but rather follows 'l'ordre logique des fondements de la névrose. C'est une genèse théorique et abstraite, une sorte de fable analytique qui déploie ... l'enchaînement rigoureux des analyes.'[40] His point is that the structure of the work is cumulative rather than successive. Lejeune's conclusion, however, is very revealing in terms of the present discussion: 'Pour l'oeuvre de Sartre, *Les Mots* sont l'oeuvre la plus "totalisante" qu'il ait jamais écrite ... Le seul à avoir réussi, par sa forme même, à totaliser une vie.'[41] This conclusion - the result of an extremely meticulous analysis - reveals the poetics-based orientation of

Lejeune's approach. In his essay, there are allusions to Gérard Genette's narratological approach in 'Discours du récit' (1972). Lejeune's whole endeavour is coloured by the narratological impetus in literary theory at that time (*Le pacte autobiographique* was published in 1975 by Seuil as part of the 'Collection Poétique'). The characteristic feature of this method is the assumption that any narrative text is capable of being 'reduced' to a totalising *schéma* of some kind. It is interesting to observe that Lejeune himself returns to the statement quoted above regarding the totalising quality of *Les Mots* in his essay devoted to the *Carnets de la drôle de guerre* in *Moi aussi* (1986). Contrasting the two autobiographical works, he describes the *Carnets* as 'un journal de recherche authentique' because 'Sartre ne connaissait pas d'avance ce que nous le voyons découvrir'; whereas *Les Mots* is a text 'fortement composé à la lumière d'une vérité acquise'. His conclusion is that 'Même si *Les Mots* sont une oeuvre plus achevée, les *Carnets* donnent peut-être une meilleure idée de ce qu'est ... la liberté'.[42]   In other words, Lejeune is valorising with some enthusiasm the apparently more existentially authentic 'carnet' form in distinction to the self-consciously literary *Les Mots*, which he still regards as a totalised work. Thus Lejeune tends to endorse the Sartrean view that the text is a further example of the progressive-regressive method.

Les Mots is an 'excessive' work in which it is the intertextual that predominates rather than the totalised. Reading the work in the light of postmodern autobiographical poetics, it becomes possible to appreciate that its potency lies in its resistance to totalisation, the manner in which it escapes the closure operated by the progressive-regressive method. Its use of parody, pastiche, quotation and self-quotation, the conflicts between the different layers of discourse, the disruption of registers, its highly problematic 'lisibilité' resulting from semantic, syntactic and narrative discontinuities place the work in a different context. As Christina Howells has argued: 'even as he rejects literature, Sartre affirms the ability of the text (and indeed the subject) to elude the totalisation threatened by his Marxist, Freudian and Structuralist opponents'.[43] Voice itself is the object of scrutiny: voices of other texts, of the discourses of bourgeois ideology. The voice of the autobiographical narrator is decentred and distanced by means of the numerous ironies which operate throughout. As we have seen, there are numerous intertextual references, pastiches, echoes and quotations. The discursive heterogeneity of the work is such that it is the mobile and plural which triumphs over the totalising straitjacket. Paradoxically, in spite of the totalising project, *Les Mots* remains closer to the contingent. The existential self emerges as a composite of texts and voices: a self composed of words.

NOTES

1   J.-P. Sartre, *Les Mots* (LM), Paris, Gallimard, 1964. All page references are to the 'Folio' edition, 1972.

2   For a discussion of the ramifications of this, see Rhiannon Goldthorpe, *La Nausée*, London, Harper-Collins Academic ('Unwin Critical Library'), 1991, pp. 52-68; 119-41.

3   For an account of the evolution of the progressive-regressive method, see Michael Scriven, *Sartre's Existential Biographies*, London, Macmillan, 1984; and Douglas Collins, *Sartre as Biographer*, Cambridge, Mass., Harvard University Press, 1980.

4   See Philippe Lejeune, 'Sartre et l'autobiographie parlée', in *Je est un autre*, Paris, Seuil, 1980. Sartre's use of the interview as an autobiographical mode is analysed in J.-P. Boulé, *Sartre médiatique*, Paris, Minard, 1993. For a discussion of the *Carnets*, see S. Doubrovsky, 'Sartre: retouches à un autoportrait', in *Autobiographiques: de Corneille à Sartre*, Paris, P.U.F., 1988, pp. 123-67; and S. Beynon John, 'Self-Image and Self-Disclosure in Sartre's Autobiographical Writings', in G. Craig and M. McGowan (eds), *Moy Qui Me Voy*, Oxford, Clarendon Press, 1989, pp. 147-67.

5   See R. Goldthorpe, op. cit.; and T. Keefe, 'The ending of Sartre's *La Nausée*', *Forum for Modern Language Studies*, 12, no. 3 (1976), pp. 217-35.

6   *Album Sartre*, text by A. Cohen-Solal, Paris, Gallimard ('Bibliothèque de la Pléiade'), 1991, p. 171.

7   Quoted in M. Contat and M. Rybalka (eds), *Les Ecrits de Sartre*, Paris, Gallimard, 1970, p. 386.

8   *Questions de Méthode* was first published in *Les Temps Modernes* in September and October 1957, then adopted (without major changes, but with the addition of a conclusion) as a kind of preface to *Critique de la raison dialectique I* (Paris, Gallimard, 1960). It has also been published as a separate volume by Gallimard ('Idées', 1967).

9   J.-P. Sartre, *Situations X*, Paris, Gallimard, 1976, p. 98. The first two volumes of *L'Idiot de la famille* were published by Gallimard in 1971.

10   A. J. Arnold and J.-P. Piriou, *Genèse et critique d'une autobiographie: 'Les Mots' de Jean-Paul Sartre*, Paris, Minard ('Archives des Lettres Modernes'), 1973, p. 5.

11   Quoted in *Les Ecrits de Sartre*, p. 386.

12   LM, p. 84.

13   LM, p. 22.

14   'L'Enfance d'un chef' is the final story in Sartre's collection, *Le Mur* (Paris, Gallimard, 1939).

15 In A. Astruc and M. Contat, *Sartre: un film*, Paris, Gallimard, 1977, p. 112.

16 J.-P. Sartre, *Qu'est-ce que la littérature?*, Paris, Gallimard, 1964. Originally published in *Situations II*, Paris, Gallimard, 1948.

17 P. Lejeune, 'L'ordre du récit dans *Les Mots* de Sartre', in *Le Pacte autobiographique*, Paris, Editions du Seuil, 1975, pp. 197-244.

18 S. de Beauvoir, *La Cérémonie des adieux, suivi de Entretiens avec Jean-Paul Sartre*, Paris, Gallimard, 1981; 'Folio' edition, 1991, p. 307.

19 Ibid., p. 306.

20 LM, p. 140.

21 Quoted in *Les Ecrits de Sartre*, p. 387.

22 *Situations X*, p. 94.

23 LM, p. 36.

24 LM, p. 124.

25 J. Lecarme, '*Les Mots* de Sartre: un cas limite de l'autobiographie', *Revue d'Histoire Littéraire de la France*, 75, 1975, pp. 1047-61; p. 1058. Geneviève Idt discusses the self-parody, in 'L'autoparodie dans *Les Mots* de Sartre', *Cahiers du 20ème siècle*, 6, 1976, pp. 55-86. P. Lejeune scrutinises the references to childhood reading in *Les Mots* in 'Les souvenirs de lectures d'enfance', in C. Burgelin (ed.), *Lectures de Sartre*, Presses Universitaires de Lyon, 1986, pp. 51-88.

26 LM, pp. 104-05.

27 *La Cérémonie des adieux*, p. 306.

28 LM, p. 132.

29 Arnold and Piriou, op. cit., p. 5.

30 M. Scriven, *Sartre's Existential Biographies*, p. 46.

31 C. Howells, *Sartre. The Necessity of Freedom*, Cambridge, Cambridge University Press, 1988, p. 180.

32 So far only two volumes of this trilogy have been published: *Le Miroir qui revient*, Paris, Editions de Minuit, 1984; and *Angélique, ou l'enchantement*, Paris, Editions de Minuit, 1987. For a discussion of the relationship between the 'nouveau roman' and Sartre, see my chapter 'The Nouveau Roman: Modernity and Postmodernity', in E. J. Smyth (ed.), *Postmodernism and Contemporary Fiction*, London, B. T. Batsford, 1991, pp. 54-73.

33 In J.-P. Sartre, *Oeuvres romanesques*, Paris, Gallimard ('Bibliothèque de la Pléiade'), 1981, pp. xv-xxxiii; and '*Les Chemins de la liberté*: les toboggans du romanesque', in *Obliques*, M. Sicard (ed.), 18-19, Paris, Editions Borderie, 1979, pp. 75-94.

34 LM, p. 43

35 J. Lecarme, op. cit., p. 1058.

36 LM, p. 130.

37   LM, p. 13.
38   LM, p. 120.
39   LM, p. 125.
40   P. Lejeune, *Le Pacte autobiographique*, p. 209.
41   Ibid., p. 243.
42   P. Lejeune, *Moi aussi*, Paris, Editions du Seuil, 1986, pp. 134-35.
43   C. Howells, op. cit., p. 193.

Sartre, Orphan Playwright: The Place of the Father in *Bariona, Les Mains sales,* and *Les Séquestrés d'Altona*

BENEDICT O'DONOHOE

The impact of Sartre's fatherlessness upon his own psyche, or personality, can be shown to be revealed through the moral and emotional attitudes of certain of his dramatic heroes. Here we shall investigate the question via Sartre's comments on his father's death and his memory in the autobiographical *Les Mots*, and then seek to interpret the legacy of this infantile bereavement by analysing the theme of the father-son relationship in three plays where it figures prominently. The plays, *Bariona* (1940), *Les Mains sales* (1948), and *Les Séquestrés d'Altona* (1960),[1] represent roughly the beginning, the middle, and the end of Sartre's playwrighting career.

Remembering his father, and his father's death in *Les Mots*, Sartre adopts a facetious and playful tone in keeping with that of the first half of the book, 'Lire', which deals with his early childhood. Yet the reader wonders whether this denotes a real insouciance on Sartre's part, or whether, on the contrary, his seeming levity enables him to disclose ironically the enormity of this event, thereby discreetly mitigating its results as he perceived them some fifty years later. His first reference to his father, Jean-Baptiste Sartre, is as one of three 'enfants du silence' of a miscalculated marriage of convenience between a country doctor and the daughter of a supposedly wealthy landowner in the Périgord. Apparently, Doctor Sartre's resentment expressed itself in sullen silence, and the unhappy Jean-Baptiste sought to escape the mute misery of his parents' relationship by going to sea, but his flight was to prove, literally, short-lived:

Jean-Baptiste voulut préparer Navale, pour voir la mer. En 1904, à Cherbourg, officier de marine et déjà rongé par les fièvres de Cochinchine, il fit la connaissance d'Anne-Marie Schweitzer, s'empara de cette grande fille délaissée, l'épousa, lui fit un enfant au galop, moi, et tenta de se réfugier dans la mort.[2]

The laconic delivery of this account scarcely disguises the momentous nature of these events for Sartre. The idea that Jean-Baptiste should 'take refuge in death', as if to have fathered Sartre were a sin to be expiated or a fate worse than death itself, is a mock-comic prelude to a trauma that had bitter-sweet consequences for the child Sartre.

However, 'Mourir n'est pas facile', Sartre continues, explaining that the ailing Jean-Baptiste then lingered for several months, cared for by his dutiful wife, Anne-Marie, and by his father, the good Doctor Sartre. Thus, whereas the imminence of death reunited Jean-Baptiste with his father, the same event separated the young Jean-Paul not only from his father but also - and this is an additional blow - from the attentions of his mother: 'Les veilles et les soucis épuisèrent Anne-Marie, son lait tarit, on me mit en nourrice non loin de là et je m'appliquai, moi aussi, à mourir: d'entérite et peut-être de ressentiment'.[3] There is a double resentment here, against mother and father, which anticipates and no doubt underpins the sense of abandonment in childhood that haunts some of Sartre's dramatic heroes, particularly Oreste in his first major play, *Les Mouches* (1943).

But for Sartre, as for Oreste, this 'délaissement' was both a bane and a blessing:

> Moi, je profitais de la situation: à l'époque, les mères nourrissaient elles-mêmes et longtemps; sans la chance de cette double agonie, j'eusse été exposé aux difficultés d'un sevrage tardif. Malade, sevré par force à neuf mois, la fièvre et l'abrutissement m'empêchèrent de sentir le dernier coup de ciseaux qui tranche les liens de la mère et de l'enfant; je plongeai dans un monde confus, peuplé d'hallucinations simples et de frustes idoles. A la mort de mon père, Anne-Marie et moi, nous nous réveillâmes d'un cauchemar commun; je guéris. Mais nous étions victimes d'un malentendu: elle retrouvait avec amour un fils qu'elle n'avait jamais quitté vraiment; je reprenais connaissance sur les genoux d'une étrangère.[4]

There are, then, several movements that are dialectical, and even contradictory, in the impact of Jean-Baptiste's death, or rather in the mature Sartre's analysis of the infant's reaction to that event. First, the resentment that Sartre alleges is ambivalent, because, as Arnould and Piriou have pointed out, 's'il en veut à sa mère de l'avoir abandonné, il ne peut pas ne pas en vouloir également à son père dont la maladie fut la principale cause de cet abandon'.[5] Second, the baby Sartre's own illness (enteritis), is perhaps the male child's confused response to the male parent, part-emulation, part-rejection (antithetical attitudes which, as we shall see, characterise the heroes of *Les Mains sales* and *Les Séquestrés d'Altona*). Third, Sartre credits his father's illness (and therefore, obliquely, his father) with having hastened the severance of the umbilical cord and yet with having, simultaneously, dulled the pain of that separation. The disadvantage of this dubious benefit, however, is that Sartre and his mother emerge from this ordeal as the 'victims of a misunderstanding', as he delicately puts it, with the result that this 'stranger' becomes in time a surrogate 'elder sister'.[6] There is a sense in which Sartre, before his second birthday, had lost not one, but both of his parents.[7]

Sartre then recalls how Anne-Marie's return to the family home with a child, but no husband, brought down greater opprobrium upon her head than if she had been an unmarried mother. She had, after all, committed a serious error of judgement and her family had been spurned: 'Mais l'insolent trépas de mon père avait désobligé les Schweitzer: il ressemblait trop à une répudiation'.[8] The unhappy Anne-Marie was regarded by her mother alternately as a parasite and as a usurper, and was treated by her father as a wayward teenager. For her child Jean-Paul, however, the effect was rather the reverse: 'La mort de Jean-Baptiste fut la grande affaire de ma vie: elle rendit ma mère à ses chaînes et me donna la liberté'.[9]

Sartre expands upon this claim, attributing his sharp sense of freedom to the absence of his father and, in effect, congratulating him for having died when he did:

> Il n'y a pas de bon père, c'est la règle; qu'on n'en tienne pas grief aux hommes mais au lien de paternité qui est pourri ... Eût-il vécu, mon père se fût couché sur moi de tout son long et m'eût écrasé. Par chance, il est mort en bas âge; ... j'ai laissé derrière moi un jeune mort qui n'eut pas le temps d'être mon père et qui pourrait être aujourd'hui mon fils. Fut-ce un mal ou un bien? Je ne sais; mais je souscris volontiers au verdict d'un éminent psychanalyste: je n'ai pas de Sur-moi.[10]

Sartre's light-hearted allusion to Freud pokes fun (and, indeed, pun) at the theory of the super-ego, and disingenuously leaves aside the pervasive influence of the maternal grandfather, Charles Schweitzer, to say nothing of the despised step-father, Joseph Mancy (of whom Sartre says, at this point, precisely nothing). Sartre caricatures the former as 'le patriarche [qui] ressemblait tant à Dieu le Père qu'on le prenait souvent pour lui'.[11] This patriarch was a largely worshipful demiurge, according to Sartre's account, because the miraculous child was not his creation, but, as it were, a pure gift from heaven:

> M'eût-il engendré, cependant, je crois bien qu'il n'eût pu s'empêcher de
> m'asservir: par habitude. Ma chance fut d'appartenir à un mort: un mort
> avait versé les quelques gouttes de sperme qui font le prix ordinaire d'un
> enfant; j'étais un fief du soleil, mon grand-père pouvait jouir de moi sans
> me posséder: je fus sa 'merveille' ... Il fut le Dieu d'Amour avec la barbe
> du père et le Sacré-Coeur du Fils.[12]

While we can perhaps understand Sartre's naïve sense of triumph at having
been spared the imposition of the super-ego, the question of whether his father's
premature death was a good or a bad thing receives no explicit answer.
Nevertheless, the manner in which he speaks of his father, although facetious,
expresses not only a gratitude (which is arguably ironic) but a kind of wistful,
even affectionate, nostalgia for the mythic being from whom he sprang. He
credits his father with having known how to die 'on time', something which, he
had argued in L'Etre et le Néant,[13] could never be done, since it is in the nature
of death to be fortuitous and absurd: 'On meurt toujours trop tôt ou trop tard', as
Inès tells Garcin in the wartime play Huis Clos.[14] Jean-Baptiste Sartre's
impeccable timing endowed his only child with the intriguing air of mourning
and mystery, while exempting him from the guilt experienced by the 'orphelin
conscient [qui] se donne tort': 'Moi, j'étais ravi: ma triste condition imposait le
respect, fondait mon importance; je comptais mon deuil au nombre de mes
vertus. Mon père avait eu la galanterie de mourir à ses torts'.[15] This flippant
self-congratulation on his orphanhood does not contradict the touching
peroration around the father whom his grandparents chose to forget, and who
had even denied Sartre 'le plaisir de faire sa connaissance': 'Aujourd'hui encore,
je m'étonne du peu que je sais sur lui. Il a aimé, pourtant, il a voulu vivre, il s'est
vu mourir; cela suffit pour faire tout un homme'.[16]

This simple but elegant tribute to his unknown father is a pre-echo of Sartre's
own epitaph in Les Mots: 'Tout un homme, fait de tous les hommes et qui les
vaut tous et que vaut n'importe qui'.[17] And it is coloured by an ineffable sense of
regret at the loss of the relationship that might have been.[18] Sartre implicitly
reproaches the Schweitzers for having witheld from him any knowledge of his
father:

> Mais de cet homme-là, personne, dans ma famille, n'a su me rendre
> curieux. Pendant plusieurs années, j'ai pu voir, au-dessus de mon lit, le
> portrait d'un petit officier aux yeux candides, au crâne rond et dégarni,
> avec de fortes moustaches: quand ma mère s'est remariée, le portrait a
> disparu.[19]

In this way, the neglect exhibited by his mother's family towards his father was compounded by the second death that they inflicted upon Jean-Baptiste by removing his portrait. Whatever memories Sartre might have had of his father as a flesh-and-blood individual were vetoed by the way in which the Schweitzers deliberately cast Jean-Baptiste into oblivion:

> s'il m'a aimé, s'il m'a pris dans ses bras, s'il a tourné vers son fils ses yeux clairs, aujourd'hui mangés, personne n'en a gardé mémoire: ce sont des peines d'amour perdues. Ce n'est même pas une ombre, pas même un regard: nous avons pesé quelque temps, lui et moi, sur la même terre, voilà tout. Plutôt que le fils d'un mort, on m'a fait entendre que j'étais l'enfant du miracle. De là vient, sans aucun doute, mon incroyable légèreté.[20]

The tone of these lines is palpably different from that of Sartre's first, seemingly disrespectful mention of the little sailor who 'made a baby at full-tilt and tried to take refuge in death'. We shall go on to show that the sadness and bereavement implicit in these later passages had already announced itself years before *Les Mots*, in a number of plays where the dramatist explores the grief of his orphanhood by making the father-son relationship the central topos of the play and by causing the mind-set, and especially the moral stance, of the central figures to hinge upon that crucial human affinity that Sartre claimed to have been spared.

In Sartre's first play, *Bariona, ou Le Fils du tonnerre*, the filial status of the eponymous hero is embedded not only in the title, but also in his very name, which Sartre chooses to reduce to the patronymic: (Simon) bar-Jonah. This son of Jonah is a leader of men, a village chief in the occupied Palestine of the Roman empire. Threatened with further exploitation - a new tax is imminent - Bariona decrees that his people should resist not by some bloody and futile rebellion, but by gradual self-extinction, by refusing to procreate: 'Or la chose était déjà telle du temps de nos pères: le village agonise depuis que les Romains sont entrés en Palestine et celui d'entre nous qui engendre est coupable car il prolonge cette agonie'.[21] Bariona urges the villagers to chant a solemn oath to this effect: 'devant le Dieu de la Vengeance et de la Colère, devant Jéhovah, je jure de ne point engendrer'.[22] As he does so, however, his own wife, Sarah, announces her pregnancy. This ill-timed news places Bariona in an impossible dilemma, for he has just sworn himself publicly to a political renunciation of paternity, taking no account of his, and his wife's, personal impulses towards parenthood. Initially, the political commitment to passive resistance commands his loyalty, and he reiterates his oath and insists upon Sarah's obedience.

Bariona's moral position is deeply ambiguous here: the political act contradicts the instinctual tendency to reproduce and perpetuate life and hope, which Sarah represents, and places him, by contrast, on the side of despair and death. The tale of the Messiah's birth, told first by the shepherds and then by the Magi, merely strengthens Bariona's resolve to hasten the Jewish extinction, the more so when a soothsayer's accurate prophecies of Jesus's mission foretell resignation, suffering and apparent defeat. Whereas Sarah and the other villagers set out for Bethlehem to adore the divine child, Bariona himself intends to take a quicker route in order to murder the Messiah and snuff out the false hopes of the Jews.

In the event, Bariona is dissuaded from this drastic course of action by reason of the heart more than by reason itself. Neither the political meanderings of the Roman functionary, Lélius, nor the more cogent philosophical and moral arguments of the Magus Balthazar (played, in the prisoner-of-war camp in which it was written, by Sartre) manage to deter him. Rather, he finds, unexpectedly, that his paternal feelings are touched when he sets eyes upon the nativity scene, in which it is above all the aspect of Joseph that holds his attention:

> La femme me tourne le dos et je ne vois pas l'enfant: il est sur ses genoux, j'imagine. Mais je vois l'homme. C'est vrai: comme il la regarde! Avec quels yeux! Que peut-il y avoir derrière ces deux yeux clairs, clairs comme deux absences dans ce visage doux et raviné? Quel espoir? Non, ce n'est pas de l'espoir. Et quels nuages d'horreur monteraient du fond de lui-même et viendraient obscurcir ces deux taches de ciel s'il me voyait étrangler son enfant? Bon, cet enfant, je ne l'ai pas vu, mais je sais déjà que je ne le toucherai pas. Pour trouver le courage d'éteindre cette jeune vie entre mes doigts, il n'aurait pas fallu l'apercevoir d'abord au fond des yeux de son père.[23]

Joseph's clear eyes are those of Jean-Baptiste Sartre: the orphan playwright evokes a scene which he cannot say took place in his own childhood, yet for which he is nostalgic. Bariona, potential father, empathises with Joseph, actual father: it is Joseph's joy that he cannot contemplate destroying, his misery that he cannot unleash, the image of life in the mirror of his eye that he cannot bear to expunge. The child is sanctified and made invulnerable because he is beheld by the eyes of his father. This look of the paternal other confers the gravity, the necessity of being that Sartre himself was denied.

It is only a matter of time before Bariona's head follows where his heart has already gone. Balthazar's philosophising about the nature of human freedom, and the Christ's (foretold) summons to assume it, reinforced by Sarah's exultation in the birth that adumbrates her own motherhood - all of these galvanise Bariona into armed resistance, rallying his villagers and calling upon them to sacrifice themselves in defence of the child now threatened by Herod's intended slaughter. At the same time, he avows his own fatherly feelings and exhorts Sarah to raise their son with the memories that Sartre himself never had:

> J'aimerais vivre et jouir de ce monde qui m'est découvert et t'aider à élever notre enfant ... Elève-le sans rien lui cacher des misères du monde et arme-le contre elles. Et je te charge d'un message pour lui. Plus tard, ... beaucoup plus tard, lorsqu'il sentira son immense solitude et son délaissement, lorsqu'il te parlera d'un certain goût de fiel qu'il aura au fond de sa bouche, dis-lui: ton père a souffert tout ce que tu souffres et il est mort dans la joie.[24]

There is a clear process of idealisation at work here, and this is not uncommon in Sartre's treatment of his dramatic heroes. Playwrights are nothing if not 'forgers of myths', as the title of one of his major lectures on the theatre declares.[25] Here the mythification is of the father, especially of the *absent* father, as hero: Bariona, like Jean-Baptiste, will be unknown to his son except through the memory of others, and it is important to him that he be remembered as an example; which suggests that the process of memorising and transmitting father to son is of real importance for the real son and author of the play, Sartre, whose own father had been consigned to oblivion. This idyllic mixture of ideal father and absent hero is poetically evoked by the 'Montreur d'images', a kind of choral commentator, a blind man who paints a purely verbal picture of the scene in the nativity stable:

> Et Joseph? Joseph, je ne le peindrai pas. Je ne montrerai qu'une ombre au fond de la grange et deux yeux brillants. Car je ne sais que dire de Joseph et Joseph ne sait que dire de lui-même. Il adore et il est heureux d'adorer et il se sent un peu en exil. Je crois qu'il souffre sans se l'avouer ... Joseph et Marie sont séparés pour toujours par cet incendie de clarté.[26]

It is not difficult to re-read these lines substituting the name Jean-Baptiste for Joseph: the shadowy figure with the bright adoring eyes, more absent than present, mute and exiled, separated eternally from his wife by the advent of the child. All of this parallels the evocation of Sartre's father in *Les Mots*, intimating that this play was, among other things, a means for Sartre to pursue that elusive image which had vanished from above his bed twenty-five years before.

In the second play to be examined, *Les Mains sales*, the theme of fatherhood is not so explicitly relevant to the action of the play as in *Bariona*, but it is scarcely less important for our understanding of the psychology of the central character, Hugo Barine. This young intellectual is a staunch party member in the state of Illyria during the Second World War. Because he wants to be involved in 'direct action', he volunteers to become secretary to the party boss, Hoederer, whom he is supposed to assassinate on the order of the party's hardliners. Once in post, however, Hugo gradually falls under the political and, more especially, the emotional influence of the older man. His wife Jessica is also drawn towards this powerful and impressive figure. At last, having passed up several opportunities to commit the assassination, Hugo shoots Hoederer only when he surprises him in an embrace with Jessica.

The nub of the plot in *Les Mains sales* is to know *why* Hugo kills Hoederer, whether out of political conviction or sexual jealousy: 'Un acte, ça va trop vite. Il sort de toi brusquement et tu ne sais pas si c'est parce que tu l'as voulu ou parce que tu n'as pas pu le retenir. Le fait est que j'ai tiré'.[27] This remark, which Hugo makes at the beginning of the play (since most of the action is presented in flashback), poses the question that is to remain unanswered. For even when he has told the whole story, he still says: 'Je ne sais pas pourquoi j'ai tué Hoederer mais je sais pourquoi j'aurais dû le tuer: parce qu'il faisait de mauvaise politique, parce qu'il mentait à ses camarades et parce qu'il risquait de pourrir le Parti'.[28] But to know what his motives ought to have been is not the same thing for Hugo as knowing what they were. We shall argue that Hugo's slaying of Hoederer is a delayed and displaced Oedipal reflex, a vicarious parricide.

Hugo has been raised in, and profoundly marked by, the stifling atmosphere of a comfortable bourgeois household, dominated by an overbearing paterfamilias (who recalls the patriarch of *Les Mots*). He bitterly remembers the struggles to give him an appetite, the indignity of being forced to swallow bull's blood and cod liver oil.[29] His revolt against his family has been both political and personal: he has subscribed to a political party representing that level of society at which hunger is a daily reality and not a luxury that has to be artificially acquired; and he has deliberately become reckless of that life which his father had striven insistently to nurture: 'Je n'ai pas envie de vivre',[30] he announces in Act I, and we see elsewhere that he *blames* his father for having given him life:

> *Karsky*: - J'ai rencontré votre père la semaine dernière. Est-ce que ça vous intéresse encore d'avoir de ses nouvelles?
> *Hugo*: - Non.
> *Karsky*: - Il est fort probable que vous porterez la responsabilité de sa mort.
> *Hugo*: - Il est à peu près certain qu'il porte la responsabilité de ma vie. Nous sommes quittes.[31]

Hugo's sardonic contempt for his own existence embraces, and is conflated with, an equally potent disdain for his father's, and this is crucial to an understanding both of the murder he commits, and of his subsequent virtual suicide. (On his release from prison, the Party, which has in the meantime adopted Hoederer's policies of accommodation with the Right, offers Hugo the chance of rehabilitation. He refuses, knowing that he will in turn be shot by the Party's executioners.)

Hugo is haunted by the childhood he loathed and by the domineering father who controlled it. He carries photographs of himself at various ages, as if to reassure himself that he has in fact grown up.[32] He studies his face in the mirror, musing upon the degree of resemblance he bears to his father.[33] Not least, he recalls with anger his father's patronising attitude towards his social conscience and consequent political commitment:

> *Hugo*: - Je n'aime pas mon père.
> *Jessica*: - On le sait.
> *Hugo*: - Il m'a dit: 'Moi aussi, dans mon temps, j'ai fait partie d'un group révolutionnaire; j'écrivais dans leur journal. Ça te passera comme ça m'a passé.'[34]

Hugo is anxious to distance and differentiate himself from the father whom he both resembles and detests. He wants to pass from intellectualism to action and to grow into a mature political commitment. It is wishful thinking on his part when he jokes with Jessica that he has a guilty secret, namely that he is not who she takes him to be:

> *Hugo*: - Je ne suis pas le fils de mon père.
> *Jessica*: - Comme ça te ferait plaisir, mon abeille. Mais ce n'est pas possible: tu lui ressembles trop.
> *Hugo*: - Ce n'est pas vrai! Jessica. Tu trouves que je lui ressemble?[35]

Hugo fears a moral more than a physical resemblance. Unlike Sartre (if he is to be believed), he has felt the weighty father crushing the life out of him, and is determined to undo the 'identification' which super-ego exacts from ego:[36] '[La jeunesse] c'est une maladie bourgeoise. (*Il rit*.) Il y en a beaucoup qui en meurent'.[37] Such cynicism discloses that there is an important sense in which Hugo's oft-repeated death wish expresses as much the will to parricide as to suicide.[38] It might almost appear to Hugo that his only possible liberation will be found in his own or his father's death (and the same unresolved Oedipal syndrome recurs in *Les Séquestrés d'Altona*).

Like the orphan playwright himself, Hugo seeks a lovable, if necessarily idealised, alternative to the unlovable real father: there is an inevitability in the fascination he will feel for Hoederer, the older man who is paternalistic but not patronising. He often addresses Hugo and Jessica as 'mes enfants', 'mon petit', and so on, but at the same time he treats them as adults: 'J'ai confiance en toi, mon petit, mais il faut que tu sois réaliste'.[39] Trust, tempered with realism, freely given: this is a new experience for the young idealist who is understandably moved by the 'density' and 'vitality' of the candid pragmatist.[40]

As Hugo's admiration for Hoederer develops into a kind of affection, so a new relationship holds out the promise of maturity for Hugo and a concomitant equality between the two men - what Jessica ironically calls 'votre amitié d'hommes'.[41] Hoederer, who claims to have gone straight from childhood to manhood,[42] offers to help Hugo make that difficult transition from youthful resentment and idealism to a mature realism. This is an essentially fatherly gesture, to bring the boy to manhood by *believing* in him, a thing which neither his own father, nor his adopted family (the Party) had ever done: 'Tu peux penser ce que tu veux de Hoederer, mais c'est un homme qui m'a fait confiance. Tout le monde ne peut pas en dire autant.'[43] This remark, which he makes to Olga, his confidante in the Party, reveals the extent of Hugo's attachment to Hoederer before the assassination.

But if he is emotionally susceptible to Hoederer, Hugo does not immediately share his political convictions, refusing to accept that accommodation and compromise are legitimate tactics in the strategic objective of bringing about a socialist regime. Hoederer's dismissal of the younger man's rigid idealism is, therefore, more hurtful to Hugo affectively than intellectually, the more so as he unwittingly uses the phrase of Hugo's father: 'C'est vrai, tu as des idées, toi. Ça te passera.'[44] This *faux pas* upsets the delicate balance of equality that had begun to establish itself between boss and secretary, and Hoederer progressively talks down to the stubborn bourgeois idealist: 'Comme tu as peur de te salir les mains. Eh bien, reste pur!'[45] Hugo's anger explodes in a petulant admission that he prefers ideas to people because he has no reason to love the latter: 'Les hommes? Pourquoi les aimerais-je? Est-ce qu'ils m'aiment?'[46] Hoederer's astute analysis of this childish misanthropy makes it clear again how important he is to Hugo's very survival: 'Les hommes, tu les détestes parce que tu te détestes toi-même; ta pureté ressemble à la mort'.[47] Once the paternal insight, the trust and affection of Hoederer are withdrawn - or felt by Hugo to have been so - the boy once more becomes volatile and dangerous. Conscious (like the young Sartre) of his lack of justification and his lightness of being, Hugo tends again towards the destruction of the surrogate father, his project sanctioned by an ideological rationale which is in fact a mere pretext.

Fathers and sons can love one another in spite of philosophical and even moral differences. Questioned by Jessica, Hoederer implies his affection for Hugo.[48] Hugo, for his part, is more explicit about his emotional dependence on Hoderer: 'je sais à présent que je ne pourrai jamais tirer sur vous parce que ... parce que je tiens à vous'.[49] Paradoxically, this strengthening bond of filial affection makes Hoederer more, not less, vulnerable to the mortal threat from

Hugo, for the younger man's whole emotional life is now at issue, and it is in this sense that Hugo's assassination of his mentor is, in the final analysis, more a crime of passion than a political act.

'Crime passionnel', in the usual acceptation of the phrase, has little meaning according to Sartre, for whom a man killing in passion does so because he believes he is within his rights: 'Car qu'est-ce que c'est que la passion? Un jaloux, par exemple, qui essaie de vider un revolver sur son rival, tue-t-il par passion? Non, il tue parce qu'il croit qu'il est dans son droit.'[50] Henri Rabi has rightly noted that 'pour la première fois, devant ce spectacle *trivial* de Jessica dans les bras du chef, Hugo se sentait une supériorité évidente. Le bon droit était de son côté. Enfin il se trouvait une raison apparemment valable d'agir.'[51] For once Hugo has, as he himself puts it, 'le plaisir de voir Hoederer déconcerté',[52] and his sudden moral ascendancy enables him to look Hoederer in the eye and to take aim without flinching. Hoederer, the admired, even beloved, father figure, is discovered to have feet of clay, to be not only amenable to the modest sexual attributes of a mere girl, but (and this is more important) apparently capable of deceiving his protégé simply to satisfy his lust. The fatherly hand extended to Hugo seems to have disguised less honourable and more selfish motives. When Hugo admits, as he analyses the assassination years later, that he was: 'Jaloux? Peut-être. Mais pas de Jessica',[53] he is alluding to, and implicitly asserting, his right to the adult, masculine affection that Hoederer had offered to him. By appearing to renege on that offer, to betray the trust of the adopted son for the surrogate father, Hoederer unleashes all the repressed hatred that Hugo feels for the real father. As he rehearses the fatal act, Hugo scornfully mimics the most paternalistic of Hoederer's promises: '"Je t'aiderai, je te ferai passer à l'âge d'homme." Que j'étais bête! Il se foutait de moi.'[54] As Pierre Verstraeten has observed, Hoederer had become an idealised incarnation of paternity, and Hugo *wants* to have shot him for political motives in order not to destroy that idyll of fatherhood.[55] In fact, it is because the adoptive father turns out (so it seems) to have been every bit as cynical and treacherous as the real father that Hugo is at last emboldened to destroy him.

Les Mains sales can be seen, therefore, both to progress from and to riposte to *Bariona, ou le Fils du tonnerre* in this respect. In the earlier play, fatherhood is vindicated and the myth of the absent but heroic father is propagated; the context is that of the Nativity, observed with the eyes of the father-to-be, for whom the son is a beloved but as yet unseen focus. In the later play, the relationship of paternity ('rotten through and through') is indicted; found guilty in the case of Hugo's father, who is physically absent throughout, yet a potent emotional presence in his son, it is temporarily redeemed in the person of Hoederer, the substitute father who completely supplants the real one, assuming the risks that that entails, and becoming the object of the child's resentment as much as of his affection. By virtue of Hoederer's betrayal (as Hugo interprets it), the myth of the father-hero is completely dissipated: Hugo's hatred of his own father is reaffirmed and he feels justified in eliminating the deceiving surrogate. Hugo's assassination of Hoederer is for him an Oedipal catharsis, achieved in the absence of the real father. The paternal optimism of *Bariona* is therefore countervailed by the filial despair of *Les Mains sales*: the paternal idyll is slain because it is fatally flawed. The father figure, Hoederer, is rendered absent (like his real counterpart) by death. The ideal father cannot bear much reality: by definition mythical, he is also by definition elsewhere.

In his last original play, *Les Séquestrés d'Altona*, Sartre returns to the father-son theme in a manner more overt, yet more complex and more intriguing than in these earlier plays. Ostensibly, the action concerns the attempts of an ageing German industrial magnate, Von Gerlach, to see his beloved elder son once more before he dies. (The father is terminally ill with cancer and intends to take his own life.) The reunion he craves is surprisingly difficult to achieve because the son in question, Frantz, has incarcerated himself in an upstairs room for the past fifteen years, since the end of the Second World War, and admits no one except his sister Leni (with whom he is having an incestuous love affair). In his self-sequestration, Frantz imagines himself making a defence of war crimes (which he and others committed in Nazi uniforms) before the tribunal of history. Von Gerlach convokes the family - Leni, his younger son Werner and Werner's wife Johanna - and asks them to swear not to leave Altona so long as Frantz is alive. Leni, sensing that, if father and son meet, some cataclysm will occur, and spying a chance to claim Frantz permanently for herself, swears Von Gerlach's oath. Werner and Johanna, by contrast, loath to surrender their freedom in this way, and hopeful of a resolution if a meeting takes place, bend their efforts towards a reunion of father and son.

This inadequate summary does not begin to do justice to the scope and complexity of *Les Séquestrés d'Altona*, but it gives some indication of the centrality of the father-son relationship to all the issues raised in the play, which include power and violence, means and ends, pragmatism and compromise versus principle and idealism, and, above all, the nature of action and the moral and existential status of the agent. Indeed, one could say that the drama appears in some degree as a kind of experiment, whose purpose is to show what becomes of these universal questions when the individual child is wholly subjugated by the male parent. For Von Gerlach is the super-ego writ large, a veritable monster of domination and control, who has imposed his will and his vision of the order of things upon his two sons (in particular) to such an extent that he has turned both of them into futile and impotent beings, a fact that the whole family acknowledges. Werner complains of having been transformed into a 'pot de fleurs'.[56] Johanna explains Frantz's resentment by the fact that he realised at an early stage that 'on lui permettait tout parce qu'il ne comptait pour rien',[57] an analysis with which Von Gerlach readily concurs. And Sartre himself pithily characterised Frantz as 'un homme voué à l'impuissance par la puissance de son père'.[58]

In the course of the play we learn that Frantz twice struggled to assert himself as a moral being independent of this father, performing (in his perception) momentous, heroic, world-changing acts in order to convince himself of his autonomy. Yet as each of these episodes (recounted in flashback) unfolds, it emerges that, despite his best efforts, Frantz's intentions were determined or distorted, his acts flawed or subverted, their consequences (for subject and object alike) altered and even reversed by the intervention at some stage of his father: 'Savez-vous ce que je me reproche: je n'ai rien fait ... Rien! Rien jamais!'[59] Since, according to the central precept of Sartre's ethics, human beings are neither more nor less than what they do, it follows that Frantz is nobody: 'Celui qui ne fait pas tout ne fait rien: je n'ai rien fait. Celui qui n'a rien fait n'est personne. Personne? (*Se désignant comme à l'appel.*) Présent!'[60] And his father ruthlessly reinforces this conclusion: 'Ta vie, ta mort, de toute façon, c'est *rien*. Tu n'es rien, tu ne fais rien, tu n'as rien fait, tu ne peux rien faire.'[61] For Sartre, Frantz's superimposed impotence and the living death to which he condemns himself for fifteen years are analogous; or, more precisely, Frantz's sequestration is a concretisation, a physical acting-out of his moral constriction.[62] Moreover, there is a logical, even a causal link between this living death of impotence and the suicide that he finally shares with his father: 'Il ne se suicide pas parce qu'il a tué ou torturé', says Sartre, 'mais parce qu'il a découvert qu'il ne peut plus rien faire. C'est son impuissance qui le tue.'[63]

In short, *Les Séquestrés d'Altona* presents a father-son dynamic that is wholly negative: the over-bearing super-ego crushes and castrates the ego of the son, coercing it into an 'identification', until at last the son revenges himself by destroying, in a sense 'assimilating', the father in his turn.[64] This necessarily entails his own destruction, since he is, in any case, a mere extension of his father: 'Vous, c'est moi', Frantz tells him.[65] Mutual annihilation is the only destiny possible for this couple united in a reciprocally aggressive symbiosis. As Michel Contat writes, in his illuminating study of this play: 'La conscience lucide de leur nullité fait de leur double suicide le seul acte que puissent encore accomplir ces deux hommes d'action. De cette façon, Frantz, dans la mort, se résorbera en son père et celui-ci aura été sa cause et son destin jusqu'au bout'.[66] Frantz, it is true, seizes the initiative by stampeding his father into a more precipitate suicide than he had planned, disconcerting the old man and thereby salvaging a scrap of autonomy at the eleventh hour. Nevertheless, this is an undeniably Pyrrhic victory, since, for Sartre, suicide is always and inescapably the most contradictory, self-deceiving and absurd of human actions.[67]

There is a progression of sorts - albeit somewhat discouraging - from the father-son relationship depicted in *Bariona*, through that found in *Les Mains sales*, and on to the one we have just discussed in *Les Séquestrés d'Altona*. In the Nativity play, fatherhood is idealised and mythified by virtue of its present and future *absence*: Joseph, the shadowy figure with the brilliant, adoring eyes, is only lightly sketched as a kind of spirit of paternal love: his child is the offspring of a greater and more perfect father, the father of fathers and of all mankind. Joseph appears as an explicit reflection of the divine super-ego, the role that all fathers, however reluctantly, inherit. Bariona himself is a father-to-be, as yet absent to the child, as the child is, and will remain, absent to him. This very absence enables him to project an heroic image for the benefit of the child to come, whose existence will (he supposes) coincide with his own disappearance. There is a parallel between Bariona's heroic self-projection and the young Sartre's imagining of his own missing father. And there is another, stronger parallel between Bariona *qua* 'son of thunder' and Jean-Paul *qua* 'miracle child', the son of nobody, the creation *ex nihilo*. If only we all created ourselves, literally, we would all be God (as Sartre defines him in *L'Etre et le Néant*), that is the being which is his own sole cause, *ens causa sui*. In which case, we would exemplify the perfection of the Father.

This idealisation of the father-son nexus in *Bariona*, made possible only by the absence of the filial factor of the equation, undergoes a reversal in the second of these three plays. In *Les Mains sales*, there is a distance between father and son, but it does not amount to a real absence - or, rather, it is a real absence mitigated by two other kinds of presence, namely inheritance and surrogacy. Because the point of view is predominantly that of the son, it is inevitable that the father be already present in him (just as Jean-Baptiste is ineradicably present in Jean-Paul). We have seen how this inheritance manifests itself in Hugo's memories of the imperious, condescending father, and in his ambivalent anxiety to resemble and not to resemble the progenitor, physically, morally or politically. Thus, his father's influence, the interiorised super-ego, conditions him, albeit by reaction against. Equally, we have seen how Hoederer becomes the surrogate father and, simultaneously, the object of an idealisation. Hugo credits him with the qualities of warmth and humanity, of density coupled with vitality, above all of understanding and generosity of spirit, all of which he found wanting in his natural father. But because it is idealised, i.e. unrealistic, Hugo's filial relationship to Hoederer founders at the first emotional disappointment. There is no logic in supposing that Hoederer's momentary surrender to the sexual advances of Jessica is in any way connected with his expressions of confidence in Hugo: they are, in fact (as we the audience know), two quite separate matters, which is why the assassination has to be explained away as a banal crime of passion: 'Je couchais avec la petite',[68] Hoederer lies with his dying breath. What has really occurred is that Hugo's overwhelmingly affective attachment to the older man has been dissolved in an irrational and childlike intuition that he has been betrayed, so that all the resentment that he feels towards his real but absent father is transferred to the idealised surrogate and discharged in the act of shooting. Unfortunately for Hugo, the extent of his identification with his fathers, real and ideal, is such that the death of Hoederer entails his own destruction. When Hugo opts to face the party's clean-up squad rather than compromise his principles, he is both dying in solidarity (emotional rather than intellectual) with his adoptive father, and justifying by self-punishment the parricide of the real father; there is a parallel to be drawn here, perhaps, with Oedipus plucking out his eyes.

In *Les Séquestrés d'Altona*, the absence and presence of father and son to each other alternate until the final apocalyptic interview in which their mutual presence leads inexorably to their mutual self-destruction. Both are victims of the dialectical father-son process (as Sartre conceives it), a dynamic that each of them had tried at different moments to arrest precisely because of its destructive force. This having proved impossible, Frantz deliberately created his own absence, both as a means of annihilating the father (whose inherent judgemental role is taken over by the tribunal of crabs), and as a means of revenging himself - the latter purpose contradicting the former, of course, since it presupposes some degree of the father's presence, a presence that obsesses Frantz in spite of himself. Equally, Frantz, though incommunicado to all but Leni, is present in his absence: a huge portrait of him dominates the living room; Von Gerlach senior sits downstairs at night and listens to the beloved son pacing the floor of his prison. This graphic representation of the radical failure of the 'lien de paternité' shows forth Sartre's most pessimistic analysis of the human relationship that he never personally experienced.

This fact possibly explains why the Von Gerlachs are victims of a failed idealisation on both parts. Like most sons, Frantz had imagined his father to be strong, powerful, and good. In the various episodes of their interaction before and after the war, he found him out to be bullying, unprincipled, potentially wicked, a fully paid-up member of the guilty generation. Worse still, Gerlach respected his son so little as to interfere in his every bid for responsibility and to transform (as he puts it himself) all his 'acts' into 'gestures'. So far from nurturing Frantz into a manager and leader, the natural heir to his industrial empire, he succeeded rather in crushing the life out of him, in turning him into a war criminal whose desperate acts of torture were displaced acts of defiance against the oppressive father:

> *Frantz*: - J'irai jusqu'au bout. Au bout du pouvoir! (*Au Père, brusquement.*) Savez-vous pourquoi?
> *Le Père*: - Oui... Une fois dans ta vie, tu as connu l'impuissance.[69]

So thorough a job has this particular super-ego done of stifling the ego that for years Frantz had experienced himself as a figment of the father's imagination more than an individual in his own right. Their shared suicide is for Frantz the culmination of what has been a living death, and at the same time the ideal consummation of their abstract relationship, an ultimate mythification that renders both of them absent:

> *Frantz*: - Je pensais: s'il trouvait moyen de la rattraper, cette image rebelle, de la reprendre en moi, de l'y résorber, il n'y aurait jamais eu que lui.
> *Le Père*: - Frantz, il n'y a jamais eu que moi.
> *Frantz*: - C'est vite dit: prouvez-le. (*Un temps.*) Tant que nous vivrons, nous serons deux ... Votre image se pulvérisera avec toutes celles qui ne sont jamais sorties de votre tête. Vous aurez été ma cause et mon destin jusqu'au bout. (*Un temps.*)
> *Le Père*: - Bien. (*Un temps.*) Je t'ai fait, je te déferai. Ma mort enveloppera la tienne et, finalement, je serai seul à mourir.[70]

The apotheosis of father and son involves the assimilation of one into the other by way of the annihilation of both.

One possible interpretation of the self-destructive resolutions of the Oedipal complex chosen by Hugo and Frantz is that the father-son bond, whatever form it appears to take, is always essentially negative: Hugo is rejected by and rejects his father; Frantz, morally castrated by his father, repudiates him in turn. This inherently flawed relationship can only be resolved by being dissolved: Hugo shoots Hoederer, Frantz accelerates Von Gerlach's suicide. But this rupture ineluctably implies the destruction of both parties: Hugo sacrifices himself, Frantz shares the fatal car ride to the 'Devil's Bridge'. The only positive picture of paternity emerges from *Bariona*, in which the idealisation process is unimpeded by any real presence.

Another possible interpretation of these catastrophic rivalries is that Sartre was, like many cradle Catholics, in thrall to Judaeo-Christian theology, according to which it appears that father and son are inseparable, and that the latter can only be legitimised in acts of self-immolation destined to placate the former. Whether we consider the Old Testament story of Abraham and Isaac, or the New Testament parable of the prodigal son, we find at the heart of them the same theme of filial submission to paternal authority, self-abnegation even to the point of self-sacrifice, the purpose of which is ultimately repossession, reappropriation or 'assimilation' of the son by the father. This theme finds its apogée, of course, in the case of Jesus himself, whose flesh-and-blood father is marginalised by the insistence upon his mother's virginity - Joseph could not even claim, like Jean-Baptiste, to have 'spilled the few drops of sperm that are the usual price of a child' - thus leaving the way clear for the Holy Spirit to perform the miraculous insemination. Here we have the circular perfection of the triune deity *qua* Father *begetting himself* as Son, in order the more completely to submit himself to his father's (i.e. his own) will. 'Let this cup pass from me', prays Jesus on the eve of his passion, 'yet not my will but thy will be done.' Here, the mysterious duality of the father and son is simultaneously asserted and transcended, as it is again when, with his last breath, Jesus cries out the terrible question: 'Father, father, why have you forsaken me?' This agonising self-doubt is re-enacted and revenged, in modern and secular mode, by the apocalyptic and self-liberating parricides and suicides of Hugo and Frantz.

Sartre's reflections upon his father in *Les Mots*, to which in conclusion we return, are more like a resurrection than a revenge, much less a parricide. Infantile resentment and facetious self-congratulation are more than counterbalanced by a sense of nostalgia for, and reconciliation with, the frank but enigmatic stranger whose portrait had for years watched over his sleep, and who, in spite of his absence, had been a 'whole' man. It is as if Sartre's anger had been exorcised by the awful self-wounding of father and son in the plays we have discussed, allowing him to play freely over the residue of relief and regret that his orphanhood bequeathed him. On the one hand, Jean-Baptiste's death left his son light and free; on the other, it deprived him of the usual *raison d'être* that legitimates the existence of the bourgeois (and no doubt of any) offspring:

> Je vécus dans le malaise: au moment où leurs cérémonies me prouvaient que rien n'existe sans raison et que chacun, du plus grand au plus petit, a sa place marquée dans l'Univers, ma raison d'être, à moi, se dérobait, je découvrais tout à coup que je comptais pour du beurre et j'avais honte de ma présence insolite dans ce monde en ordre.[71]

This is a telling piece of self-analysis, which discloses intimate emotional sources for the basic tenets of Sartrean philosophy: the contingency of the world and of ourselves in it; the sense of non-existence generating the need to create ourselves by what we do; the exhilarating and alarming sense of freedom; the necessity we encounter to invent our own values. At the same time, Sartre cannot help wondering whether he would not have been spared these intimations of absurdity and the anxiety they bring, had he only had a father:

> Un père m'eût lesté de quelques obstinations durables; ... il m'eût habité; ce respectable locataire m'eût donné du respect pour moi-même. Sur le respect j'eusse fondé mon droit de vivre. Mon géniteur eût décidé de mon avenir; polytechnicien de naissance, j'eusse été rassuré pour toujours. Mais si Jean-Baptiste avait connu ma destination, il en avait emporté le secret; ma mère se rappelait seulement qu'il avait dit: 'Mon fils n'entrera pas dans la Marine.' Faute de renseignements plus précis, personne, à

commencer par moi, ne savait ce que j'étais venu foutre sur terre. M'eût-il laissé du bien, mon enfance eût été changée; je n'écrirais pas puisque je serais un autre. Les champs et la maison renvoient au jeune héritier une image stable de lui-même; ... je n'étais maître de personne et rien ne m'appartenait ... je restais abstrait. Au propriétaire, les biens de ce monde reflètent ce qu'il est; ils m'enseignaient ce que je n'étais pas: *je n'étais pas* consistant ni permanent; *je n'étais pas* le continuateur futur de l'oeuvre paternelle, *je n'étais pas* nécessaire à la production de l'acier: en un mot, je n'avais pas d'âme.[72]

In short, the legacy of his father's non-existence was, for Sartre, a powerful sense of his own concomitant non-existence. His options appeared to be either to complete that sense of abstractness by himself retreating into death, or to assume the entire responsibility for his life. He had attempted the former as a baby, and continued to be a delicate and sickly child, reminding the grown-ups that 'j'avais pensé mourir à ma naissance'.[73] This retreat into death is the course ultimately chosen by Hugo and Frantz. Sartre himself, by contrast, opted for life, ridding himself of the paternal ghost by working through the scenarios of repression, rebellion, and self-destruction that *Les Mains sales* and *Les Séquestrés d'Altona* undoubtedly are. These are the sentiments that Sartre imagines he might have felt had his father lived, but which, paradoxically, he only feels because his father died, depriving him all at once of loving affirmation, castrating judgement, and *raison d'être*: hence the anguished obligation to be *ens causa sui*.

The mature Sartre was not so naive as to aspire to that perfected, impossible, divine status. However, he derives an affecting satisfaction from feeling able to claim, at the end of his autobiography, that he has attained at least the same measure of completeness as that which he ascribed to his late father:

Si je range l'impossible salut au magasin des accessoires, que reste-t-il? Tout un homme, fait de tous les hommes et qui les vaut tous et que vaut n'importe qui.[74]

Jean-Baptiste was also 'tout un homme'. Consciously or otherwise, Sartre's autobiographic epitaph reunites him with his father in an abstract perfection that recuperates the violent climaxes of Bariona, Hugo, and Frantz, and implies a possibility of harmony in this most fraught and dangerous of human connections - provided, always, that the son is *free*. By implication, Sartre exhorts us to *behave as if fatherless*, even if we have the mixed fortune not to be. Tragedy resides not in orphanhood, but in believing that we are any less alone, any more justified by the presence of the father. What Sartre has learned empirically is, he wants to say, generally true: fatherless or not, we are all thrown back on our own resources and inventiveness, radically alone, a prey to our inescapable freedom and, *malgré nous*, masters of our destiny.[75] To be fathered makes no difference, except insofar as it makes self-delusion, or 'mauvaise foi', about one's place in the world possible, and even likely. The trick is to be *as if fatherless* and to choose freedom and life *nevertheless*: only thus can 'n'importe qui' become 'tout un homme'.

NOTES

1   *Les Mains sales* (MS) of 1948, *Les Séquestrés d'Altona* (SA) of 1960, and *Les Mots* (LM) of 1964 are all published by Gallimard (Paris) in the NRF/'Collection blanche' series, and these are the editions to which page numbers in these notes refer. *Bariona, ou le Fils du tonnerre* was not published until 1970, in the bibliographical study, *Les Ecrits de Sartre*, edited by Michel Contat and Michel Rybalka (Paris, Gallimard), where it occupies pages 565-633.

2   *Les Mots* (LM), p. 8.

3   LM, pp. 8-9.

4   LM, p. 9.

5   A. J. Arnould and J.-P. Piriou: *Genèse et critique d'une autobiographie, Les Mots de Jean-Paul Sartre*, Paris, Minard ('Archives des Lettres Modernes'), 1973, p. 32.

6   LM, p. 13.

7   Resonances of these ambiguities can be found again in *Les Mouches*, where the ruthless Oreste murders his mother, Clytemnestre, despite the pleas of his sister, Electre, because he holds his mother truly responsible for the death of his natural father, Agamemnon.

8   LM, p. 9.

9   LM, p. 11.

10   LM, pp. 14-15.

11   LM, p. 14.

12   LM, pp. 14-15.

13   *L'Etre et le Néant*, Paris, Gallimard, 1943 (references are to the 'Collection TEL' edition of 1976), pp. 594-95.

14   In Jean-Paul Sartre, *Théâtre I*, Paris, Gallimard, 1947, p. 179.

15   LM, pp. 11-12.

16   LM, p. 12.

17   LM, p. 213.

18   This regret finds voice also in the comment Sartre makes on the relationship that might have existed between himself and God, the ultimate super-ego (LM, p. 83).

19   LM, p. 12.

20   LM, pp. 12-13.

21   *Bariona* (B), p. 579.

22   B, p. 581.

23   B, p. 620.

24   B, pp. 631-32.

25   'Forgers of Myths: the young playwrights of France' (1946), in Jean-Paul Sartre, *Un Théâtre de situations* (ed. M. Contat and M. Rybalka), Paris, Gallimard (Collection 'Idées'), 1973, pp. 56-67.

26   B, p. 617.

27   *Les Mains sales* (MS), p. 33.

28   MS, p. 256.

29   For striking parallels with Sartre's own experience, see *Les Mots*, pp. 70 ff.

30   MS, p. 44.

31   MS, p. 145.

32   MS, pp. 70-71.

33   MS, p. 42.

34   MS, pp. 42-43.

35   MS, p. 68.

36   'The basis of the process is what is called an "identification" - that is to say, the assimilation of one ego to another one, as a result of which the first ego behaves like the second in certain respects, imitates it and in a sense takes it up into itself' - Sigmund Freud, 'The Dissection of the Psychical Personality', in *New Introductory Lectures on Psychoanalysis*, Harmondsworth, Penguin ('The Pelican Freud Library', vol. 2), 1973 , p. 94.

37   MS, p. 142.

38   MS, pp. 45, 142, 228, 232.

39   MS, p. 102.

40   MS, pp. 116, 120.

41   MS, p. 137.

42   MS, p. 142.

43   MS, p. 164.

44   MS, p. 206.

45   MS, pp. 208-09.

46   MS, p. 211.

47   MS, p. 211.

48   MS, p. 220.

49   MS, p. 233.

50   'Théâtre épique et théâtre dramatique', in *Un Théâtre de situations*, p. 135.
51   Henri Rabi: 'Les thèmes majeurs du théâtre de Sartre', *Esprit*, 18, no. 10 (October 1950), p. 443.
52   MS, p. 240.
53   MS, p. 243.
54   MS, p. 240.
55   See Pierre Verstraeten: *Violence et éthique*, Paris, Gallimard, 1972, p. 96.
56   *Les Séquestrés d'Altona* (SA), p. 23. Sartre describes his own futility in the same terms (see *Les Mots*, p. 72).
57   SA, p. 56.
58   'Entretien sur *Les Séquestrés d'Altona*', in *Un Théâtre de situations*, p. 308.
59   SA, p. 172.
60   SA, p. 186.
61   SA, p. 214.
62   See *Un Théâtre de situations*, pp. 350-52.
63   Ibid., p. 352.
64   See note 36 above.
65   SA, p. 51.
66   Michel Contat, *Explication des 'Séquestrés d'Altona'*, Paris, Minard ('Archives des lettres modernes', 89), 1968 , p. 63.
67   See my article 'Sartre's Theories on Death, Murder, and Suicide', *Philosophy Today*, no. 25, 1981, pp. 334-56.
68   MS, p. 241.
69   SA, p. 205.
70   SA, pp. 217-18.
71   LM, pp. 69-70.
72   LM, pp. 70-71.
73   LM, p. 71.
74   LM, p. 213.
75   See, for example, *Un Théâtre de situations*, p. 57.

Autobiography and Biography: Simone de Beauvoir's Memoirs, Diary and Letters

TERRY KEEFE

There are at least three different forms of writing by Simone de Beauvoir about her own life: her memoirs, her diaries, and her letters to Sartre. A great deal is to be gained from an examination of some of the problems to which the co-existence of these different kinds of text gives rise, and it is of particular interest to see what emerges when we try to put all three forms together in order to make some kind of patchwork autobiography, or, indeed, to construct parts of a biography.

One fairly brief, sixteen-month period is covered in one way or another by all three major forms of writing, namely the period between Sartre's mobilisation in September 1939 and the end of January 1941, less than two months before his release from the prisoner-of-war camp in Trier in March. The simple fact is that we have three detailed accounts of her day-to-day or week-by-week life during that period written by Beauvoir herself; two written at the time and the third composed some twenty years later, with the aid of one or both of the earlier forms. However, both of the first two sets of texts are incomplete, in that some of the letters and diary-entries that Beauvoir wrote are lost, or have not been published. And while the relevant section of *La Force de l'âge* (which is the volume of her memoirs in which she deals with the period concerned)[1] cannot be said to be incomplete, when it reproduces the text of her diary it does so only on a selective basis.

Indeed, we can look first at the way in which Beauvoir uses her diary in *La Force de l'âge*. Some of the things to be said about this could have been said long ago, as soon as *La Force de l'âge* was published, but of course it has only recently become possible - since the publication of Beauvoir's *Journal de Guerre*[2] in 1990 - to look at the extracts in *La Force de l'âge* in relation to a fuller text of the diary.

In a brief preface, Beauvoir begins Part II of *La Force de l'âge* by mentioning her first novel *L'Invitée*,[3] in order to say that one does not find in its pages 'la trace des jours où je les écrivis: ni la couleur des matins et des soirs, ni les frémissements de la peur, de l'attente, rien'.[4] One might suppose, then, that this is at least part of what she wishes to convey in *La Force de l'âge*. And since within a few pages she is simply reproducing text from her war diary, this reproduction may be taken to be part of that process. On the thematic level, however, Beauvoir goes on to claim that the early years of World War II changed her attitude towards the quest for personal happiness, and, without mentioning the source, she quotes from her diary in September 1939 to confirm this.[5] She also quotes an entry from January 1941, to the effect that changes in the world have caused her to abandon almost completely her earlier idea of happiness.[6] But finally Beauvoir somewhat qualifies the view expressed in her diary in 1941 by saying that in fact she never escaped entirely from her pre-war conception of happiness.

In other words, before the beginning of the text proper of *La Force de l'âge* Part II, Beauvoir has already given her reader two indications of how to receive the diary extracts that will follow: they will convey 'la couleur des matins et des soirs ... les frémissements de la peur, de l'attente', but they also need to be seen as expressing views of twenty years before, views that can now be seen in a different perspective.

It was on 1 September 1939, when Sartre's departure for the war was imminent, that Beauvoir began keeping a war diary. She introduces the extracts from it in *La Force de l'âge* - extracts that are uninterrupted and constitute the whole text of *La Force de l'âge* for the following fifty pages - in the following way:

> Et puis un matin, la chose arriva. Alors, dans la solitude et l'angoisse, j'ai commencé à tenir un journal. Il me semble plus vivant, plus exact que le récit que j'en pourrais tirer. Le voici donc. Je me borne à en élaguer des détails oiseux, des considérations trop intimes, des rabâchages.[7]

She prefers reproducing the diary, then, to using it as the basis for telling a story ('le récit que j'en pourrais tirer'), but we are bound to be wary about the announced excising of 'des considérations trop intimes'.

There is, of course, the question of the sensitivities of others. When she published some of Sartre's letters in 1983 (more than 20 years after *La Force de l'âge*), Beauvoir said: 'Elles se rapportent à un passé récent ... pour ne pas gêner certains tiers - ou leurs proches - j'ai supprimé des passages, changé des noms'.[8] The same would apply with even greater force to *La Force de l'âge*, and it is difficult to find anything to say against Beauvoir's scruples on this count. This matter, however, overlaps awkwardly with the question of whether Beauvoir is omitting from *La Force de l'âge* intimate details of her *own* feelings and actions. One might say that every autobiographer without exception omits *some* intimate details, and that in most but not all cases this is because those details are considered, in some sense, too intimate. One could also say that at least Beauvoir is honest about what she is doing. Yet what is distinctive about this particular case is that we are for once in a position to see exactly what the autobiographer chose to omit, and to judge for ourselves what the significance of the omissions is.

Take, for instance, the case of Jacques-Laurent Bost, 'le petit Bost'. Because of the content of *L'Invitée*, it is easy to forget that the affair between Beauvoir and Bost, which began in 1937, was not public knowledge at the time of publication of *La Force de l'âge*. In fact, it was probably first revealed in print in the biography of Beauvoir by Claude Francis and Fernande Gontier in 1985.[9] In any case, for whatever reason, Beauvoir still felt obliged to hide the nature of this relationship from the reading public when she wrote *La Force de l'âge*. Hence anything in the war diary that would point to such a relationship has to be omitted from the reproduced diary in *La Force de l'âge*.

Now, this is not nearly as simple a matter as it may sound. It is not at all akin, as we might loosely suppose, to merely taking one name off a list, or to deleting particular paragraphs from a text on a word processor. First of all, Beauvoir does not wish to delete Bost from the diary altogether, so that she has to disentangle the passionate strand of her relationship with him from other strands. Secondly, there are extensive and quite complicated sets of *consequential* amendments that need to be made. Two major ones, in particular, are worth mentioning.

Beauvoir's affair with Bost had begun *after* the beginning of his relationship with Olga Kosakievicz, the third member of the notorious 'trio' that Sartre and Beauvoir tried to form in the mid-1930s. For some time, then, Beauvoir was hiding from Olga her affair with Bost. The diary makes this clear, but since *La Force de l'âge* suppresses the affair with Bost, it must *also* suppress the passages describing how she hid the affair from Olga. As a matter of fact, this is no more than the tip of an enormous iceberg, for the record of Beauvoir's relations with Olga as a whole in the diary extracts in *La Force de l'âge* is a considerable distortion, by omission, of the record of that relationship in the diary itself. The diary proper shows the Beauvoir-Olga relationship to be a very close and complex one, but very little of this is allowed to come through the extracts in *La Force de l'âge*.

This in turn is bound up with complications concerning Olga's sister Wanda.

Sartre at the time was engaged in a peculiarly intense and convoluted affair with Wanda, which again Beauvoir wants to keep out of *La Force de l'âge* (Wanda is referred to, in a distant way, as 'la soeur d'Olga'). This, too, has consequences for the sifting of material from Beauvoir's diary, since there are many passages referring to the two sisters together. The excising or pruning of these in itself impoverishes and distorts the material on Olga.

This can bring us back to Bost, for the second noteworthy feature of how he is treated in the diary extracts in *La Force de l'âge* is very similar. Quite naturally, in her diary Beauvoir very frequently refers to Sartre and Bost together: they are both away at war and she is anxious, sometimes distraught, at what may happen to them. But hiding her affair with Bost means, for her, hiding also the intensity of her worries about him. Omitting expressions of these worries, therefore, also tends to involve omitting from *La Force de l'âge* many expressions of her feelings about Sartre to be found in the diary. In one way, this may not matter too much, because there is so much *else* retained about her feelings for Sartre. Yet in another way it matters a great deal, since, according to the diary, these constant worries are a major feature of Beauvoir's state of mind during the beginning of the Phoney War, but they are not properly represented in the extracts. There is something particularly ironical about this point, for we began by noting that what Beauvoir was setting out to do in *La Force de l'âge* was to describe 'les frémissements de la peur, de l'attente'.

Moreover, there is possibly another aspect to these particular omissions and some related ones. The fact is that at many points the text of the diary shows Beauvoir to be utterly bound up with, not to say devoted to, Sartre and Bost. One does just wonder whether, in writing *La Force de l'âge* ten years after *Le Deuxième Sexe*, with a growing sense of that book's importance and impact, Beauvoir was not inclined to make her diary show her to be rather less dependent psychologically on her male companions than in fact she was at the time.

The more one thinks about this, the more complicated the matter becomes. Principally because of her anxiety about Bost and Sartre - and it has to be said that the anxiety over Bost is greater, since he seems to be in more danger - Beauvoir can be seen in her diary to undergo periods of deep depression in the early weeks of the war. Neither the depth nor the frequency of these moods can be allowed to come through in *La Force de l'âge*, for the reasons mentioned, so that this also means that Beauvoir has to suppress the ups that regularly follow the downs! Hence one really does begin to doubt whether the text of *La Force de l'âge* can sensibly be taken as an accurate record of her state of mind at the time, or of 'la couleur des matins et des soirs'. It is not enough to bury these doubts within general theoretical views on the selective nature of all autobiography. The fact is that the account in *La Force de l'âge* can be *seen* to be selective in specific ways, and yet it is given a certain spurious authenticity by the presentation of the diary entries as almost complete.

Our doubts, in any case, are greatly reinforced when we remember that Bost, Olga and Wanda are by no manner of means the only intimates of Beauvoir who have to be handled in a special way as she prunes her diary entries. Beauvoir did not, of course, wish her lesbian relationships of this period to be recorded in *La Force de l'âge*. Indeed, she seems to have continued to try to cover them up for most purposes until her death.[10] Her way of covering them up in *La Force de l'âge*, consisted in removing altogether from the text of her diary numerous references to Nathalie Sorokine and Bianca Lamblin,[11] as well as recasting other references to them and modifying whole entries where they bulked large. We may also suppose that some of the coyness that we have mentioned in Beauvoir's references to Olga in *La Force de l'âge* stems from the fact that this relationship, too, had been a sexual one at some stage. Nor is this the end of the matter, for there are evidently aspects of her long-standing relations with, for instance, Fernando Gérassi - with whom it turns out that she had some sort of affair - and Mme Morel that cause her to feel the need to excise many references to them from the diary extracts reproduced in *La Force de l'âge*.

An interesting measure of the significance of all of this relates to the fact that near the beginning of October 1939 Beauvoir made an entry in her diary that summarised the six phases that she had passed through in the five weeks since Sartre's departure - just the kind of entry, one would have thought, that would have had a very useful place in *La Force de l'âge*. However, she omits it from the extracts, almost certainly because one of the phases is based on her anguish over Bost, another on the period when she was sharing a flat with Olga ('Kos' in the diary), and another on a period spent in Quimper with Bianca. She simply cannot foreground these factors at this point, having been playing them down in the earlier entries.

Beauvoir breaks off the continuous use of extracts from her diary after her return to Paris following her clandestine visit to Sartre near the war front at the beginning of November 1939. She claims: 'De retour à Paris, j'ai continué à tenir ce journal, mais sans conviction. J'étais installée dans la guerre: la guerre s'était installée dans Paris'.[12] It is certainly true that seeing Sartre constituted some kind of watershed in her early wartime life. On her return, she is no longer anxious about him (nor anxious about Bost, for that matter), and her life does settle into a certain routine. She scarcely leaves Paris now, and this is why, when she includes two further extracts from her diary, saying, 'Dans cette existence, monotone jusqu'à l'austérité, la moindre diversion prenait une grande importance. Je détache encore de mon journal ces deux récits',[13] one of them relates to a rare trip out of Paris.

The second extract[14] is of interest in two ways. Firstly, thematically, since its subject - the way in which Colette Gibert fantasises about Louis Jouvet's feelings for her - parallels quite interestingly the mental battle between Beauvoir and

Olga over the absent Bost (which in turn, of course, underlies the ending of *L'Invitée*). And secondly, because what is presented as a single diary entry for 8 December is in fact a blending of material from that date and from the entry on 13 November. There is no great harm in this, of course, but it is another reminder of the fact that what we do *not* have in *La Force de l'âge* is entirely authentic text from Beauvoir's war diary. It can be shown that there are other examples - if fairly trivial ones - of transpositions in the quoted extracts. There are also countless examples of what are broadly stylistic changes from one text to the other, and a few cases where Beauvoir 'tidies up' events recorded in the diary, to the point of saying things about her movements in the extracts that are not literally true.

It is also the case, in general, that Beauvoir's diary between her visit to Sartre in Brumath in November 1939 and their next meeting during his leave in Paris at the beginning of February 1940 has less variety and breadth than before November. But there is nonetheless some disingenuousness about Beauvoir's comments on her diary at this juncture in *La Force de l'âge*. The fact is that her life and her diary - apart from a Christmas break, spent skiing in Megève - were utterly dominated on a day-to-day basis by her relations with Olga, Nathalie and Bianca in particular. For all of the reasons discussed earlier, it simply would not have been possible for Beauvoir, in any case, to reproduce substantial extracts from her diary to cover this period. There is, in fact, only one other extract from the period, in addition to the two just mentioned, and that is a very brief paragraph describing a rehearsal of Dullin's production of *Richard III* (that it is dated 10 January instead of 16 January should probably be ascribed to printer's error or Beauvoir's handwriting, rather than to more sinister motives!).

When, at the end of 1939, she re-read all of her diary notebooks for the first four months of the war, Beauvoir made the following comment: 'il n'y a pas grand-chose à en penser, celui de septembre est intéressant, à cause des événements, et puis il est fait soigneusement; et puis ça va en décroissant parce que ma vie est devenue si sage'.[15] Certainly changes in the diary are noticeable after November, as has been indicated, but there is another dimension to the way in which they relate to changes in the pattern of Beauvoir's life and writing, for it is at this point that something needs to be said about how Beauvoir's *Lettres à Sartre*[16] fit into this picture as a whole.

They certainly constitute, of course, the *longest* of the three records we have. The period that we are focusing on is covered in 115 pages in *La Force de l'âge*; the war diary is around 350 pages long; but there are over 540 pages of letters from Beauvoir to Sartre over the same period. Distinctions are hard to draw, but, for our present purposes, some of the material in the letters can be regarded as irrelevant, since we are homing in on the sequences where Beauvoir is recounting her day-to-day life, rather than those where she is, say, responding to points in Sartre's letters or sorting out with him questions of money and parcels to be sent. Nevertheless, the account of her life in the letters is, in general, fuller than the account in the war diary. That is to say that most commonly the letters give more detail on any particular topic than the diary.

There are some exceptions to this in the very earliest letters of the period, that is in the phase said by Beauvoir in her diary to be characterised by 'une grande horreur, une fuite vaine et perpétuelle ... Et des peurs folles.'[17] In the last letters written during this phase, just before Olga comes back to Paris to be with her, Beauvoir certainly plays down the extremes of anxiety recorded in her diary concerning the fate of Sartre and Bost. She contemplates the possibility of the deaths of Sartre and Bost, but does not mention this in her letters; nor does she repeat what appears to be a hint of suicide: 'que cette phrase puisse se dire, s'écrire: "le petit Bost est mort", ça donne envie de se sauver en criant. "Sartre est mort", je sais que cette phrase-là je ne la dirais à personne.'[18] In short, she is probably protecting Sartre from the very deepest of her depressions.

There is nothing remarkable about this, but it is worth making the point that in this particular respect the diary is richer and fuller than either the letters, where she is protecting Sartre, or *La Force de l'âge*, where she is unable to own up to the depth of her feelings about Bost and therefore omits the whole sequence. It is equally worth noting that there are some items of the latest war news recorded in the diary but not in the letters, if only because this reminds us that Beauvoir was conscious that her letters to Sartre might be censored by the army. We know, of course, that when it came to referring to Beauvoir's proposed illegal visit to Sartre near the front, they both used a code in their letters.[19]

Returning to the point that in general it is the letters that are fuller than the diary, we should perhaps pause for a moment over the quite complex implications of this. What strikes one especially is that there is rather more detail about individuals and Beauvoir's relationships in the letters than in the diary. At first, one is tempted to say that this is natural, that the people concerned are known to both of them, so that Beauvoir was bound to dwell at more length on the details in writing to Sartre. But this is based on certain presuppositions regarding what is appropriate to letters and diaries, and there are some unusual circumstances in this particular case. For one thing, Beauvoir intends from the first that Sartre shall read her diary, so that it is not altogether wrong to say that she writes it for him, or at least with him in mind: 'je tiens facilement ce journal, il est déjà très épais et je vous le ferai lire tout au long'.[20] This raises some interesting questions. We might, for instance, need to go back to the matter of her keeping things from Sartre in letters, and perhaps think, rather, in terms of her expecting to keep a few things from him just for a short time. Certainly, one major motivation behind Beauvoir's diary is the keeping of a record that Sartre will eventually be able to consult.

But there is also the curious matter of the enormous overlap between the diary and the letters. We have so far concentrated on differences, but what is most extraordinary, in the end, is that Beauvoir should have spent so much time and gone to so much trouble recording exactly the same things twice, often in exactly the same terms. She may, of course, have feared that her letters might go astray. Occasionally, she thinks this has happened, but almost always the letters turn up in the end. In any case, she never *says* that this is why she keeps a diary as well. On the other hand, to suggest that she keeps it in order to have her *own* record of the war years would be to beg a few questions, since it does not quite fit with the idea that she writes the diary in some sense for Sartre. Equally, it forces us to ask, on the literary level, what are the conventions that Beauvoir recognises and adopts when she begins keeping a diary. Is she filtering the material she includes according to certain perceived standards and traditions governing the diary form? It might actually be possible to arrive empirically at some kind of answer to this question by examining, in a broadly stylistic context, the nature of the differences between the diary and the relevant parts of the letters.[21]

On the other hand, there is some sort of cross-contamination between one genre and another. At some stages Beauvoir acknowledges that she is using pre-existing diary entries when she writes her letters. Thus, for instance, early on, immediately after saying that Sartre must read the diary, she says: 'je ne le recopie pas, mais je m'en sers en ce moment pour vous écrire afin de ne rien oublier'.[22] And later: 'Heureusement que j'ai tenu sagement mon petit carnet cette semaine avec espoir de vous le montrer: je vais donc le recopier à peu près'.[23] But later on, perhaps after Christmas 1939 in particular, for at least some of the time she undoubtedly gave first priority to her correspondence, so that one finds references in the letters to her need to catch up with entries in the diary. This is a useful reminder that, while in general a letter written under one dateline will indeed have been written on that date, some diary entries under a particular date will actually have been written much later (occasionally Beauvoir registers this fact by grouping a number of retrospective entries under a particular dateline). In any case, in view of the fact that the letters are fuller than the diary, it is now clear that we are sometimes dealing with additions to the original diary material, and sometimes with omissions from the original letter material.

The very practicalities of the writing of both letters and a diary containing much the same material are intriguing, for the actual time of day at which the writing takes place comes strongly into play. In her letters Beauvoir is often writing primarily about the events of the previous day, although on many occasions when she is writing in the middle of the day she brings events right up to date. However - perhaps, again, for reasons relating to her conception of what a diary is - she does not, as she might have done, break up her diary entries in the same way, even though we know that the actual writing process sometimes took place in the middle of the day. One imagines that it would be rare for letters - which tend, after all, to be sent off soon after they are written - to serve as a text to be copied into a diary, yet, as we have seen, this certainly happened on some occasions in Beauvoir's case. It would be interesting to know how often, and a close study of all of her explicit references to the moments when she was writing her letters and her diary might cast more light on the matter.

From Christmas 1939 onwards, the keeping of a diary looks very much like an activity secondary to Beauvoir's letter-writing. Yet we know that the whole period from November to February was dominated by the intimate relationships that she excludes from *La Force de l'âge*. (It is also marked to some extent by her work on *L'Invitée*, which for some reason she also omits from the memoirs.) The events of February 1940, in any case, bring some relationships to a head in such an extraordinary way that the consequences for Beauvoir's autobiographical writings are extreme ones.

Sartre and Beauvoir had devoted much time and thought to planning Sartre's leave in Paris, largely because it involved deceiving, in one way or another, most of the people anxious to see him - his mother, Bianca, Wanda, etc. - and involving others, like Beauvoir's sister, in the deceptions. To make matters worse, Bost was due to arrive on leave at around the same time: 'je me noie dans des combinaisons pour que ces deux permissions collent bien ensemble';[24] 'Ça va être encore compliqué à arranger tout ça, quelle vie en casse-tête'.[25] This, in turn, involved deceiving still other people, notably Olga. It is difficult to know what exactly all of the arrangements were in the end for the leave, but the flavour of the whole occasion can be gained from a brief extract from a letter where Beauvoir is doing her planning:

> Ecoutez - le petit Bost dit qu'il arrive vers mercredi, il va deux jours à Taverny, il me verra sans doute vers le vendredi; mais ce n'est pas sûr. Je préférerais de beaucoup le voir au début de sa permission, ça me serait désagréable qu'il voie Kos. avant moi, mais bien entendu je veux aussi vous voir deux jours au moins avant de vous laisser à Wanda - à la rigueur je m'accommoderais de 2 j. (en cachette) - 3 jours Wanda - 2 j. (officiels) et encore 4 j. en cachette - seulement entre cette combinaison 2-3-6 et l'autre 6-3-2 ça fait pour vous un décalage de 4 j. touchant Wanda qui peut être gênant. Pouvez-vous la laisser dans le vague?[26]

We can form the same impression from an excerpt from her diary relating to a day when Sartre's presence in Paris was actually officially known to all concerned (Beauvoir has just been listening to Olga's confidences about how another woman has thrown herself at her!):

Elle est encore là quand frappe Sorokine qui se sauve en déroute; je lui dis de revenir dans 5 mn et Kos. se sauve aussi en déroute. Bientôt Sorokine revient; elle a été à 'Mistral', elle était persuadée que je voulais lui jouer un tour; je lui explique que c'est idiot, elle me tombe passionnément dans les bras. Etreintes - elle est charmante et surtout lorsque les draps rabattus soigneusement sur elle, elle me lit tous ses papiers sur Proust, et l'art et la vie; on discute, je lui explique des choses, je suis tout en tendresse avec elle; j'aurais été prise par cette fille si seulement je m'étais un peu donnée - mais je n'ai aucune envie de me donner, je me sens même un peu noire là-dessus. Elle achève de se peigner quand Sartre vient: nouvelle déroute.[27]

Sartre's leave took place between 4 and 15 February 1940. Obviously, he and Beauvoir had no need to exchange letters during this period, and Sartre made no entries in his notebooks during his leave. Hence the only substantial record of his stay written by either of them is that offered by the entries in Beauvoir's *Journal de Guerre*. These entries - the first seven or so of which are written retrospectively at one go, as Beauvoir admits - are scarcely longer (at just over thirteen pages) than equivalent entries elsewhere, but again they are a record against which the account in *La Force de l'âge* can be compared.

This account is a very brief and revealing one. It is predictable by now that she should omit all reference to their intimate friends, and understandable that she gives half a page to their discussion of Sartre's latest ideas on morality and commitment. But it seems a little odd that she should devote the last half-page to a quotation from a subsequent letter from Sartre to Brice Parain. She describes the discussion with Parain about generations and Drieu la Rochelle that gave rise to the letter as 'assez vive',[28] but in her diary she calls it a 'conversation ennuyeuse'.[29] What is happening here is confirmed by the fact that Beauvoir ends the account of Sartre's leave in *La Force de l'âge* by reproducing a vivid and memorable entry from the diary, which describes the scene at the station with mothers, wives and girl-friends saying goodbye to their loved ones. That is, she is making retrospective selections from the events of the leave in relation to what can now, in 1960, be seen to have some historical significance. Again, this is perhaps inevitable and certainly unexceptionable in itself, but some of its interest derives once more from the point that it is based on assumptions about what is appropriate to *La Force de l'âge*. It is in this area that the debate about the significance of calling Beauvoir's volumes 'memoirs' rather than 'autobiography' might take place.

Needless to say, in *La Force de l'âge* Beauvoir also savagely prunes and plays down the account of Bost's leave in her diary and letters. Their eagerly-awaited reunion came the very day after Sartre's departure and was quite dramatic, whereas *La Force de l'âge* casually introduces the five-sentence account by saying: 'Bost vint en permission par une de ces journées glacées'.[30]

With February 1940, in any case, we begin to run into problems of a very different kind concerning Beauvoir's autobiography and biography. The precise significance of the last ten days or so of February is very difficult to establish, for no letters that Beauvoir wrote between 20 and 26 February inclusive are in the published collection. We know from her diary that she wrote to Sartre on 20, 21, 22 and 23 February, and there is no reason to suppose that she did not write on the other three days too. Furthermore, although there was irregularity in the timing of the post, it seems pretty clear that nothing from Beauvoir actually failed to reach Sartre during this time. It is curious, then, that the editor of the letters, Beauvoir's adopted daughter, Sylvie Le Bon de Beauvoir, does not draw attention to, much less explain, this gap. All the more curious as she took the trouble to point out that the lack of letters between 3 and 16 February is to be explained by Sartre's leave in Paris! Moreover, Le Bon insists in her preface to the two volumes that 'On trouvera donc ici les lettres adressées par le Castor à Sartre, depuis 1930 jusqu'en 1963, dans leur intégralité'.[31] And again 'Cette correspondance est intégrale. Les raisons qui pouvaient en 1983 justifier des coupures n'existant plus, je n'en ai pratiqué quasi aucune'[32] - although one is bound to wonder about the significance of 'quasi'. Why, then, does Le Bon not at least signal that some seven letters are missing here? The point is that these missing letters would have been of particular interest, since rather extraordinary psychological dramas were being played out during the days concerned, and we know that at least one of the unavailable letters written by Beauvoir was an extensive commentary on those events.

A few days after the end of Sartre's leave, Wanda learned of letters that Sartre had written to a young drama student, Colette Gibert, with whom he had had a brief affair in the summer of 1938 (described in graphic physical detail in his letters to Beauvoir at the time).[33] Sartre's quite remarkable reaction to Wanda's furious letter to him is revealed in his account to Beauvoir of what he has already said to Wanda and what Beauvoir must do to repair matters.[34] The letter that Sartre sent Wanda to read before posting it on to Gibert must be one of the nastiest that he ever penned: 'Je ne t'ai jamais aimée, je t'ai trouvée physiquement plaisante quoique vulgaire, mais j'ai un certain sadisme que ta vulgarité même attirait. Je n'ai jamais - et cela du premier jour - entendu avoir avec toi autre chose qu'une brève aventure ...'[35] Furthermore, a breathtakingly insensitive side to Sartre's nature continues to show itself, for he calmly tells Beauvoir that in rebutting the charge of a 'mystical' relationship with her, he has said to Wanda: 'Tu sais bien que je passerais sur le ventre de tout le monde (même du Castor malgré mon "mysticisme") pour être bien avec toi'.[36]

It is intensely frustrating, then, that the last of Beauvoir's missing letters is one dated 26 February, in which she presumably reacted to the news of what Sartre had told Wanda. He had, in any case, explicitly asked for Beauvoir's opinion on a number of points, including his womanising. We know that there was severity in Beauvoir's reply, because Sartre subsequently refers to her 'état (justifié) de sévérité envers moi',[37] and to her 'lettre sévère',[38] a phrase that Beauvoir herself uses.[39] And we can directly infer from other comments by Sartre that she strongly criticised his character and conduct, taking him to task, in particular, for the vile letter to Gibert.[40]

It is important to recognise just how unusual such a letter from Beauvoir to Sartre is. At one point he virtually quotes it - 'Ce qui m'a surtout frappé c'est ce que vous dites que je m'accorde une prépondérance sur les gens et que je trouve que ce qui est mensonge pour moi est bien une assez bonne vérité pour eux'[41] - and it is clear that the letter would risk striking a very dissonant chord indeed in what is the characteristic tone of their relationship in the rest of the published material. It even looks at one stage as if Beauvoir may have given Sartre some kind of ultimatum, for he says: 'Pour conclure, je crois que ce que vous pensez c'est 1^0 que j'ai fait vis-à-vis de Bourdin une saloperie gratuite ... - 2^0 qu'il faut désormais faire en sorte que jamais plus ces histoires ne se reproduisent dans notre vie. Est-ce ça? Je souscris à tout. Je vous promets qu'il n'y aura plus aucune histoire d'ici longtemps ...'[42] In short, the circumstances are very remarkable and extreme ones. Sartre says on 29 February: 'en ce moment je suis dans un drôle d'état, je n'ai jamais été si mal à l'aise dans ma peau depuis que j'ai été fou ... une sorte de déséquilibre affectif et moral que je n'avais pas connu depuis ma folie'.[43] It is therefore all the more striking that Sylvie Le Bon does not even note that certain letters are missing from exactly this time.

Since Le Bon's collection resumes just at the point where Sartre begins to be relieved at Beauvoir's reaction, following what appears to have been a number of harsh letters - 'J'ai votre lettre de mardi et je suis rudement soulagé. Mais il ne faut pas trop craindre que vos lettres sentent un peu bien fort le blâme, vous devez me mettre le nez dans ce que j'ai fait'[44] - one begins to wonder whether the unavailability of the letters concerned is more than a coincidence. Because the published letters already show Beauvoir criticising Sartre severely for his conduct concerning Bianca, any suppression of letters that may have taken place seems likely to be for reasons relating specifically to Sartre's relationship with Wanda. It also appears more likely to have been perpetrated by Beauvoir herself than by Sylvie Le Bon. One is bound to be struck by the parallels with rather unedifying aspects of Beauvoir's reactions near the end of Sartre's life. We need to remember, too, that Beauvoir claimed that Sartre's letters were lost, yet eventually published them; and that she frequently claimed her own were lost too; Sylvie Le Bon's account is that she found them in one of Beauvoir's cupboards, after her death, in 1986.

There are other problems about Beauvoir's texts. Her diary entries break off, in a slightly abrupt way, on the very day when Sartre sent Beauvoir the letter announcing Wanda's fury and his own desperate reaction to it. There is then a gap in the diary of about three and a half months, unaccompanied once more by any explanation by Sylvie Le Bon, who, before the only other such break, notes: 'Ce carnet s'interrompt ici'.[45] It looks, however, as if the diary may indeed have stopped at this time, for Beauvoir notes in a letter of 3 March that she is so far behind with her diary that she thinks she will stop keeping it.[46] She wants to put the time into her letter-writing. One hypothesis, then, is that the personal events of late February were exceptional and traumatic enough to cause Beauvoir to neglect her diary *and*, eventually, to destroy certain key letters. It is not quite clear what reasonable alternative explanations can be entertained.

The letters to Sartre continue until 23 March, that is until he is about to come back to Paris for his second leave. For a period, then, it is just these letters and not Beauvoir's diary that we are able to measure *La Force de l'âge* against. *La Force de l'âge*, in fact, passes from Bost's leave in mid-February to Sartre's second leave at the end of March in two brief steps, one involving some general comments on the state of the war, and the other dwelling for the first time - with material transposed from a slightly earlier period - on her relationship with Nathalie Sorokine. (At a later stage of *La Force de l'âge*, Beauvoir again elects to dwell on this relationship, perhaps largely because Sorokine is essentially youthful, lively and a relief from ominous political circumstances.) Needless to say, she feels, as ever, only able to record relations with Sorokine selectively, by omitting their intimate, sexual side. Equally, *La Force de l'âge* omits all reference to a rather dramatic visit that Beauvoir paid to Bost near the front in the middle of March, a visit that actually caused Sartre to delay his second leave a little.

A point of interest here is that as early as 1945 Beauvoir published a fictionalised version of this visit in *Le Sang des autres*. There is actually a whole story still to be told about Beauvoir's direct use of incidents from her life in her fiction. It seems that Nelson Algren, for one, never forgave her for describing their affair in such detail in *Les Mandarins*. It is quite certain, too, that some accounts of the origins of *L'Invitée* now need to be re-examined in the light of the letters and diary. If we were inclined to think, for instance, that Françoise's discovery of the illusory nature of her belief in a symbiotic relationship with Pierre ('on ne fait qu'un') stems from Beauvoir's similar disillusionment at the time of the trio with Olga, we need to think again. Beauvoir had exactly this belief (using exactly the same phrase)[47] in 1939, long after the trio with Olga. It is worth remembering that *L'Invitée* was actually dedicated to Olga, and worth taking seriously Beauvoir's reported remark to Deidre Bair: 'too many people ... entirely overlooked the fact that the most unpleasant aspects of Xavière came from my prickly relationship with Wanda'.[48] Wanda is little more than a shadowy figure in *all* of Beauvoir's autobiographical writings: it is only by doing some reading between the lines and, above all, reading Sartre's letters that one comes to see how much impact

Wanda had, indirectly, on Beauvoir's life.

From near the end of March, we do not have even Beauvoir's letters to enable us to reconstruct her life. Unfortunately, Sylvie le Bon's note after Beauvoir's letter of 23 March scarcely provides a coherent explanation of the gap:

> Ici advient une interruption de trois mois dans la correspondance. Deux raisons à cela: lettres écrites ont été perdues, et d'autre part, vu les événements, il n'était plus nécessaire ou plus possible d'écrire.[49]

It is fairly plausible that Sartre should have brought Beauvoir's letters back to Paris during his second leave and left them there, but that those written to him after his leave should have been lost during the Defeat. But Le Bon comes close to implying that Beauvoir scarcely wrote to Sartre after 23 March. In fact, she probably wrote to him daily between 9 April and the middle of June. One can directly infer from references in Sartre's own correspondence that she sent at least nearly fifty letters during this time.

Because for a period of some two and a half months we have no letters by Beauvoir, no diary, and an account in *La Force de l'âge* that understandably concentrates on the broad events of the war, we know little about Beauvoir's personal life just before the Defeat. We are, therefore, doubly unfortunate in one respect, for there is a curious replay of the earlier Wanda incident in the middle of May, when Sartre coolly announces that he has decided to marry Wanda, who may be ill:

> Je viens de lui écrire que si elle veut et si les délais ne sont pas trop longs, j'étais prêt à l'épouser pour avoir trois jours de permission. Je pense que ça ne vous sera pas agréable, bien que ce soit purement symbolique, ça fait 'engagé jusqu'au cou'. Moi ça me déplaît très fort, pas tant à cause de ça, qu'à cause de ma famille à qui je dois le cacher et qui l'apprendrait sûrement un jour. Mais je vous l'ai dit et j'y suis décidé: je veux faire tout ce que je peux pour T. à partir de maintenant. En compensation, je prendrai tout de même une petite journée pour vous voir.[50]

Again, one would have dearly loved to see Beauvoir's reply to this news. Not only is the letter not available: neither is Sartre's letter where he probably reacted to her reply. Sartre's letter to Beauvoir on 15 May is mysteriously missing from the collection that Beauvoir herself published!

But it is true that by this time personal relationships and incidents were rapidly paling into insignificance as the German army began to advance. Beauvoir again kept a diary record of her life from 9 June onwards, and this is how she introduces extracts from it in *La Force de l'âge*: 'J'ai rédigé vers la fin de juin un récit de ces journées et je le transcris, en me bornant, comme pour mon journal de guerre, à y pratiquer quelques coupures'.[51] Fascinatingly, she reminds us in *La Force de l'âge* that the diary stops between 13 and 28 June: 'J'ai à peu près raconté dans *Le Sang des autres*, en attribuant cette expérience à Hélène, comment les journées suivantes se sont passées',[52] so that we come back to the point that there really are moments of Beauvoir's life described in more detail in her fiction than in her autobiographical writings as such.

When it comes to the return to Paris, from 28 June onwards, Beauvoir again reverts to the text of her diary in *La Force de l'âge*: 'de nouveau, je préfère recopier ici le récit de ce retour, tel que je l'écrivis sur le moment'.[53] The following 14 pages or so of *La Force de l'âge* consist of continuous extracts, and this is to prove the last time that she uses her war diary in this way. All of the comments previously made about the excision of references to aspects of her personal relationships could be repeated here, but there is now an additional political dimension to her tinkering with the original text, since she is dealing with the uniquely sensitive subject of the Occupation and the reaction of French people to it. It is understandable, perhaps, that she should omit a reference to her parents' attitude towards the Germans, which rather unflatteringly shows their confusion and a touch of resignation,[54] but what is of more interest is how Beauvoir manipulates her own reactions to German soldiers and to the Occupation experience.

She does two things in particular. Firstly, she weakens or excises altogether those references to her state of mind in the earliest stages of the Occupation which indicated that she was rather excited by the experience and regarded it as something of an adventure ('Rarement j'ai passé des jours plus intéressants et forts que ces deux-là').[55] And she also quite systematically takes out of her original text those references to the German soldiers that she met and saw around her which are naturally construed as favourable, or at least as showing that she was not without sympathy for them and to some extent tried to put herself in their place:

> il y avait beaucoup de soldats tout souriants et heureux et jeunes et souvent assez beaux ... ils m'ont paru d'une autre espèce et je sentais quelle formidable aventure ça devait être pour un jeune Allemand de se trouver en France en vainqueur, d'avoir traversé indemne un mois de guerre, d'être bien vêtu, bien nourri et de se sentir d'une race élue ... Mais c'était aussi passionnément intéressant. Nulle part je n'ai senti [mieux] ce que ce pouvait être pour les Allemands que la victoire, on la touchait du doigt; chaque regard, chaque sourire, c'était la victoire, et il n'y avait pas un visage français qui ne fût une défaite vivante.[56]

She even says of certain German soldiers: 'Il faut dire qu'ils étaient beaucoup plus proches, on avait la vie mêlée à la leur, on se sentait solidaires'.[57]

However innocuous the personal reactions that Beauvoir has just been shown deleting from her diary in *La Force de l'âge*, it is clear that they would have risked clashing with the strong anti-fascist emphasis that she goes on to give as characterising her attitude from July onwards, when she stops using the text of her diary; and when, indeed, she stops keeping the diary again. She says that fascism 'contredisait toutes les valeurs sur lesquelles s'était bâtie ma vie. Et chaque jour m'apportait de fraîches raisons pour le détester.'[58] Once Beauvoir is out of the diary mode, she is able to look back, for instance, on views that she held on Jews not long before and say how inadequate they were. In many ways, then, the distinction between the diary extracts and the rest of the text of *La Force de l'âge* is a very sharp one.

She says that she stopped keeping her diary in the middle of July because she no longer had anything to say, and that reminds us that she had taken it up again with Sartre in mind: 'j'ai fait un carnet détaillé de tout ce qui m'est arrivé depuis un mois, c'est comme une grande lettre qui vous est destinée'.[59] Once regular two-way contact by letter is again established with him, she has no need of a diary and prefers to put her energy into her correspondence.

During the relatively brief period in July when accounts in letters and diary again overlap, we find similar patterns of omissions and additions to those noted before the Defeat. Perhaps unsurprisingly, the general picture is much the same as in September 1939, with Beauvoir leaving out of the letters accounts of her deepest depressions, yet adding a few personal details of other kinds in the letters. The threat of censorship - now German and not French Army censorship, of course - looms very large and many references in the diary to the war and German soldiers have to be dropped. It is interesting to recognise that such references are dropped from *La Force de l'âge* for one reason and from the letters for quite another.

Beauvoir takes up her war diary once more, beginning 'C'est une lettre que je commence pour vous - peut-être l'aurez-vous dans un an',[60] when she hears the harrowing news that Sartre is being transferred from a prisoner-of-war camp in Baccarat to one in Germany. But she does not have the courage to continue with it. There are a few more desultory, near-suicidal entries in November 1940, when Beauvoir is still out of touch with Sartre; then three from January 1941, when she is at last back in contact through brief 25-line letters on regulation German-army paper and is reading philosophy again and finishing off *L'Invitée*. Because these last letters are severely limited in form and content, they complement the sections of *La Force de l'âge* that lead up to the permanent return of Sartre to Paris in March 1941 in a fairly straightforward way, containing personal material but of a non-scandalous kind.

On the basis of our scrutiny and comparison of three forms of writing, we can end by making one or two general points about Beauvoir and the autobiographical process.

We must not neglect the full significance of the fact that we have been dealing with a case where there is earlier material that can be compared with the later memoirs. Passing over the point that the earlier material is published by someone other than the author and is therefore *potentially* pruned by two people not one, we might want to suggest that if there are those who first live their lives then write their autobiography, Beauvoir belongs to a quite different category of people, whose lives actually *consist* in large part of writing about their own lives. Yet that is not quite appropriate, in spite of the fact that Beauvoir kept a diary, on and off, from childhood onwards. She did not come to autobiography proper until the classic age of around 50, and it needs to be remembered that the 18 months or so that we have been concentrating on is entirely atypical, by virtue of the separation from Sartre. Nevertheless, the use of multiple forms of autobiography is striking. And, certainly, for a reader to use any one type of source only, in the case of Beauvoir, is to risk gaining a very limited and potentially distorted picture of her life. It is clear that *La Force de l'âge* (and indeed the later volumes of memoirs) are *so* selective in their treatment of personal relationships - and especially of sexual relationships: Beauvoir acknowledged late in her life that she wished that in her memoirs she had offered a more frank account of her sexuality - that they are very much less of a full and frank record than Beauvoir's apparent openness had long led many to suppose. It is also clear that we are dealing with a case where it is impossible to make sense of one person's autobiography without reference to the biography, or even autobiography, of someone else.

This leads back to our earlier point that both letters and diary can be seen as being written *for Sartre*. At one point in the letters Beauvoir goes so far as to say: 'Tout ce que je vis, je le vis pour vous raconter, pour que ça fasse un petit enrichissement de votre propre vie'.[61] To this degree, the key distinction between the memoirs on the one hand and both the letters to Sartre and the war diary on the other may be that the former were written for posterity rather than for Sartre. In this respect, it would be interesting to consider the place of *La Cérémonie des adieux*[62] in relation to Beauvoir's other autobiographical writings. But, in any case, some fascinating questions arise here concerning the importance of readership.

There is also the related issue of whether the deeply personal nature of much of the material of the *Journal de guerre* and the letters to Sartre may not, in the end, constitute autobiography in the fullest sense at all. Is it too simple to suggest that Beauvoir is in a sense too close to the material; that there is a certain lack of perspective, of the general kind sometimes provided, precisely, by her memoirs, for all their omissions? We noted earlier that she says she prefers to use the diary as it is rather than telling a story based on it, but at least from time to time she has a sense of the limitations of the diary procedure itself, even while she is engaged in it. As early as December 1940, we find her commenting: 'En relisant les premiers carnets j'ai compris combien on faussait le sens d'une journée en la racontant dans son présent, ce qui en fait le prix et la signification c'est souvent son rapport avec l'avenir'.[63]

Perhaps, then, some kind of combination of authentic, original, diary-type material and later comment is especially viable as autobiography. But one cannot help thinking that the style of combination in *La Force de l'âge* is unsatisfactory. What is remarkable, perhaps, is that, in spite of her opening remark on happiness, Beauvoir does not actually make retrospective or corrective comments on the diary entries that she uses. (It would be useful to compare *La Force de l'âge* and *La Force des choses*[64] in this respect, since in the latter Beauvoir uses her diary of the Algerian War, apparently in much the same way.) She seems to think that allowing the diary to speak for itself gives it a special kind of authority. Yet that authority is seriously undermined once we recognise that she tinkers with her text in order to produce the effect that she wants, or to take out effects that she does not want. More radically undermined, perhaps, than if Beauvoir had been seen to distance herself deliberately from the content.

Finally, it is certainly worth re-registering the fact that, in spite of the obvious difficulties involved, autobiographical material in Beauvoir's fiction must sometimes be acknowledged to be as telling, or as 'accurate', as material presented in non-fictional form. The notion of '*the* truth' about Beauvoir's life (or anyone else's) is undoubtedly problematical, but the fact remains that some things said about Beauvoir's life are true and others are not. It is equally evident that some things that Beauvoir herself says about her life - whether in autobiographical writings or works of fiction - are true, while others are not. The great difficulty of checking should not deter us: we can make a certain progress in distinguishing one from the other by comparing different autobiographical writings, as has been done here. We also make *some* progress with the more complicated process of interpreting omissions. At least, we are able to *locate* omissions, and while their significance will sometimes be a controversial matter, precisely nothing is gained by throwing up our hands and declaring that *all* autobiography is selective (is anyone impressed by the point that all photographs have edges?). Later in her career Beauvoir herself was a good deal more sensitive than she had been earlier to the significance of what is *not* in any given text. One of her aims in her last two works of fiction was, as ours has been here, to 'faire parler le silence'.

NOTES

1   *La Force de l'âge* (FA), Paris, Gallimard, 1960 (all page-references are to the two-volume 'Folio' edition, 1980).

2   *Journal de Guerre* (JG), Paris, Gallimard, 1990.

3   *L'Invitée*, Paris, Gallimard, 1943.

4   FA, p. 423.

5   FA, p. 424. (Beauvoir's reference is to JG, p. 54, although she does not actually quote from the diary itself, but, rather, from the reproduction of the relevant entry in *La Force de l'âge* (FA, p. 454). In the reproduction she has already amended the original entry in certain minor but not entirely insignificant ways, and, curiously, at FA, p. 424 she amends the amended entry still further!)

6   FA, p. 424. (The reference here is to JG, pp. 362-63, and the quotation incorporates only one minor amendment to the original entry.)

7   FA, p. 433.

8   *Jean-Paul Sartre. Lettres au Castor et à quelques autres* (LC), Edition établie, présentée et annotée par Simone de Beauvoir, Paris, Gallimard, 1983, two volumes; vol. I, p. 7. The manuscripts recently deposited in the Bibliothèque Nationale show that Beauvoir's cuts are in fact very extensive and often significant.

9   *Simone de Beauvoir*, Paris, Perrin, 1985.

10   Deirdre Bair, whose long biography of Beauvoir (*Simone de Beauvoir. A Biography*, Jonathan Cape, 1990) came out within weeks of the publication of Beauvoir's diary and letters, appears to have been taken in by both Beauvoir herself and the editor of the letters and diary, Beauvoir's adopted daughter, Sylvie Le Bon de Beauvoir.

11   Nathalie Sorokine is referred to as Lise Oblanoff in Beauvoir's memoirs. Bianca Lamblin, called Bianca in the memoirs but Louise Védrine in the letters, has recently published her own account of her relationship with Sartre and Beauvoir: *Mémoires d'une jeune fille dérangée*, Paris, Balland ('Le Grand Livre du Mois'), 1993.

12   FA, p. 483.

13   FA, p. 485.

14   FA, pp. 487-88.

15   JG, p. 218.

16   *Simone de Beauvoir. Lettres à Sartre* (LS), Edition présentée, établie et annotée par Sylvie Le Bon de Beauvoir, Paris, Gallimard, 1990, two volumes.

17   JG, p. 69.

18   JG, p. 27.

19   See, for instance, LS, vol. I, pp. 156-57.

20 LS, I, p. 86.

21 The status of the letters in particular has recently been discussed by Geneviève Idt and Jean-François Louette: 'Sartre et Beauvoir épistoliers en guerre: "Voilà de la lettre ou non?"', *Etudes Sartriennes 5: Itinéraires, Confrontations*, Université Paris X (RITM, 5), 1993.

22 LS, I, p. 86.

23 LS, II, p. 75.

24 JG, p. 268.

25 JG, p. 278.

26 3 February 1940; LS, II, pp. 74-75.

27 10 February 1940; JG, p. 274.

28 FA, p. 492.

29 JG, p. 273.

30 FA, p. 494.

31 LS, I, p. 10.

32 Ibid.

33 14 July 1938 onwards; LC, I, pp. 184-200.

34 23 February 1940; LC, II, pp. 88-89.

35 23 February (?) 1940; LC, II, pp. 90-92.

36 24 February 1940; LC, II, p. 94.

37 LC, II, p. 108.

38 LC, II, p. 109.

39 LS, II, p. 92.

40 28 February 1940; LC, II, p. 104.

41 LC, II, p. 110.

42 LC, II, p. 111.

43 LC, II, pp. 108-09.

44 LC, II, pp. 110-11.

45 JG, p. 351.

46 LS, II, p. 104.

47 LS, I, p. 99.

48 Bair, op. cit., p. 231.

49 LS, II, p. 151.

50 LC, II, p. 220.

51 FA, p. 501.

52 FA, p. 507.

53 FA, p. 511.

54 JG, p. 326.

55 JG, p. 315.

56 JG, pp. 317-18.

57 JG, p. 320.

58   FA, p. 526.
59   LS, II, p. 152.
60   JG, p. 355.
61   LS, I, p. 124.
62   In *La Cérémonie des adieux suivi de Entretiens avec Jean-Paul Sartre, août-septembre 1974*, Paris, Gallimard, 1981.
63   JG, p. 219.
64   Paris, Gallimard, 1962.

Daughters and Desire: Simone de Beauvoir's *Journal de Guerre*

EMMA WILSON

Simone de Beauvoir writes in *La Force de l'âge* of her desire to create a fictional self: 'je rêvais à me dédoubler, à devenir une ombre qui transpercerait les coeurs et qui les hanterait'.[1] This chapter will be concerned with doubling and duplicity, as well as with the haunting shadow of a textual Beauvoir with which readers have to contend. Toril Moi notes that 'many critics first reduce every text by Beauvoir to her own persona'.[2] But conversely it is possible to take one of Beauvoir's most personal texts and analyse its fictional construction, and its conscious creation of a narrating self. This reading will concentrate on her recently published *Journal de Guerre*,[3] not giving an overview of the text, but rather focusing specifically on the journal's description of Beauvoir's relationship with Nathalie Sorokine. Analysis of the ambiguous nature of these relations, and of Beauvoir's troubled narration of her own involvement, will lead to a broader discussion of the female-female couple in Beauvoir's texts, which has been an area of particular concern to feminist readers. Discussion will centre on how Beauvoir constructs herself with relation to a female other. In a letter of 16 October 1939 Sartre writes to Beauvoir: 'Votre histoire avec Sorokine est curieuse. Quelle part y prenez-vous?'[4] This is precisely the question that will be raised here.

Nathalie Sorokine was a student of Beauvoir's at the Lycée Molière. They met in 1938 when Sorokine was 17 and Beauvoir was 30. Sorokine is renamed Lise Oblanoff in *La Force de l'âge*, where Beauvoir describes her in the following terms: 'cette année-là, ma meilleure élève était une Russe blanche. Dix-sept ans, blonde, avec une raie au milieu qui la vieillissait, de gros souliers, des jupes très longues. Lise Oblanoff m'amusa tout de suite par son agressivité.'[5] Beauvoir details, somewhat obliquely, the circumstances in which she became increasingly intimate with Sorokine. She tells of meeting the girl on the metro station at Trocadéro, of the girl's compliments about her classes, of their repeated meetings in the metro and the gradual, insistent courting of the teacher by the pupil. Read in the context of the rest of *La Force de l'âge* this could be seen as another schoolgirl crush. Indeed in the accounts of her existence as teacher Beauvoir perpetuates an image of a heady romantic world reminiscent of Colette's *Claudine à l'école* or Leduc's *Thérèse et Isabelle*.[6] In *La Force de l'âge* Beauvoir tells of the lesbian advances made by Mme Tourmelin,[7] of the 'nombreuses flammes' she and Colette Audry inspired at the Lycée Corneille in Rouen,[8] and of her own 'grande affection' for her student Olga.[9] The *Journal de Guerre* suggests, however, that Beauvoir's relationship with Sorokine crossed the boundaries of the schoolgirl crush and it is this transgression that makes it so very interesting.

Even in *La Force de l'âge* Beauvoir registers, however implicitly, some trouble over her relationship with Lise Oblanoff. There is a tone of justification in her statements: 'j'avais le coeur vague, et la solitude me pesait: c'est pourquoi je ne résistai que mollement aux efforts que fit Lise pour s'infiltrer dans ma vie'.[10] Beauvoir's attitude to Lise here appears at best ambivalent; she analyses apparently candidly why she succumbed to Lise's affections, saying: 'le besoin qu'elle avait de moi me toucha',[11] and she goes on to illustrate very neatly the rhythm of their relationship: 'elle m'excédait, je m'irritais, elle ricanait, pour finir elle se mettait à pleurer et je me radoucissais. Elle paraissait si vulnérable que, devant elle, je me sentais tout à fait desarmée.'[12] It is this self-confessed disarming of Beauvoir which is unusual and which makes her relationship with Sorokine all the more compelling. It may also make her readers turn to her *Journal de Guerre* with increased curiosity. The *Journal de Guerre* covers the period from September 1939 to January 1941. Parts of it already appear in *La Force de l'âge*, and as an introduction to these edited sections from her journal Beauvoir writes: 'Je me borne à en élaguer des détails oiseux, des considérations trop intimes, des rabâchages'.[13] These have been saved up indeed to illuminate her posthumous existence; as Margaret Crosland puts it: 'If Beauvoir's death was an irreparable loss, these posthumous publications have allowed deeper insight into her personality and relationships'.[14] The questions addressed here will concern the deeper insights that Beauvoir's *Journal de Guerre* offers into her relationship with Sorokine, and the way in which the posthumous text allows us to re-read those that have gone before.

First of all we should consider the conditions of production and reception of the *Journal de Guerre*. Where one might think of a diary as a private document, it appears that Beauvoir's journal was intended to be read by Sartre. Margaret Crosland comments: 'even the journal was intended for him, he was its first reader'.[15] And Beauvoir embeds within her narrative the tale of its own reading (notably, for example, in the entry of 3 November 1939). She writes in the abbreviated version that appears in *La Force de l'âge*: 'Je montre mon journal à Sartre. Il me dit que je devrais développer davantage ce que je dis sur moi. J'en ai envie'.[16] Sartre is privileged as the analyst and interpreter of Beauvoir's written existence. What is telling, however, is that, although Beauvoir's journal was apparently intended for Sartre, she also wrote him copious letters that recount the same events as the diary entries, but with frequent differences. While Beauvoir is engaged in the continual textualising of her existence (she writes indeed: 'je voulais encore que ma vie fût "une belle histoire qui devenait vraie au fur et à mesure que je me la racontais"'),[17] the narrations she creates are perhaps deliberately differing and varied. It is an irony that the reader intent on finding the 'truth' behind the fictional autobiography *La Force de l'âge* should again be faced with gently divergent accounts in Beauvoir's journals and letters.[18] These posthumous texts provide us with further narrative, with new and haunting fictions of Beauvoir which tend to supersede those previously known.

The question of the journal and letters as narrative is itself relevant to the issue of Beauvoir's relations with Sorokine. In a letter of 23 December 1939 Sartre writes to Beauvoir: 'Vous m'amusez avec votre harem de femmes'.[19] Is Beauvoir's narration of her love affair with Sorokine, at least in part, aimed at exciting or intriguing the distant Sartre? This leaves aside, of course, the question of the extent of Beauvoir's involvement in, and enthusiasm for, real relations with Sorokine. Yet it seems important to discuss the impact of Sartre's reception on the texts as they stand. Beauvoir herself writes to Sartre: 'Tout ce que je vis, je le vis pour vous raconter, pour que ça fasse un petit enrichissement de votre propre vie'.[20] Whether or not there is much truth in this statement, the point that it frames Beauvoir's narration of her encounters with Sorokine is highly significant, and leads us to wonder constantly how far these intimate moments are concocted and narrated for the (voyeuristic) delectation of the male reader. And if this should be the case, what conclusions can we draw about Beauvoir's relations with other women?

We can look now in greater detail at the presence of Nathalie Sorokine within the *Journal de Guerre*, and compare some of its entries with Beauvoir's parallel letters to Sartre. The *Journal de Guerre* consists of seven notebooks in all. The first, covering the period from 1 September to 4 October 1939, contains little reference to Sorokine who was working as an au pair in the Pyrenees at the time; Beauvoir merely charts the receipt and writing of letters. It is in the second notebook, covering the period from 5 October to 14 November 1939, that the narration of Sorokine's relations with Beauvoir starts in earnest. Beauvoir begins painstaking accounts of her own feelings and of the role she was apparently being led to play. These initiatory encounters are particularly interesting both for their immediacy, and for the intellectual analysis that Beauvoir immediately offers.

Sorokine returned to Paris on 9 October 1939 and went to see Beauvoir at about 5 pm. They go out for a glass of wine, and in her journal Beauvoir tells how: 'elle me prend le bras d'un geste gauche et plaisant, mais je reste embarrassée sans savoir quoi lui dire'.[21] The anecdote is related in almost the same words in a letter to Sartre written later the same evening, yet in the letter Beauvoir goes further, analysing her experience and dwelling on the ambiguity of the situation. She writes: 'je me fais l'effet d'un séducteur embarrassé devant une jeune vierge, mystérieuse comme toutes les vierges; seulement le séducteur a du moins une consigne claire qui est de séduire et de percer le mystère, si j'ose dire - tandis que moi, c'est moi qui suis en même temps la proie, c'est une situation des plus incommodes et exclusivement reservée aux pièges'.[22] It seems possible to argue that Beauvoir was drawn precisely to the difficulty of the situation. Her diary entries and letters which follow appear to rehearse the problem of being a woman caught between the roles of subject and object of desire. Over and over again Beauvoir stresses the trouble her relations with Sorokine cause her, yet she seems reluctant to abandon them.

An equivalent double-bind may be perceived in Beauvoir's attitude to physical passion with women. A sexual relationship of a kind begins between the two women on 11 October 1939, Beauvoir writes in her journal: 'elle s'est écroulée dans mes bras comme en juillet et on a échangé des baisers passionnés; il m'a semblé qu'elle cherchait des caresses précises, je lui en ai fait quelques-unes'.[23] The same appears to happen on 12 October 1939, when Beauvoir writes: 'Je m'assieds à côté d'elle sur le lit, et la console, et tout de suite, étreintes, baisers passionnés'.[24] These blow-by-blow accounts are hardly erotic, yet Beauvoir reveals some warmer feelings when she describes Sorokine as 'charmante, souvent avide et nerveuse, mais si plaisante dans la tendresse';[25] when she writes to Sartre of 'des moments de tendresse noyée et plaisante';[26] and when she admits in her journal: 'je me sens vraiment tendre pour elle'.[27] Beauvoir confesses to Sartre: 'elle est charmante quand elle est comme ça, le visage tout transfiguré, et enfantine, et pathétique, et tout et tout'.[28] Beauvoir seems drawn to Sorokine's vulnerability and dependence, yet simultaneously to shy away from responsibility. Her detachment is emphatically expressed as she states: 'je ne sais que faire et je suis emmerdée',[29] and writes to Sartre: 'me voilà embringuée dans une histoire et comme elle a l'air exigeante et autoritaire comme tout, ça m'ennuie assez'.[30] And in this letter to Sartre she adds a detail (significantly?) absent from her journal: 'Naturellement, pour moi, j'étais un morceau de bois, je serai un être asexué à la fin de la guerre'.[31]

As the second notebook continues, Beauvoir's stated lack of desire becomes more questionable. On 14 October 1939 they again spend the evening together and Beauvoir writes in her journal: 'pour la première fois elle accepte une complicité tendre avec moi',[32] and in her letter to Sartre the next day she details what she finds attractive in Sorokine: 'une manière de me toucher furtivement la main, de tendre la joue'.[33] Beauvoir seems particularly taken with Sorokine's childlike qualities: her tartan hair ribbon, her 'air d'une petite fille trop poussée'.[34] Repeatedly she stresses Sorokine's tenderness, her charm, yet their relations remain troubled and begin to take on a pattern of rejection, tears and reconciliation.

Beauvoir sets limits on the relationship which Sorokine resents. She writes for example: 'Elle pleure quand je dis que je la verrai seulement deux fois par semaine'.[35] Beauvoir's position appears entirely ambiguous, as she herself is ready to admit. She notes in her journal: 'je suis bien gentille, mais dans l'ensemble, la pauvre chienne, je ne la traite pas trop bien',[36] and this analysis is nuanced two days later when she writes: 'je suis gentille avec elle autant que je peux'.[37] Beauvoir constructs a scenario where she bestows affection and where Sorokine, 'revendicante comme toujours',[38] always asks for more. And this analysis of events is accepted by commentators on the relationship.[39] Margaret Crosland describes Sorokine as 'troublesome' and 'unpredictable';[40] Deirdre Bair speaks of her invading Beauvoir's life and writes: 'she became moody and threw tantrums, then clung like a barnacle'.[41] Bair goes on to quote Beauvoir in interview: 'Natasha was so charged with emotion that one had to be careful with her. One had to be on guard, because she had a tendency to consume people. She was like violent, destructive weather: beautiful to look at if you were not subject to it, leaving horrible destruction and desecration in its wake. Still, I liked her very much. She was a very good friend to me. I just had to be careful to keep our friendship under my control.'[42]

It can be argued, however, that the relationship with Sorokine continually slips out of Beauvoir's control; and this, indeed, makes Beauvoir's journal all the more interesting to read, since the text of order, veracity and control is cross-cut with anxiety, indecision and desire. In fact, one might wonder if this is not precisely the qualm Beauvoir has on re-reading the first three notebooks of her journal at the end of December 1939. She writes at the beginning of the fourth: 'En relisant les premiers carnets j'ai compris combien on faussait le sens d'une journée en la racontant dans son présent, ce qui en fait le prix et la signification c'est souvent son rapport à l'avenir'.[43] Beauvoir's words here appear to invert the opening lines of Sartre's *La Nausée*: 'Le mieux serait d'écrire les événements au jour le jour. Tenir un journal pour y voir clair.'[44]

In this way Beauvoir registers dissatisfaction with the genre of the 'journal intime' as such. Philippe Lejeune specifies that an autobiography differs from a 'journal intime' in terms of the 'perspective rétrospective du récit'.[45] And although she writes a daily journal Beauvoir manifestly favours this retrospective perspective. As Terry Keefe shows in his article 'Simone de Beauvoir's Second Look at Her Life', in *Tout Compte fait* Beauvoir seeks a new perspective even on the memoirs she had already written, since 'aspects of her past took on greater significance to her when she was no longer trying to re-live or re-create it, but deliberately reflecting upon it'.[46] Beauvoir rejects the unguarded immediacy of diary writing. As she re-reads her journal, we might diagnose a telling reluctance on Beauvoir's part to see clearly into her own relations with Sorokine.

These become more complex, and Beauvoir's feelings more complicated, in the third and fourth notebooks. The third covers the period from 15 November to 25 December 1939 and contains the most extensive references to Sorokine. In the very first entry Beauvoir writes: 'je m'y attache de plus en plus'.[47] This growing attachment becomes evident to Sartre also, who gives his blessing in several letters written in December. He writes: 'Je suis heureux que vous vous attachiez à Sorokine';[48] 'j'aime bien vos rapports avec Sorokine';[49] and 'je vous encourage fort à bien aimer votre petite Sorokine, qui est toute charmante'.[50] In this period Beauvoir and Sorokine kiss, argue, make it up, Sorokine brings Beauvoir 'bouchées au chocolat' and caramels. Beauvoir is sometimes cold and shuts Sorokine out: 'Je la laisse mijoter', but then: 'Au bout d'un moment je pense comme elle sera triste si elle part vraiment, et j'ai honte, j'ouvre la porte et je lui dis d'un ton bourru de remonter'; and 'la séance de baisers'[51] begins again.

There appears to be a continual contest in Beauvoir as to how far she will concede to what she constructs as Sorokine's desire. While on 6 December she writes: 'je suis émue de Sorokine et j'essaie d'être la plus gentille possible',[52] on 7 December she attempts again to retain control and writes: 'elle me dit qu'elle est si contente parce que ça a fait tant de progrès entre nous en 3 mois; mais quand je dis que c'est à son maximum, elle proteste, elle attend encore plus'.[53] In a letter of the same evening Beauvoir expresses her troubled state to Sartre, saying: 'Que ferai-je d'elle? Je ne sais.'[54] And she develops the problem further a week later when she writes again to Sartre: 'Il n'y a rien à faire, elle veut coucher avec moi', and continues: 'Il faudra coucher avec elle. Que faire? je suis bien ennuyée et assez fort prise par cette petite personne - mais quoi?'[55] The impersonal imperative gives way to a more perplexed and then confessional tone. The controlled and controlling Beauvoir admits to being 'assez fort prise' by Sorokine. And in the next week, in her journal, she gives way to a cautious fantasy about a fullblooded relationship with her: 'j'ai presque envie d'une vraie histoire avec elle; toute la soirée je repense légèrement à sa tendresse charmante',[56] and the next day she says: 'j'ai un peu envie d'une passion avec elle, d'une histoire avec elle parce qu'elle me charme tout à fait'.[57] To Sartre she writes: 'je l'aime de plus en plus - je suis tentée de faire de la passion avec elle, de la voir un peu beaucoup, etc. Mais je ne sais si je céderai.'[58]

Beauvoir seems to make a conscious decision to succumb in the following January as we discover in the fourth notebook, which covers the period from 26 December 1939 to 19 January 1940. In early January Beauvoir comes to admit: 'moi je veux bien pousser les choses'.[59] That night she describes the experience of holding Sorokine naked in her arms and her letter to Sartre the next day is notably ambiguous; she claims to have slept with Sorokine 'sans aucun désir, mais par scrupule',[60] yet she comments, too: 'moi, j'étais charmée d'elle, vraiment je l'aime beaucoup'.[61] Beauvoir is caught indeed in a double-bind of conflicting passions. She at once lives out a relationship with Sorokine, whilst simultaneously denying any desiring involvement. On 13 January she returns to the question of who is seducing whom, as she says: 'j'ai absolument l'idée d'une "initiation", ce qui me ferait honte si je n'étais profondément prise dans l'instant'.[62] She describes herself again as bound up in the situation and speaks also of 'nouvelles étreintes, et avec réciprocité'.[63] Throughout this month Beauvoir's involvement and interest seem at their most intense. She admits to 'un goût vif pour son corps'[64] in a letter to Sartre, and while she seems still to refuse to acknowledge desire for Sorokine, she notes in the fifth notebook: 'elle me plaît physiquement de plus en plus'.[65]

Yet this fifth notebook, covering the period 20 January to 23 February 1940, begins to show a slight decrease in interest in Sorokine. Instrumental in this might be the return of Sartre on leave in February 1940. Beauvoir notes on 11 February: 'Ça me fait un peu étrange de retrouver un amour plein',[66] and speaking here of her female lovers Sorokine and Louise Védrine, she says: 'je ne comptais pas au besoin qu'elles ont de moi'.[67] Beauvoir here quickly rejects her own growing desire and involvement and denies the 'réciprocité' she herself had described the month before.

Tantalisingly the journal breaks off between March and June 1940. The sixth notebook covers the period from 9 June to 18 July. Here Beauvoir appears for the most part to feel invaded by Sorokine, who has been staying with her. Beauvoir complains about not getting enough sleep with Sorokine in her bed; she craves solitude and despairs at Sorokine's continued presence. In the seventh notebook, which is only very brief, although it covers the period from 20 September 1940 to 29 January 1941, Sorokine is not mentioned. Beauvoir in *La Force de l'âge* and Deirdre Bair in her extensive biography both follow through the end of Beauvoir's relations with Sorokine and describe the vestiges of friendship which remained between them. This is not our concern here, for our central argument relates not to what really happened between them (who desired whom? who seduced whom? was Beauvoir a lesbian?). What is far more relevant is the specificity of the text Beauvoir has produced in writing her journal and the questions of sexual identity that it would seem to raise.[68]

We prefaced our reading of the *Journal de Guerre* with a reminder that it was intended to be read by Sartre and it is, paradoxically, with reference to the figure of Sartre that we may come to a better understanding of the roles Beauvoir plays in her relations with Sorokine. 'Paradoxically', because these events were taking place, for the majority of the time, in Sartre's absence and, moreover, he had thus far never met Sorokine. Although the two were later to sleep together, at this time Sorokine seems to have felt herself very much Sartre's rival.

So did Beauvoir replace Sartre with Sorokine? Did Sorokine become the 'petit compagnon'[69] Sartre envisaged for Beauvoir? Was she the replacement to be sacrificed at the end of the war?[70] For the most part this is not the case. Sorokine played a very different role for Beauvoir: it seems that she played Simone to Beauvoir's Sartre. And to substantiate this point of view we may refer to Michèle Le Doeuff's reading of *Le Deuxième Sexe* in *L'Etude et le rouet* before returning to look in further detail at Beauvoir's journals.

In the second part of *L'Etude et le rouet*, Le Doeuff tackles the issue of self and other in *Le Deuxième Sexe*. She notes: 'l'homme est le Même, la femme est l'Autre',[71] and she shows how Beauvoir, whilst conceding this point, would also seem to challenge its immutability. As Le Doeuff says: 'elle réintroduit un élément qui rouvre l'espace d'un problème - la réciprocité'.[72] Reciprocity undermines the hierarchical dualism of self and other. But Le Doeuff continues on a more negative note saying: 'entre les sexes cette réciprocité n'a pas été posée, parce que les femmes n'ont pas (encore) rendu la pareille à ceux qui les posent en Autres'.[73] Le Doeuff reveals that Beauvoir's contribution to the question is in expanding the concept of alterity; as she says: 'Pour tel groupe, tel autre est l'Autre', and '[Beauvoir] pluralise patiemment cette catégorie monolithique de "l'Autre"'.[74]

It seems possible to argue that Beauvoir created, at least in her journal, an alternative relation of female self and female other. Elizabeth Fallaize argues that this is the case in *Le Sang des autres* also and writes most persuasively: 'In so far as the Blomart-Hélène relationship has an autobiographical base, it echoes the structure not of the Beauvoir-Sartre model but of the encounter which Beauvoir had during Sartre's absence with Nathalie Sorokine, to whom the novel is dedicated'.[75] Fallaize goes on to show how Beauvoir allowed her fictional self to adopt the male subject position: 'Given that Sartre was largely absent from Paris during the period to which this novel essentially relates, and that the pattern of pursuit and flight was actually enacted between Beauvoir and another woman, it becomes apparent how Beauvoir was able for once to eject the ubiquitous Sartre-model male from her fiction and create a male figure in whom her own experience was partly embodied'.[76]

The evidence of the *Journal de Guerre* shows further, I think, that Beauvoir wanted not only to eject the Sartre-model male, but to usurp his position as well. The similarity of Sorokine's relation to Beauvoir and Beauvoir's to Sartre is quite striking. A pertinent example in this context is that of the keeping of a journal. Where Beauvoir kept the journal ostensibly for Sartre, she notes of Sorokine: 'Elle sort un petit carnet où elle note ce qu'elle a à me raconter et à me dire et elle me raconte sa vie'.[77] Beauvoir seems touched by Sorokine's offering up of the details of her life. She likes, too, Sorokine's evident interest in her own journal: 'De mon côté je lui lis des passages de ce carnet, et je suis touchée de voir à quel point elle s'intéresse, à quel point elle cherche à me connaître moi, dans mon intimité, et pas seulement en tant qu'objet qu'elle aime'.[78] She comments on this in a letter to Sartre the next day (21 December 1939) saying: 'comme vous disiez de vous et Wanda, W. vous aime parce que c'est vous - et Sorokine, moi'.[79] In February 1940, when Sartre is with her in Paris, Beauvoir writes: 'on cause tendrement, plaisamment sur Sorokine, Védrine, Wanda, etc.'.[80] Sartre and Beauvoir chat about their mistresses together. A female lover gives Beauvoir access to identity as male self rather than female other.[81] What we may go on to discuss here is the way in which this construction of lesbian relations would appear to be problematic, both to Beauvoir herself and to her readers.

Throughout our reading of the *Journal de Guerre* we have stressed the trouble that relations with Sorokine gave Beauvoir. This trouble was not merely caused by the fact that Sorokine was probably difficult and demanding, but also as a result of the very ambivalent position in which Beauvoir found herself. Indeed, Beauvoir's ambivalent attitude to lesbianism itself is felt very strongly in her chapter within *Le Deuxième Sexe*. 'La Lesbienne' is in some ways very inspiring. Beauvoir speaks of lesbianism as 'une attitude choisie en situation, c'est-à-dire à la fois motivée et librement adoptée'.[82] She denies the idea of a 'destin anatomique',[83] and addresses instead the issue of women contesting their role as object with regard to a male subject. As her argument becomes more detailed, and more specific, comparison with the *Journal de Guerre* becomes more telling. Beauvoir concentrates first on adolescence, claiming that the female body is frequently an object of desire for the female adolescent. She writes that '[amours saphiques] apparaissent souvent chez l'adolescente comme un ersatz des relations hétérosexuelles',[84] and she adds 'c'est une étape, un apprentissage'.[85] With her thoughts of initiation and seduction, this indeed appears to be how she constructs her relations with Sorokine in the *Journal de Guerre*.

However, as she continues her argument in 'La Lesbienne', Beauvoir comes to reject her idea of a continuum between homosexual and heterosexual relations and to maintain absolute difference between the two. She creates images of lesbian relations dependent on doubles and mirroring: 'c'est seulement quand ses doigts modèlent le corps d'une femme dont les doigts modèlent son corps que le miracle du miroir s'achève'.[86] She continues in this slightly idealistic vein: 'Entre femmes l'amour est contemplation; les caresses sont destinées moins à s'approprier l'autre qu'à se recréer lentement à travers elle'.[87] For Beauvoir, in theory, like gender makes for reciprocity (exactly the word she touches on at the height of her relations with Sorokine): 'dans une exacte réciprocité chacune est à la fois le sujet et l'objet, la souveraine et l'esclave; la dualité est complicité'.[88] Yet this is precisely the way in which Beauvoir seems not to have allowed her relations with Sorokine to develop. The pupil-teacher, lover-beloved dyad is scrupulously inscribed in the text however much we may begin to doubt the real role Beauvoir played.

Beauvoir tries to construct herself as constantly 'sujet' and 'souveraine'. In this way the relationship never reaches the doubling reciprocity Beauvoir imagines in lesbian relations, but always remains in effect an inferior copy of a heterosexual model. This is in keeping with Beauvoir's highly favourable attitude to heterosexuality as expressed in 'La Lesbienne'. In the midst of this chapter Beauvoir makes the surprisingly sweeping statement that in lesbian relationships 'la volupté a un caractère moins foudroyant, moins vertigineux qu'entre l'homme et la femme',[89] and she comes to uphold the unquestionable superiority of the heterosexual couple, where female emotion is tempered by 'le calme masculin'.[90]

Beauvoir perpetuates this privileging of heterosexuality in her interviews with Alice Schwarzer, collected in *Simone de Beauvoir aujourd'hui*. Alice Schwarzer asks Beauvoir in 1982: 'vous n'avez jamais eu de relations amoureuses avec une femme?', to which Beauvoir replies: 'Non, jamais. J'ai toujours eu de très grandes amitiés avec des femmes. Très tendres, parfois même avec une tendresse caressante. Mais ça n'a jamais éveillé en moi de passion érotique.'[91] I think it is questionable whether the publication of the *Journal de Guerre* necessarily contradicts this statement. It seems indeed that the implications of the appearance of this text are more subtle.

In the 1970s and 1980s, in the midst of the feminist movement, Beauvoir was asked not infrequently about her attitude to lesbianism. In 1972 Alice Schwarzer asks Beauvoir particularly about lesbian separatism. Hélène V. Wenzel, in her interview published at the front of *Simone de Beauvoir: Witness to a Century*, asks Beauvoir quite insistently about her friendships with women and about what Wenzel describes as women's enabling/writing relationships. (Here she refers specifically to the role Beauvoir played in enabling the writing of Violette Leduc.[92])

The issue of Beauvoir's relationships with women has surfaced again and again in feminist criticism and biographies. Frequently Beauvoir is described as mother: Alice Jardine calls her 'my own first feminist mother';[93] Yolanda Astarita Patterson writes: 'several articles which appeared after Simone de Beauvoir's death on April 14, 1986 proclaimed her the mother of the women's movement, the mother of all liberated women, whether or not they know her name or her work'.[94] Penny Forster and Imogen Sutton have even called their book of interviews with women about Beauvoir *Daughters of de Beauvoir*.[95] It seems a necessary desire on the part of the daughters of Beauvoir that their mother should be not only maternal but also seductive.[96]

Deirdre Bair in a chapter of her biography entitled 'The Friendships of Women' looks particularly at relations between Beauvoir and her adoptive daughter Sylvie Le Bon. Bair comments that 'the relationship of the women has been the suject of intense speculation ever since Beauvoir made it public in 1972'.[97] Margaret Crosland comments more aggressively: 'This relationship inevitably intrigued the voyeurs who would later question both Beauvoir and Sylvie with crude persistence about its exact nature: were they lesbians, were they mother and daughter?'.[98] It is noteworthy, too, that both Bair and Crosland appear to feel compelled to add their own assessment of the situation. Bair seems inclined to suggest that Beauvoir and Sylvie did have a lesbian relationship; she writes: 'the question of a lesbian relationship made both women angry, but each addressed it. Beauvoir was furious whenever scholars, writers and political activists urged her to proclaim a lesbian identity, not for herself but because she feared personal embarrassment and possible professional reprise for Sylvie, who made one cryptic remark on the subject: '[Beauvoir would only say] that we were good friends because I didn't want her to say anything more, for many reasons, many bad reasons'.[99] Crosland, on the other hand, follows Beauvoir's own line, when she quotes her arguing that this was not lesbianism or a mother-daughter relationship, but something else with an emotional and intellectual centre.[100] Elaine Marks adds her analysis, saying: 'Sylvie Le Bon, it would seem, is more of a "double" than she is a disciple, a friend, a lover, or a daughter, although elements of these categories may be read into their relationship'.[101] Sylvie Le Bon, in an interview appropriately included in *Daughters of de Beauvoir*, speaks of herself as a replacement Zaza, saying of Beauvoir : 'I think she had a kind of nostalgia for a close, intimate relation with a woman'.[102]

What are we to make then of the *Journal de Guerre*, published posthumously and edited by Sylvie Le Bon de Beauvoir, whom readers have been keen to position somewhere, ambiguously, between daughter and lover? It seems as if the relations between Beauvoir and Sylvie provided the perfect conditions for the publication of a narrative of relations between Beauvoir and Sorokine. Indeed the Beauvoir-Sorokine relationship is viewed, by Margaret Crosland, for example, as hovering between the sexual and the maternal-filial.[103] This view is only compounded by *Les Mandarins*, where Nadine, Anne's daughter, is based on Sorokine.[104] What is Beauvoir's intention in allowing the publication of these intimate journals? Or as Wenzel puts it: 'did Simone de Beauvoir have ... difficulty reconciling writing and truth and fiction when she readied her journals for publication?'.[105]

Michèle Le Doeuff makes much of the posthumous publication of Sartre's *Lettres au Castor et à quelques autres* and shows how they are essential to the re-reading of Beauvoir's memoirs. She comments on Sartre and Beauvoir's excessive narration of their personal lives, saying: 'Eu égard à la notion de témoignage, Sartre et Simone de Beauvoir ont cru bon d'assumer publiquement leurs moindres faits et gestes, invitant aussi à doter les aléas les plus quotidiens de leurs rapports d'une signification ayant valeur pour l'humanité toute entière'.[106]

If the publication of Beauvoir's *Journal de Guerre* is making any particularly significant statement about relations between women, and we have argued that it is, then the statement is essentially about difficulty and about role play. Eve Kosofsky Sedgwick writes at the beginning of her book *Between Men*: 'At this particular moment, an intelligible continuum of aims, emotions and valuations links lesbianism with other forms of women's attention to women: the bond of mother and daughter, for instance, the bond of sister and sister, women's friendship, "networking", and the active struggles of feminism'.[107] Beauvoir herself acknowledges the proximity between close friendship and lesbian relations. She says in interview with Hélène Wenzel: 'Yes, I think there are very, very easy movements between the two. From physical tenderness to lesbianism, per se. I think one could very easily slide from one to the other, there aren't the same barriers as between a man and a woman.'[108] It seems, however, that this easy sliding caused Beauvoir many problems, as expressed in the *Journal de Guerre*. And the evidence of Beauvoir's difficulty may lead us to think again about the ease of female homosocial bonding. Beauvoir seems on the whole to have perceived and named herself heterosexual and, as Mary Evans writes, for Beauvoir, 'sexuality is essentially organized as heterosexuality'.[109] This need not be challenged in the light of our reading of the *Journal de Guerre*, since, as Judith Butler argues powerfully: 'Is it not possible to maintain and pursue heterosexual identifications and aims within homosexual practice?'.[110]

This would seem an apt explanation of Beauvoir's case. She says in interview with Schwarzer: 'En soi, l'homosexualité est aussi limitante que l'hétérosexualité: l'idéal devrait être de pouvoir aussi bien aimer une femme qu'un homme, n'importe, un être humain, sans éprouver ni peur, ni contrainte, ni obligations'.[111] Beauvoir herself appears to have felt under no obligation to name her relations with Nathalie Sorokine a lesbian affair. Does she merely seek to avoid limitation through naming?[112] Or by doing this does she in fact manage to maintain the heterosexual identification present throughout the text of the *Journal de Guerre*, where she not only writes for Sartre's consumption but constructs herself as his double in her relations with a woman?

As a whole the *Journal de Guerre* is emphatically ambiguous: Beauvoir both describes and denies lesbian desire. She develops a scenario whereby Beauvoir the lesbian becomes a fantasy projected by her pupil and lover Nathalie Sorokine. And we may note, moreover, that this is also a fantasy for Beauvoir's readers who themselves become her desiring daughters. What the *Journal de Guerre* reveals that is most surprising, perhaps, is Beauvoir's evident complicity with the existence of this illusory self.

NOTES

1   *La Force de l'âge* (FA), Paris, Gallimard, 1960, p. 418. All page-references are to the two-volume 'Folio' edition (1980).
2   *Simone de Beauvoir and French Feminism*, Oxford, Blackwell, 1990, p. 28.
3   *Journal de Guerre* (JG), Paris, Gallimard, 1990.
4   Jean-Paul Sartre, *Lettres au Castor et à quelques autres* (LC), Paris, Gallimard, 1983, two volumes; vol. I, p. 356.
5   FA, p. 396.
6   Colette, *Claudine à l'école*, Paris, Albin Michel, 1900; Violette Leduc, *Thérèse et Isabelle*, Paris, Gallimard, 1966. For a study of Beauvoir's role as teacher, see Catherine Portuges, 'Simone de Beauvoir: Feminist as Teacher', in Patricia De Meo (ed.), *Perspectives sur Sartre et Beauvoir, Dalhousie French Studies*, 1986 (numéro spécial), pp. 107-16.
7   FA, pp. 112-15.
8   FA, p. 188.
9   FA, p. 262.
10   FA, p. 495.
11   FA, p. 496.
12   FA, pp. 496-97.
13   FA, p. 433.
14   *Simone de Beauvoir: The Woman and her Work*, London, Heinemann, 1992, p. 14.
15   Ibid., p. 259.
16   FA, p. 479.
17   FA, p. 414.
18   Terry Keefe makes a revealing comment on the reliability of Beauvoir's memoirs when he says: 'By omitting all reference to certain phenomena, it is possible to avoid telling lies, but only at the risk of making a great deal of what one does say a distortion of the truth', *Simone de Beauvoir: A Study of her Writings*, London, Harrap, 1983, pp. 48-49.
19   LC, I, p. 503.
20   *Simone de Beauvoir, Lettres à Sartre* (LS), Paris, Gallimard, 1990, two volumes; vol. I, p. 124.
21   JG, p. 82.
22   LS, I, p. 173; 'piège' is a term used by both Sartre and Beauvoir to denote 'homosexual'.
23   JG, p. 84.
24   JG, p. 86.

25   JG, p. 84.
26   LS, I, p. 178.
27   JG, p. 86.
28   LS, I, p. 180.
29   JG, p. 84.
30   LS, I, p. 178.
31   LS, I, p. 178.
32   JG, p. 92.
33   LS, I, p. 191.
34   JG, p. 134.
35   JG, p. 97.
36   JG, p. 108.
37   JG, p. 111.
38   LS, I, p. 246.
39   For a more glowing account of Sorokine, see Oreste F. Pucciani, 'Natasha: 1921-1968', in Patricia De Meo (ed.), op. cit., pp. 5-6.
40   Margaret Crosland, op. cit., p. 230 and p. 271.
41   Deirdre Bair, *Simone de Beauvoir: A Biography*, London, Jonathan Cape/Vintage, 1991, p. 236.
42   Ibid., p. 237.
43   JG, p. 219.
44   Jean-Paul Sartre, *La Nausée*, Paris, Gallimard ('Folio'), 1938, p. 11.
45   Philippe Lejeune, *Le Pacte autobiographique*, Paris, Seuil, 1975, p. 14.
46   Terry Keefe, 'Simone de Beauvoir's Second Look at her Life', *Romance Studies*, no. 8 (Summer 1986), pp. 41-55; p. 43.
47   JG, p. 157.
48   LC, I, p. 453.
49   LC, I, p. 497.
50   LC, I, p. 503.
51   JG, p. 166.
52   JG, p. 185.
53   JG, p. 186.
54   LS, I, p. 333.
55   LS, I, pp. 351-52.
56   JG, p. 206.
57   JG, p. 209.
58   LS, I, p. 378.
59   JG, p. 230.
60   LS, II, p. 18.
61   LS, II, p. 243.
62   JG, p. 240.

63   JG, p. 241.

64   LS, II, p. 42.

65   JG, p. 258.

66   JG, p. 276.

67   JG, p. 276.

68   For the reader, Beauvoir's life may be seen as that recounted in the journal. As Philippe Lejeune says: 'Pour le lecteur, qui ne connaît pas la personne réelle, tout en croyant à son existence, l'auteur se définit comme la personne capable de produire ce discours, et il l'imagine donc à partir de ce qu'elle produit', op. cit., p. 23.

69   LC, I, p. 453.

70   LC, I, p. 503.

71   Michèle Le Doeuff, *L'Etude et le rouet*, Paris, Seuil, 1989, p. 124.

72   Ibid.

73   Ibid.

74   Ibid., p. 125.

75   Elizabeth Fallaize, *The Novels of Simone de Beauvoir*, London, Routledge, 1988, p. 63.

76   Ibid.

77   JG, p. 137.

78   JG, p. 206.

79   LS, I, p. 370.

80   JG, p. 280.

81   Beauvoir says of Sartre: 'Il était le double en qui je me retrouvais', in Josée Dayan, *Simone de Beauvoir* (un film de Josée Dayan et Malka Ribowska), Paris, Gallimard, 1979, p. 18.

82   *Le Deuxième Sexe*, Paris, Gallimard, 1949, two volumes; 'Idées' edition, vol. I, p. 510.

83   Ibid., I, p. 481.

84   Ibid., p. 486.

85   Ibid.

86   Ibid., p. 499.

87   Ibid.

88   Ibid.

89   Ibid., p. 504.

90   Ibid., p. 505.

91   Alice Schwarzer (ed.), *Simone de Beauvoir aujourd'hui*, Paris, Mercure de France, 1984, p. 118.

92   Hélène V. Wenzel (ed.), *Simone de Beauvoir: Witness to a Century*, *Yale French Studies*, no. 72, 1986. See Isabelle de Courtivron, 'From Bastard to Pilgrim: Rites and Writing for Madame', ibid., pp. 133-48.

93 Alice Jardine, 'Death Sentences: Writing Couples and Ideology', *Poetics Today*, vol. 6, nos. 1-2 (1985), pp. 119-31; p. 125.
94 Yolanda Astarita Patterson, 'Simone de Beauvoir and the Demystification of Motherhood' in Wenzel (ed.), op. cit., pp. 87-105; p. 90.
95 Penny Forster and Imogen Sutton (eds.), *Daughters of de Beauvoir*, London, The Women's Press, 1989.
96 Catherine Portuges links the mother-daughter paradigm with that of sisterhood too; see 'Attachment and Separation in *The Memoirs of a Dutiful Daughter*' in Wenzel (ed.), op. cit., pp. 107-18.
97 Deirdre Bair, op. cit., p. 508.
98 Margaret Crosland, op. cit., p. 414.
99 Deirdre Bair, op. cit., p. 510.
100 Margaret Crosland, op. cit., p. 414.
101 Elaine Marks, 'Transgressing the (In)cont(in)ent Boundaries: The Body in Desire' in Wenzel (ed.), op. cit., pp. 181-200; p. 198.
102 Forster and Sutton, op. cit., p. 125.
103 Margaret Crosland, op. cit., p. 224.
104 Simone de Beauvoir, *La Force des choses*, Paris, Gallimard, 1963, two volumes; 'Folio' edition, vol. I, pp. 361-62.
105 Wenzel, op. cit., p. x.
106 Michèle Le Doeuff, op. cit., p. 198.
107 *Between Men: English Literature and Male Homosocial Desire*, New York, Columbia University Press, 1985, p. 2.
108 Wenzel, op. cit., p. 23.
109 *Simone de Beauvoir: A Feminist Mandarin*, London and New York, Tavistock, 1985, p. 128.
110 Judith Butler, 'Imitation and Gender Insubordination' in Diana Fuss (ed.), *Inside/Out: Lesbian Theories, Gay Theories*, London and New York, Routledge, 1991; pp. 13-31; p. 17.
111 Alice Schwarzer, op. cit., p. 82.
112 For further discussion of naming and identity, see Judith Butler, op. cit.

Part II

Nizan, Camus, Leduc, Genet and Guibert

Commitment and the Self in the Writing of Paul Nizan

MARY ORR

If Nizan is known at all, it is for his political commitment, energy and activism, a self-expression through action rather than through writing. Although prolific in literary, critical, journalistic and fictional production, Nizan left no autobiography as such. He seems always, and in this league particularly, to be overshadowed by both Sartre and Beauvoir. But we shall seek to show here the extent to which Nizan's expression of the existential self outstrips in authenticity those more widely-known, but later, representatives of the genre, *Les Mots* and *Mémoires d'une jeune fille rangée*. These share with Nizan's work preoccupations with subjects such as the family, education, the role of the writer, and with questions of literary 'engagement' and 'mauvaise foi'. What they singularly fail to do is question the genre of autobiography itself as the supreme seat of 'embourgeoisement'. It is this issue that Nizan can be shown to be addressing with particular pertinence and avant-garde acuity.

Special focus will be placed here on his novel *La Conspiration*,[1] to highlight where Nizan is particularly aware of the problematic presentation of the authentic, Marxist-existentialist and proletarian self. We shall first outline the ways in which Nizan's novels may be seen to be autobiographical in conventional terms. Then we shall investigate his new, revised version of the genre itself, before examining the structural and structuring procedures that this entails. And, finally, the style and stance of his mode of autobiographical expression will be considered. Questions concerning the definition of autobiography itself will then be reopened. Suffice it to say here that they will relate not to a Lejeunian 'pacte autobiographique' or 'autobiocopie',[2] so much as to a more secret, radical 'conspiration', a devious plotting between the socio-political, committed self and the writing self.

Why, though, has Nizan's work received so little attention in relation to the autobiographical project? Annie Cohen-Solal's *Paul Nizan: Communiste impossible*[3] uses much corroborated evidence from Henriette Nizan's accounts to place Nizan the person against his writings, particularly events, descriptions and people in the novels. Most critics study his works chronologically against Nizan's biographical details, be they investigating Nizan the writer, Nizan the Communist or Nizan the traitor. Throughout, there is a collision between the writer and his characters, often with totally misjudged equations such as the Pluvinage-Nizan mask in *La Conspiration*. Such a conflation smacks of undergraduate naïveté, yet in Nizan studies it has been acceptable. The better critics, like Steel,[4] stress the concatenations of real and fictional representations of the self, and opt for the more sophisticated persona of Bloyé as a kind of Nizan-alibi. Only one contribution to the Nizan colloquium of 1987 in Lille, Deguy's 'L'Ecriture du *Je* dans *La Conspiration*',[5] treats the subject overtly. However, even here, Deguy slips into the truism of the writer behind any novel, setting up self in Nizan's third-person, fictional 'roman à clef' or 'roman à thèse', this calqued onto Flaubertian or Gidean use of first-person narrative devices, such as the diary and letters. What we may suspect is that because Nizan chose not to write first-person narratives (the normal viewpoint of traditional autobiography), critics have not asked why this is so, and hence not opened up the opus to revised standards for the autobiographical genre itself.

A related barrier to anything but conventional response to the contemporaneity and documentary tone in Nizan's writing is its 'realist' thrust. Normative readings of the journalistic and propagandist in Nizan are the result, without critics being aware that these elements too may be more to do with the subject and the subjective than with the historian-journalist's so-called objectivity. It is precisely in the fold or overlap between the propagandist social realism of his novels and the personal convictions of the correspondent that the autobiographical voice of Nizan is to be found. His writings were formed by an education in opinion-trading, evaluation and informed consciousness-raising activities.[6] Let us now chart, but not in lengthy discussion of his 'biographemes', the aspects of Nizan's work that match the criteria for the standard autobiography.

Autobiography is accepted as the genre that tacitly expounds the dignity of personhood against the background of a particular time and place, but is also open to universal issues of selfhood and self-expression for posterity. Right at the heart of the existentialist project is this dignity, albeit momentary, of the enlightened self, the self faced with the void and thus with the need to confront mortality with acts confirming existence. 'Engagement' in this sense is central to autobiography, though belief in the 'être-pour-soi' may not be dressed up as such. The moment of awareness is tantamount to the 'conversion' experience of traditional autobiographers such as St Augustine or Rousseau. The unenlightened 'before' and enlightened 'after' are foregrounded in existential writing. Concomitant with this dividing moment are points of initiation - sexual encounter is the usual site of this - which trigger awareness of self. The 'être-pour-soi' versus 'être-en-soi' aspect of initiation in Nizan's narrators confirms and extends its existential significance. The individual qualities of the autobiographer as exemplar, the isolating nature of this separation from ordinary humanity, and the need to communicate the difference of individuation are paramount also in existentialist writing. Truth to oneself (authenticity) concerning right and wrong actions at the heart of existentialist novels corresponds to confessional elements in all autobiographies and enables the narrator to evoke sympathy and positive judgement from the reader. Both autobiographical and existentialist modes of writing argue a defence of self, self-defence and advocacy of a changed life-style. Old characteristics and 'mauvaise foi'-type blindness are then eschewed as the maturer self scrutinises the weaknesses of youth. As with standard autobiography, retrospective evaluations and social critiques from the personal viewpoint on family, church, and society are always blended together to contextualise the self. Various 'manies' and obsessions then distinguish and personalise for the reader the autobiographer, whose psychological investigation and introspection go hand in hand with philosophico-metaphysical *angst* undergone by the narrating subject. In existentialist works, this *angst* is the expression of the universally experienced void. Superimposition of the wiser self on previous selves (although memory is admitted as faulty, fact a mix with fantasy, and writing itself a conscious, but unreliable, vehicle of voice) layers the work chronologically.

The above criteria for standard autobiography and its existentialist variants tally with Nizan's fictions, the only and important deviations from the norm being Nizan's consistent non-use of the first-person narrative voice and his refusal to reconstruct the past by means of, or at the expense of, the present. These features are the cut-off point marking out where Nizan, in *La Conspiration*, is establishing very different insights into the Marxist-existentialist mode of expressing the self. The rejection of the focus on the past and the 'je' is not accidental. Nizan., is fully aware of the capitalist, bourgeois implications of both of these strategies. Implicit reactionary support of the literary tradition of Western humanism and autobiographical conversatism, as well as the elevation of the entrepreneurial 'je' cannot be justified by Nizan either. A true Marxist dialectic enters the arena here, for Nizan revokes the thesis of the autobiography à la Rousseau by his antithesis of the 'non-je', the non-intimate genre. The self is exteriorised in a third person *combination* of persons. Thus, the choice is still an authentic narrative of self, but *not* the voice of the auto-self, that narcissistic, humanistic and ultimately bourgeois re-evaluation of the 'moi suprême'. Along with it, the more universalising 'nous' and 'vous' (found in Camus's *La Chute*, for example), which only mark complicity between the 'moi' and the reader, are also to be rejected. Nizan expunges all bourgeois forms of autobiographical voice, for they are inauthentic to the project of the Marxist, working-class voice of the 'on'. This has to be cut free from the traps of re-embourgeoisement, or the treachery of the working-class figure who aspires to be a petty-bourgeois hero. We can now go some way to explaining why the Marxist worker-hero is also absent from Nizan's work, for it is the Antoine Bloyés who will render this project void. Instead, the true communist workers can only appear *en masse*, in the anti-autobiography of deluded bourgeois like the protagonists in *La Conspiration*, in the gaps in the narrative that are constantly suggestive of others' presence and existence. Herewith come the necessary problems of viewpoint, style, structure, and narrative authority, together with the new advocacy of *collective* persuasion and enlightenment based on the life/lives of non-bourgeois ideologues. Hence, the persona focus is impersonal and external. Navel-gazing and psychological investigation automatically smack of bourgeois inauthenticity, and it is worth noting how often the characters in *La Conspiration* fall into that trap, mistakenly thinking they are ideologically sound!

Acts, therefore, are not the property of a single hero, but loci of *en masse* valorisation and evaluation. The outsiders to capitalism and its cultural tradition as well as its fictional and autobiographical project need, then, to enlist new generic categories in order to find a voice and a structure both existential and cultural. Socialist realism is the gateway to this genre which demands authenticity *sui generis*. Again, I think Nizan transforms its more limiting didacticism and propagandist hectoring by harnessing it to the portrayal of the authenticating self amid the scene of history, whose Other is always the relating narrator looking on and relating to the action. Past tense gives way to present-tense actualisation of the emergent self-in-community, whose future embodiment as collective is encapsulated in the accumulative, present-tense narrative. Acts impinge now and for the future, not the past, as ontogenetic, laden with the prophetic voice. Urging and urgency go together. Such separation from past tradition, then, demands the restructuring of the autobiographical genre, replacing confessions, 'journal intime', solipsistic mirror-diaries and memoirs by their inside-out reformulations. Defining these, because no term exists, can only be by coinage of hybrids such as 'notes-correspondances' or 'biojournalisme', both forms of what may be termed a wider anti-capitalistic 'autrebiographie'.

Having established why Nizan rejects the privileged subject, first-person narrative and autobiography as form, we can now examine the structural and structuring procedures that a Marxist expression of self will imply, using *La Conspiration* as example. Rupture is a key device, both in the form and content of the text. The three main but unequal segments of the novel, 'La Conspiration', 'Catherine' and 'Serge', offer three third-person narratives interlinked by character, but differing in angle of vision. The intercalated 'extraits d'un carnet noir' and 'récit de Pluvinage' suggest character introspection rather than inspection. The overall effect is a layering, but also a breaking-up of a picture where pieces and characters cannot interlock. The second structuring device is repositioning of the same character, whose role in another section is always different. This highlights the 'pour-soi' or 'en-soi' shift in value any given actant holds at a particular textual moment. The regrouping and reappraisal of character in turn questions neat causal unfolding so evident in the standard autobiography. Cause and effect *is* crucial, but as rupture, not elucidation. Effects are frequently negative in Nizan and determine a complete break with the past cause, Rosen's suicide being a key example.

Vital, too, is the rupture of a stream-of-consciousness or unified autobiographical voice. *La Conspiration* adopts narrative strategies found elsewhere. For example, Musset's *Confession d'un enfant du siècle*, an autobiographical novel of youth and immaturity, based on Musset's own turbulent affair with George Sand, and written shortly after the event, employs a third-person narrator, Octave. His contextualisation in history and as the product of an epoch at war (that is, before he was born) is used as a ploy to gain the reader's sympathy for the *circumstances* of this romantic escapist dreamer, who finds nature and love with Brigitte, after rejecting the city voices of his times and his unfaithful mistress. That the main character returns to the status quo, but as privileged narrator strengthened by his relationship with Brigitte, confirms a personal rather than a political attitude to the self. Nizan, on the contrary, takes the near-contemporary event, the quasi-pseudonymous stance and the focus on history and magnifies them. He politicises and depersonalises the notions of epoch, nation, family, love affairs, the outcome of the idealist strivings of youth faced with misunderstanding. For him, *La Conspiration* is rather his personal 'confession d'une fin de siècle' through various mouthpieces. Rupture with revolutionary romanticism is urgently required to counter its fascist potential for creating a superman mentality. It is not the ego, nor even the id that needs attention, but a politicised superego which will operate through time and history against the prevailing ethos. Hence Rosen's romantic posturing, including escapism to Naxos (Greece being the birthplace of Western civilisation), is to be read as retrogressive, a-political and narcissistic. His relationship with his sister-in-law Catherine is a pastoral idyll - as with Musset's Octave, an interlude in growing up - but in Rosen's case is exaggerated to the point of romantic extreme: suicide. His betrayal of his comrades and lost faith in the political revolt against his family is a lesser crime than his bid to keep his ego intact and take personally the guilt of bourgeois hypocrisy in a grand heroic gesture.

Where Musset provides a structural inverse model of the personal versus the political for Nizan's *La Conspiration*, Gide's *Les Faux-Monnayeurs* offers a generic stalking horse. Gide's Edouard and Nizan's Pluvinage share an interest in diary-writing. The third-person distance narrative on the interplay of characters and their plottings is a common authorial position. While Gide is constantly questioning and rupturing the seamless traditional novel and begging questions concerning the demarcation between the fictionalised and autobiographical self, Nizan's work can be said to move beyond even this by refuting the 'mise en abîme' reflections on the writing process itself. Such narrative introspection would be a further and ultimate manifestation of the same fixation on privileging self within the tradition and culture of Western capitalism. Despite the fact that Gide's characters are counterfeiters, throwing off the traces of their bourgeois fathers, they too return to a position of integration within the narrative ethos, for forgeries are but copies of the original. Nizan thus breaks with Musset and Gide, with the romantic, psychological autobiography and the capitalist realist, and anti-realist novel by attending particularly to structure itself. Self-reflecting mirrors are replaced by self-refracting ones which break the bounds of a personal optic to capture the wider field of human vision.

Rupture and repositioning work because a third structuring device is in operation: the positioning of givens as points of reference for reinterpretation. To borrow Marxist terminology, in place in the novel is an infrastructure, the economics of personhood in the form of family, education, money, society and social expectation. This is the 'basic structure of an organisation or system ... and determinant of economic growth', to quote the Collins dictionary. Replace 'economic' here by 'personal', and we have the nodal points of how self is constructed in autobiography. *Les Mots* and *Mémoires d'une jeune fille rangée* exemplify the pattern. Capitalism, embodied in the sons of the bourgeois fathers in *La Conspiration*, has reached the point of no return (rupture) and provokes overt questioning of the superstructural web governing all points of the infrastructure. Agencies of legal, political and academic institutions and their entrenched capitalist/bourgeois ideology are revealed by the particular battleground of a given character, but they are all equal as dominant modes of production of cloned bourgeois. Blocked together, they voice the unrelenting message of the abortive conspiracy. The sons are no different from their fathers, for their youthful exuberance is the natural *psychological* reaction against parents, not a political one. It is only the maturer character, Bloyé, and the voice-over narrator who point towards the ideological superstructure Nizan is actually promoting, by default: Marxism. The structural devices therefore build on norms to say the unsaid, and imply the real as against what is taken to be so but proves otherwise. Chronological outworking of the infrastructural and superstructural dimensions of the text is then not a lapse back into traditional novel forms, with chapters or diachronic autobiographical reconstructions. It is again the properly Marxist use of history in dialectical materialist terms, to kickstart a new mode of production by means of rupture with the past. Hence, the present tense is the overriding choice in Nizan's novel, one of the modes by which the new-style 'autrebiographie' takes shape on the microcosmic level. As representative of an act for the future, it is also the place that is least sifted and ordered to fit with the colonising, past-oriented dominant ideology.

Retrospection, then, has to be replaced by prospection. The position of otherness in terms of time, space and narrative is what protects the present moment from solipsism, the self from self-fulfilling prophecy. Therefore, retrospective time is kept to the minimum in the text. The context of narration is extremely close to the context of the writer. Both conjoin to focus on a non-bourgeois future learnt from the 'révoltes manquées' of Rosenthal and Pluvinage. Constantly emerging from the text is the superstructure of Marxist-informed speculation, prophecy in its political, ethical and community-centred functions, for a people, not a person. Instruction and corrective utterance behind the surface words of the infrastructural characters suffuse the text with its call to action, but to authentic non-posturing action of the background Bloyé, as opposed to the overtly flamboyant Rosenthal. To elucidate the kaleidoscopic range of viewpoint in *La Conspiration*, Nizan uses a third-person narrative that stresses the *choices* of position and the immediacy of the context.

Journalistic in its public sense, this third-person voice is no less subjective in its mode of presentation:

> le fait 'journalistique' n'obéit pas à d'autres règles que le fait proprement historique, qu'il est, exactement au même titre que lui, l'objet d'une connaissance indirecte, d'un savoir fondé sur des *traces* - sauf au cas, fort rare, où l'on est soi-même le premier témoin, ce qui suppose la plus exigeante de critiques, de soi sur soi ... Entendons que les informations chaque jour accessibles doivent se soumettre à la critique négative de 'sincérité', d' 'exactitude', qu'il faut éliminer les *erreurs* d'observation ou de tradition.[7]

> Quiconque avait le souci de combiner la fidélité à la réalité et les nécessités de l'information sentait qu'il fallait tenir compte de quelques règles de fonction et de métier devant cette histoire fulgurante et éclipsée qui ne se suspendait pas un jour, qui ne respirait pas, qui pressait et qui pourtant était *l'histoire* ... On voyait qu'il fallait risquer et décider pour une version qu'on savait sans doute au moins prématurée, entre la multiplicité des sources et des contradictions des témoignages.[8]

The reporter/documentary-compiler is always a presence at a distance in the situation, this angle of vision then determining the degree of propaganda permitted, because narrative as mono- or multivocal space is carefully controlled. At times in *La Conspiration*, for example, Nizan uses a character's words as a positive, sometimes a negative opinion: at times one which is the other's without contributing to the message. Often, however, it is the opinion of the link-person between the witnesses that carries more ideological weight. Nizan, like Flaubert before him, delights in the anonymity of the aphorism, the maxim and the totally objective voice *ex nihilo* which gives away the omnipresence of the controlling narrator. Although unnamed, this voice is paradoxically always more authoritative and informed, attributes often attached to (autobiographical) maturity. Frequently in *La Conspiration*, it clashes radically with the youthful exaggerations and simplifications of the protagonists. This overview voice (the 'autrebiographe') between the lines is the seat of 'reality', 'veracity', 'truth' in the narration, as well as coming closest to the voice of an authentic proletariat-conscious Marxist/existentialist commentator. Nizan is well aware of the advantages and disadvantages of the anonymity of this persona. Clearly, a drawback is that s/he may not be understood or even noted by readers and critics. Evidence shows that this is frequently why Nizan has been equated with one of the characters in the text, rather than with the narrator, who ties all the narrations together, and holds the metaphorical microphone in the text. The advantages, however, are precisely the non-identification of this narrator as Nizan, so that the slippage into privileging one individual subject over the others is avoided. The further advantage is that the overtly propagandist and simplistic moral/ethical/political line is not pronounced. Nizan, while a committed communist, cannot be described as a party yes-man. He did not swallow and regurgitate dogma. The narrator's presence in the text makes this subtle distinction, allowing a communist voice to predominate but not pronounce a single political ideological line.

The second mode of shifting emphasis and playing elements off against one another on the micro levels of the text is the mix of styles. The idyll of the adventure with Catherine is almost lyrical at times and contrasts sharply with the faster-moving dialogues between the conspirators. There is also the satirical and pompous 'franglais' of the Rosenthal family and Carré's strongly communist manifesto-type language, which seems more a literary than an oral pronouncement. Again, critics have often misunderstood the necessity of this mixing. It is not mere borrowing from types of narrative or intertextual reworking of Gidean or other turns of phrase because Nizan is a raw and unformed writer. The contrary is rather the case. Nizan uses intertexts as examples of narrative against which his may *act* and react in a much more engaged and political way. Therefore, certain intertexts are clearly satirically reworked, even denounced, by their juxtaposition with the less colourful aphorism and maxim-speak. Moreover, the intertextual dimension is not to show the inter-referentiality of bourgeois culture, but perhaps the need to go through this narcissistic looking-glass and smash its subjectivity. It is the patchwork of fragments of narrative style that then becomes not just a political consciousness-raiser, but a literary (anti-bourgeois) one as well. The authentic ideological style and voice will not be privileged fragments themselves, but 'correct' interpretations of the spaces between these blocks of cultural text.

However, the authentic ideological voice must not be so hidden in the textual interstices that it becomes bland, over-subtle, or worse, intellectual. Nizan juxtaposes extremely partisan, arrogant, denunciatory, self-castigating, and sardonic blocks of utterance. This overt shock-tactic (to 'épater le bourgeois') not only fits realistically with the 'us and them' mentality of youth filled with the post-conversion enthusiasm and fundamentalism of political or ideological discovery. The various tirades and set-piece pontifications or critiques from individuals allow Nizan himself the narrative space to berate and castigate capitalism from inside its self-representations as realist novel or autobiography, by exaggeration of monology, dialogue, or 'omniscient' opinion.

The most important mode of expression in *La Conspiration* to mask and reveal clashes of worldview, then, is irony. It allows criticism, commentary, questioning, distance and anonymous partisan expression. It permits intrusion into the narrative, and is a particularly valuable tool to cut into other third-person prose forms. The more one reads Nizan, the more ironic his narrative appears. Statements suddenly spring a trap, exploding previous, comfortable, affirmative positions. Positions are, as already noted, always interim and never one individual's property, not even the omnipresent narrator's. However, if there is any gauge of an authentic voice in Nizan, it is the ironic, goading commentator, seeking properly committed acts and stances. Through this, Nizan states his place with the non-particularised collective of the proletarian 'on', by whose authority he then writes. The remaining question is whether this 'conspiration' between Nizan's socio-political and writing self in this 'autrebiographie' succeeds or fails. Is *La Conspiration* a new model for proletarian, collective third-person autobiography or merely a utopian, propagandist novel?

Conspiracies connote unlawful, 'evil' political activities, often including criminal and treasonable acts. Their hatching is always from within the dominant ideology, requiring group tactics if they are to succeed. Secrecy, infiltration and active deception (cover) are their means of conduct. Plots are their method of action. The word 'conspiration', then, fits exactly with Nizan's cunning narrative tactics as just described. The plot of the novel reveals the secret plot of forming a new form of proletarian expression from within bourgeois novel/autobiography forms. Irony is the cover, and its communication infiltrates ideas through various mouthpieces. Grouping (structural) tactics are essential to act against slippage into the old ideology of self-centred writing. And successful conspiracies transform unlawfully valorised acts into lawful ones, because the superstructural mindset has been ruptured and changed. Positive conspiracy is the awareness of 'mauvaise foi' that drives towards the achievement of authenticity in all aspects of self-formation, infra- and superstructurally. Therefore, one can see the 'conspirational' textual activities at work in Nizan's last novel. It plots the contrivances, devises combinations of actions, concurs with the new ideology of self-as-cooperative, unites in design to produce new narrative ends. In the intransitive rather than transitive verbal sense of the verb 'to conspire', to 'act together towards some end as if by design', a superstructural ordering/authority principle is allowed space. For the Marxist, this is dialectical materialism, the place once occupied by the gods of capitalism. It is the force of history and change whereby Nizan might be said to justify his unlawful 'omniscience' concerning characters which intrudes sporadically in his fictions. Authority and authorship then align under powerful personal and political conviction. It is this that, in turn, renders the writer 'engagé', an actant or tool for cultural change:

> L'écrivain est celui qui a pour fonction de définir et de révéler aux hommes leurs plus hautes valeurs et leurs plus vastes ambitions: il découvre les valeurs que leur vie implique et leur fournit des justifications qu'ils puissent tous accepter, parce qu'elles vont dans le sens de la grandeur et de l'accomplissement.[9]

This task clearly is not utopian in its idealism, but practical in its real political drive to progress, and to the consciousness-raising of humankind. In *La Conspiration*, through the 'autrebiographical' stance of the writer/narrator, Nizan does indeed appear to fulfil his own Marxist/existentialist job description. The self, though idiosyncratic, has been wrested from the desire for individualism and is made universal, a voice on behalf of others.

Several questions, however, remain. The socio-political and writer 'conspiration' only works if one accepts the essentially devious ploys in the text. Even by the multiplicity of textual 'Verfremdungseffekten', this space of voice in the interstices of the bourgeois dialogues may not, for some, be sufficient to document the coming-into-being of the still-unrepresented proletariat. The fold or overlap between socialist realism and personal conviction described at the beginning relies on the outsider position of ambiguity and distance. It can be argued that Nizan belonged properly neither to the Marxist proletariat, nor to the bourgeois intelligensia, and that, instead of ambiguously straddling the two, he is a traitor to both. In the conflict of class and style, he can be said to betray both the propaganda text and proletarian 'autrebiographie' by overt intellectualism drawn from his ENS education. This makes him unable to portray authentic proletarian non-intellectuals. The counter-question in defence of our discussion of Nizan is, of course, whether so-called working-class autobiographers are not really 'Antoine Bloyés', aspiring by cultural means to rise to the bourgeoisie. Here, one must agree, Nizan has spotted the contradiction of form and content for the proletarian self in the autobiographical genre, and has acted accordingly in *La Conspiration* by excluding first-person forms, and expressly the autobiography as self-for-posterity. Hence, Nizan's record of himself is more authentic than Sartre's *Les Mots* in this existential context.

Another important issue is Nizan's iconoclasm, particularly in the light of his resignation from the Communist Party. Is such a political/ideological stance, even if Marxist, not simply individualism in another guise? Is the desire to be the privileged Seer not actually the twentieth-century political form of Romanticism? As with all prophetic pronouncements, time is often the touchstone of truth. In the light of the demise of the communist bloc, Nizan's political stance has an extremely pertinent and contemporary ring to it, whereas Sartre and Beauvoir appear more outmoded. Democratic socialism might, then, usefully find its voice through Nizan's attempts to construct 'autrebiographie'. This task for class and/or race is the same conspiracy against the capitalist, patriarchal, bourgeois autobiography that feminists have been waging more recently. Marguerite Duras in *L'Amant* uses the same third-person tactics to voice woman spaces in her story. If avant-garde in many respects, clearly with regard to women Nizan is a product of his time, for the voice of authority and call to action in *La Conspiration* is wholeheartedly male, and addressed to the male reader. Militancy, military metaphor and the conquest of women as object are clear evidence of the unquestioned phallocentrism of Nizan's portrayal of society. His 'autrebiographie' does not even contemplate the doubly-hidden female worker within expression of the non-bourgeois collective 'on', which will always slip towards the pronoun 'il'.

In conclusion, then, whatever one feels to be the authentic Nizan or the authentic voice in *La Conspiration*, this text provides clear aspirations for political and narrative change. Nizan emphasises the properly existential in the autobiographical project, in that it is a textual politics of life versus death. He especially highlights his belief in the dignity of man (*sic*), both in his writing and in his premature death in action. By actively choosing not to write a first-person, past-promoting kind of autobiography, Nizan revolutionises the genre itself, as has been shown. *La Conspiration* wrests autobiography from its bourgeois heritage by being both the fictionalised, third-person autobiography of Nizan's youth and the 'autrebiographie' of his literary and political 'engagement' in pre-war France.

NOTES

1   *La Conspiration*, Paris, Gallimard, 1938.
2   P. Lejeune, *Le Pacte autobiographique*, Paris, Seuil, 1975; and 'L'Autobiocopie' in M. Calle-Gruber and A. Rothe (eds), *Autobiographie et biographie*, Paris, Nizet, 1989, pp. 53-66.
3   A. Cohen-Solal, *Paul Nizan, communiste impossible*, Paris, Bernard Grasset, 1980.
4   J. Steel, *Paul Nizan, un révolutionaire conformiste?*, Paris, Presses de la fondation nationale des sciences politiques, 1987. Chapter 9 deals particularly with the 'semi-autobiographiques' elements of *La Conspiration*.
5   B. Alluin and J. Deguy (eds), *Paul Nizan écrivain*, Lille, Presses Universitaires de Lille, 1988.
6   See, for example, Sartre's Preface to Nizan's *Aden Arabie* (Paris, Maspero, 1967), p. 14 ff.; *Les Chiens de garde* (Paris, Rieder, 1932; reprinted, Paris, Maspero, 1976); *Chronique de septembre* (Paris, Gallimard, 1939); or his *Ecrits et Correspondance, 1926-1940* (Paris, Maspero, 1970; two vols).
7   Nizan's introduction to *Chronique de septembre*, p. 13.
8   Ibid., p. 15.
9   *Ecrits et Correspondance*, vol. II, p. 36.

Albert Camus: The Man behind the Myth

STEVE ROBSON

Camus himself warned commentators against drawing too many parallels between his own life and those of his fictional characters, when, in the essay 'L'Enigme' in *L'Eté*, he noted that:

> L'idée que tout écrivain écrit forcément sur lui-même et se peint dans ses livres est une des puérilités que le romantisme nous a léguées ... Les oeuvres d'un homme retracent souvent l'histoire de ses nostalgies ou de ses tentations, presque jamais sa propre histoire, surtout lorsqu'elles prétendent à être autobiographiques.[1]

But while his work is not explicitly autobiographical, scrutiny of his notebooks and correspondence in particular shows that it constitutes a mediated autobiography, in that it arises out of, or reflects, his struggle with his nature and his efforts to attain in public the artistic and personal ideals that he formulated in his youth.

The dichotomy between the public and private personae of Camus will be unknown to many readers of his work, and indeed is missed by his most authoritative biographer to date, H. R. Lottman. Yet a significant self-dialogue exists in Camus's journalistic writings as early as 1939 and the outbreak of war finds him commenting in *Alger Républicain*:

> Jamais peut-être les militants de gauche n'ont connu tant de raisons de désespérer. Bien des espoirs et bien des croyances se sont effondrés en même temps que cette guerre. Et parmi toutes les contradictions où le monde s'agite, contraints à la lucidité, nous sommes alors conduits à tout nier.[2]

The pessimism that such comments contain is not something commonly associated with the lucidity of the author of *Le Mythe de Sisyphe* and *L'Homme révolté*, but it tells only part of the story. Camus's notebooks suggest that he quickly rose above this despair, offering in his 'Lettre à un désespéré' (which Parker rightly sees as self-addressed),[3] the reasons for its ultimate rejection. To despair was to enjoy a private privilege that he could not allow himself. When war broke out, Camus's initial fatalism did appear to be justified and was accordingly expressed in the *Alger Républicain* editorial, but by the time of the 'Lettre', which was written in his private notebooks and not published, Camus was able to consider the situation less emotionally and hence to urge himself beyond despair, realising that he still had a role to play in continuing to struggle for peace. In later years the dialogue between the public and private sides of Camus was sustained, the difference being that never again would he make such a public outburst.

A particularly significant later example of the public-private dichotomy can be found in a letter from Camus to Jean Grenier dated 4 August 1958, which, whilst expressing Camus's personal belief that the Algerian situation at the time is beyond hope, affirms the need to project a public vision of optimism:

> Je crois comme vous qu'il est sans doute trop tard pour l'Algérie. Je ne l'ai pas dit dans mon livre parce que *lo peor no es siempre seguro* [*sic*] - parce qu'il faut laisser ses chances au hasard historique - et parce qu'on n'écrit pas pour dire que tout est fichu. Dans ce cas-là, on se tait. Je m'y prépare.[4]

Here we see once more the self-dialogue that was apparent in Camus's reaction to the outbreak of World War II. Perhaps with desperate irony, he stresses that it is the 'worst' that is not certain, rather than simply a negative outcome. Even given this view of the circumstances, he continues the struggle until the last possible moment by not declaring that 'tout est fichu'. But, aware that he can do no more to influence positively the outcome of the conflict, Camus can only wait for events to take their course and resist any temptation to prophesy catastrophe. The influential writer and journalist of the mid-fifties will not allow himself the same self-indulgence as the provincial journalist of 1939. His public explanation of his refusal of despair in 1955 was blunt and simple: 'Je prendrai parti ... contre le désespoir, puisque en Algérie, aujourd'hui, le désespoir, c'est la guerre'.[5] Yet the truth behind his willed refusal to give public expression to private pessimism is more complex than it initially appears, since it involves Camus's conception of himself as a public figure and writer.

Clues to this self-conception exist throughout his notebooks, partly in the form of reflections on authors he admires. In 1941, during the turmoil of the Occupation, he compares his own historical situation to that of other writers, all of whom are universally recognised literary giants: 'Ceux qui ont créé en pleines périodes de troubles: Shakespeare, Milton, Ronsard, Rabelais, Montaigne, Malherbe'.[6] And eight years later we can witness him making a similar comparison, in terms of the writer's suffering and commitment to his art: 'Kleist qui brûle deux fois ses manuscrits ... Piero della Francesca, aveugle à la fin de ses jours ... Ibsen à la fin amnésique et réapprenant l'alphabet ... Courage! Courage!'[7] In the same period he uses Tolstoy's achievement of his greatest work as a measure of his own artistic accomplishments, looking ahead, perhaps, to his projected but unfinished novel, *Le Premier Homme*.[8]

These comparisons tell us much about Camus's artistic aspirations and motivations, but the demonstration of such ambition was not limited to indirect literary comments. His notebooks and correspondence reveal that a definite strategy was being applied to his projected career as a writer. By 1936 he had sketched out a series of ideas for his 'oeuvre', based around 'absurdité' and 'lucidité', and in March of that year we are presented with the first example of an ascetic programme of discipline that Camus would struggle to impose upon himself each time he embarked on a new project: 'Mon livre, y penser constamment. Mon travail, l'organiser sans attendre à partir de dimanche.'[9] By May Camus was no longer considering his output as a single novel, but viewing it instead as a series of interlinked books; and nearly a year later his notebooks attest to a total of six planned projects.[10] Moreover, he was not content merely to produce an adequate first novel: it had to be a great novel. It was partly for this reason that he decided not to allow the publication of *La Mort heureuse*, and indeed his notebooks describe the iron discipline he imposed upon himself after completing the first version of that book: 'C'est pour briller plus vite qu'on ne consent pas à réécrire. Méprisable. A recommencer.'[11] And even after his major achievements of the early forties he retained his sense of discipline and drew up ever-more-ambitious agendas for his work. Indeed, such planning was to continue up until his death, being regularly noted in his *Carnets*.

The full significance of such a well-planned artistic output is revealed when we consider Camus's parallel effort to discipline himself as a writer. A 1949 notebook entry demonstrates the strict regime that he forced himself to follow whilst working on *L'Homme révolté*: 'Lever tôt. Douche *avant* petit déjeuner. Pas de cigarettes avant midi. *Obstination au travail. Elle surpasse les défaillances.*'[12] A year later he is still seeking to sustain this dedication to his work, struggling to motivate himself to a concentrated effort, even if only for a limited period. He writes of his need to achieve 'Un mois de maîtrise absolue - sur tous les plans'.[13] However, we have to wait another seven years before Camus gives his own explanation of his continual need to impose a working discipline on himself. In a notebook entry dated 8 August 1957 he writes:

> La tentation est forte de rejeter cet effort incessant qui me rend malheureux dans le bonheur lui-même, cette ascèse vide, cet appel qui me raidit vers je ne sais quoi. Je ferais du théâtre, j'écrirais au hasard des travaux dramatiques, sans me soucier, je serais libre peut-être. Qu'ai-je à faire d'un art estimable ou honnête? Et suis-je capable de ce dont je rêve? Si je n'en suis pas capable, à quoi bon rêver? Me libérer de cela aussi et consentir à rien! D'autres l'ont fait qui étaient plus grands que moi.[14]

His literary aspirations are represented here as a tyranny obliging him to give up more natural expression. His dream is to abandon the struggle for personal esteem, for personal greatness, and produce instead a less calculated work, one written 'au hasard'. In the light of this comment, we can see more clearly the pattern of psychological self-analysis in Camus's notebooks. He constantly remarks upon his natural tendency to diversions and distractions, a lack of application that he views as a weakness; and this generates a need for continual self-appraisal and self-criticism, an effort to drive himself on, give himself direction, and correct his failings.

The foundation for this personal struggle can be found in *Le Mythe de Sisyphe*, in which Camus takes up the Nietzschean idea of the need for coincidence between thought and action. He notes Nietzsche's proposition that 'un philosophe, pour être estimable, [doit] prêcher d'exemple',[15] and with respect to Schopenhauer feels that it is the 'conduite' of a philosopher which 'finit par juger son homme'.[16] It is in this context that Camus attempted to live up to the image of the artist that he had formed for himself and dominated some of the more natural, carefree, pleasure-seeking aspects of his personality. In his notebooks in 1949 we see him commenting ironically on his programme of self-discipline: 'J'ai deux ou trois passions qu'on peut juger coupables, que j'estime telles et dont j'essaie de me guérir par l'exercice de la volonté. J'y réussis parfois.'[17]

Yet in later years Camus came to recognise the regime that he imposed upon himself as the source of much of his unhappiness. Finally aware of the negative effects of his programme, he realised the need to relax, to return to the carefree joys of his youth:

> Il m'arrive de terminer certaines journées les dents serrées et j'ai souvent l'impression de marcher et de travailler par une pure volonté qui seule me tient debout. Mais dans ce cas il faut accepter d'être indulgent pour soi et pour sa propre nature. Il faut retourner à une vie plus animale, au repos, à la solitude.[18]

The return to a more natural life can be interpreted as a return to the innocence of *Noces*, to the simple pleasures of his youth, at a time when obscurity coincided with happiness.

In the foreword to the re-edition of *L'Envers et l'Endroit* in 1957, Camus was at last able to distance himself sufficiently from his experiences to analyse his reactions and his personality critically in a published piece. His insights into his behaviour reinforce many of the comments already made, since he highlights the effort towards self-improvement and self-control, the fear of failure, the desire for greatness. He had come to realise that his personal worth lay in his Algerian roots:

> Comme tout le monde, j'ai essayé, tant bien que mal, de corriger ma nature par la morale. C'est, hélas!, ce qui m'a coûté le plus cher ... Si, du moins, on pouvait vivre selon l'honneur, cette vertu des injustes! Mais notre monde tient ce mot pour obscène; aristocratie fait partie des injures littéraires et philosophiques. Je ne suis pas aristocrate, ma réponse tient dans ce livre: voici les miens, mes maîtres, ma lignée; voici, par eux, ce qui me réunit à tous. Et cependant, oui, j'ai besoin d'honneur, parce que je ne suis pas assez grand pour m'en passer.[19]

Towards the end of his life Camus appears to be coming to terms with himself as an artist, being able to distance himself a little from his obsessions and to begin to overcome the need to view himself through the historical definition of literary greatness that he had created in his formative years. We are able to witness him in May 1958 partially breaking free from his need to live up to this conception of greatness, as he prepares a freer, less politicised, but more human creation, *Le Premier Homme*:

> Etapes d'une guérison.
> Laisser dormir la volonté. Assez de 'il faut'.
> Dépolitiser complètement l'esprit pour humaniser.
> Ecrire le claustrophobe - et des comédies ... Ne serait-il pas que j'ai souffert de l'excès de mes responsabilités?[20]

It was this 'volonté', this effort to link the private man to his public image, that had resulted in the regimes of self-discipline earlier cited, an asceticism that Camus described as being contrary to his nature, but which was perhaps necessary given the distractions resulting from his commitment to political life in France. In 1959, even while working on the more personal, freer project of *Le Premier Homme*, he confessed to Jean Grenier that the monastic life of the writer was 'contraire à ma nature, si bien que le travail est une violence que je me fais. Mais il le faut.'[21] He was unable, even at this point in his life, totally to forget the ideal of literary greatness that he had formed in his youth, driving himself on to complete the next part of his 'oeuvre'.

The source of this ideal and its influence on Camus's life may have come initially from his mentor, Jean Grenier, but another influential figure from Camus's formative period already mentioned, and one who retained this position until Camus's death, was Nietzsche. Grenier himself had noted this influence, seeing it as stemming from Camus's history of illness,[22] but Camus's identification with Nietzsche was by no means limited to his own physical suffering. He quotes Nietzsche to Grenier, frequently comes back to the problem of achieving an accord between thought and action, and uses a quotation to this effect from Nietzsche as the epigraph to the third volume of his notebooks: 'Celui qui a conçu ce qui est grand, doit aussi le vivre'.[23] But clearly Camus had found himself enslaved by the conception of 'grandeur' that he had set out to live up to, and it is difficult not to see an element of ironic confession in his portrayal of Grand in *La Peste*, with the latter's dream of hearing his novel acclaimed by the exclamation of 'Messieurs, chapeaux bas!'.

Camus's failure to achieve his ideal for himself tormented him throughout the 1950s, as a number of notebook entries show. In December 1954 he confesses how he has 'toujours espéré devenir meilleur' and that he has 'toujours décidé de faire ce qu'il fallait pour cela', but that his level of success is doubtful.[24] In the summer of 1956 this expression of his failure to meet his own standards is repeated in similar terms.[25] Some seven months before his death Camus is still occupied with the same problem of self-worth, taking stock of his struggles with himself and finally coming to the conclusion that his nature cannot be changed:

> Il m'arrive de regretter de ne pas être meilleur. Quand on est jeune, on croit au progrès personnel et qu'à force de décisions ou d'emplois du temps on viendra à bout de ses défauts. Et puis, à 45 ans on se retrouve tel qu'on était au départ, ou à peu près, moins la croyance au progrès. Bref, il faut vivre avec soi-même.[26]

But, on the level of moral and political action, this is by no means tantamount to giving in to fatalism and despair. There is no reason to suppose that Camus ever went back on his early determination to go on undertaking some form of action as long as any chance of success remained, with the concomitant belief that the action itself has value even if it does not result in success. The outstanding embodiment of this stance is Rieux in *La Peste*, but Camus also makes the point in his notebooks, with regard to 'grandeur': 'La grandeur, c'est d'essayer d'être grand. Il n'en est point d'autre.'[27] For Camus, 'grandeur', in turn, is linked with a certain type of aristocracy:

> Quoi qu'il prétende, le siècle est à la recherche d'une aristocratie. Mais il ne voit pas qu'il lui faut pour cela renoncer au but qu'il s'assigne hautement: le bien-être. Il n'y a d'aristocratie que du sacrifice.

L'aristocrate est d'abord celui qui donne sans recevoir, qui *s'oblige*. L'Ancien Régime est mort d'avoir oublié cela.[28]

The key phrases in this statement, dating from 1951, are 'renoncer', 'sacrifice' and 's'oblige', demonstrating Camus's sense of personal duty. He saw such a duty as one that demanded certain sacrifices, such as his own 'bien-être'. For the aristocracy concerned, 'le devoir ne consiste ni à s'affirmer ni à se supprimer mais à faire servir ce qu'on affirme ... pour consacrer un jour une seule image supérieure de l'homme'.[29]

Camus was always acutely conscious of the impact that his writings could have on his readership and he attempted to set himself up as an example, in order to 'faire servir' his affirmations. Even before he became the influential public figure of the post-war years, he was suffering doubts about his vocation on these grounds, and questioning the value of his contribution to art and politics. He lacked confidence in himself as a writer and felt himself to be losing the 'assurance que ce qu'on sent et ce qu'on est vaut comme exemple - l'assurance qu'on est irremplaçable et que l'on n'est pas lâche'.[30] In 1943, then, marked by his experience of *Combat* and the Resistance, and developing his private preoccupation with exemplarity in the domain of art, Camus was struggling to define his own theory of artistic commitment, something not referred to since the production of *Révolte dans les Asturies*.[31] Some of his most positive, optimistic works, of course, date from the ensuing period of his career. His notebooks show that his object in *La Peste* and *Les Justes* is to instruct and to guide by offering examples of conduct through his protagonists. And they, in turn, embody in many respects the values contained in *L'Homme révolté*. None of the books concerned is unequivocally optimistic, but we come away from each with an impression of hope tempered with lucidity. There is a marked difference between the optimism of these works and those of Camus's first cycle, which centred on Absurdity.

Even in the *Lettres à un ami allemand*[32] Camus had not progressed beyond the zero point of the absurd as described in *L'Etranger*, and the final stance adopted in the fourth letter is a willed position rather than a logically defensible one. Camus places his belief in man at the centre of a refusal of the conclusions of his own philosophy. Yes, the world may be absurd, but all actions cannot be considered equivalent, since, as Cherea claims in *Caligula*, some are 'plus belles que d'autres'. The *Lettres* may be seen as a literary formulation of Camus's crisis of faith in man caused by the outbreak of World War II. In this instance, the role of 'désespéré' is taken by the German friend and the dialogue is conducted on the public stage, albeit with Camus assuming a more positive role. In a very real sense, however, it is still a dialogue with the self, with the man that Camus had once been. Indeed, he is willing to recognise in himself and his comrades a link with the German friend, which is the 'perpétuelle tentation de vous ressembler', a temptation to nihilism that he had ostensibly vanquished after the experience of September 1939.[33]

The fact is that while the ethic of Absurdity did not endorse nihilistic violence, it did not condemn it either, and left Camus unable to justify his resistance to the Nazi regime except in emotional, intuitive terms. In a letter to Jean Grenier dated May 1943, we see him reacting against the conclusions he had drawn from the Absurd. Realising that he is unable to live honourably by his ethic of lucidity alone, he describes a more fundamental and personal position:

> Tout est permis, bien entendu, mais je sais qu'il est des actions que je ne ferai pas, des paroles et des fidélités que je ne renierai pas ... et surtout des bassesses que je regretterai toujours.[34]

Camus is struggling to find reasons not only to refute the Nazi position, but also to justify his own conduct, yet he is unable to go further than a spontaneous notion of honour. The *Lettres* publicly describe this struggle, showing Camus attempting to separate himself from the German friend, just as he had separated himself from the 'désespéré' he had become in September 1939. He made this clear in his 'Défense de *L'Homme révolté*', where of the problems faced by the resistants during the Occupation years he wrote:

> Il serait juste de dire que nous savions où était le mensonge, sans encore pouvoir dire où se trouvait la vérité. Il fallut donc aller au plus pressé, fermer les yeux et lutter selon son coeur.[35]

In a footnote to this text he added that the *Lettres* 'traduisent ... l'essentiel de cette expérience'. His stance at the time, then, is an intuitive, emotional one that finds its basis in a lived experience rather than abstract philosophy. It is based on the refusal of actions opposing the deeply felt sense of personal honour that Camus gives evidence of in the letter to Grenier.

This willed refusal of nihilism should come as no surprise to us, since the same will was at work in *Le Mythe de Sisyphe*, where the maintenance of the Absurd through the refusal of suicide is effectively an arbitrary choice made by the individual, and not a logically necessary conclusion. The significance of the book lies, precisely, in the very arbitrariness of the wager on the absurd that Camus suggests we make. It is a willed position as opposed to a logical one, offering an example of hope to a generation tempted by despair. Indeed, Camus's conclusion to the book is in many ways similar in tone to his journalistic appeals. It is a motivating call, stressing the strength of man's will and tenacity in determining his fate and happiness, at the same time linking them to the Pascalian notion of a wager. The wager advocated is in a sense an extension of Camus's own personal conception of greatness. Two notebook entries written in 1943 bring this out very clearly. In the first he writes: 'Avoir la force de choisir ce qu'on préfère et de s'y tenir. Ou sinon il vaut mieux mourir.'[36] A few pages later this sense of aspiration is extended to become a duty: 'Le devoir c'est de faire ce qu'on sait être juste et bon - "préférable". Cela est facile? Non, car même ce qu'on sait être préférable, on le fait difficilement.'[37] The arbitrary choice of life over suicide is the choice of a man attempting to reach an ideal, trying to demonstrate the 'préférable' in his work as well as his life. The attempt to set an example and to write exemplary works, then, goes back much further than *La Peste* and *Les Justes*. But however much more positive and optimistic these works may be, the values that they embody still do not receive philosophical justification in Camus's writings until the formulation of 'Je me révolte, donc nous sommes' in *L'Homme révolté*.

Even after the success of *La Peste* Camus continued to harbour doubts about his personal worthiness. But his perception of the role of the artist became even clearer and in 1949 he compared his vocation to that of a priest:

> Dans un monde qui ne croit plus au péché, c'est l'artiste qui est chargé de la prédication. Mais si les paroles du prêtre portaient, c'est qu'elles étaient nourries par l'exemple. L'artiste s'essaye donc de devenir un exemple.[38]

Like the priest, Camus is seeking to preach a message of hope and lucidity, lending it weight through his own personal example. He is still haunted by the image of greatness he formed for himself in his youth and once more we witness him repeating the Nietzschean idea of an accord between philosophy and action. Hence a significant part of *L'Homme révolté* consists of an analysis of the link between philosophy and politics, showing the role of the former in determining the latter. From metaphysical revolt to historical revolt, it is the flawed philosophical basis of the various movements he describes that is said to result in their failure. He criticises in turn the dandy, the surrealist, the fascist, the Marxist, the existentialist, illustrating in each case the descent from idealism to nihilism, from emancipation to slavery. Unequivocal admiration is reserved only for the fastidious assassins, the subjects of *Les Justes*. It is true that Camus begins the book with the positive message of solidarity contained in the formula, 'Je me révolte, donc nous sommes', but he fails to describe in any detail a political system that could be set against those he criticises. Even his formula is born of the arbitrary choice not to commit suicide expressed in *Le Mythe de Sisyphe*.

If the book finishes on a positive, optimistic note, with Camus elucidating his theory of measure, and concluding with the image of the arc of an arrow flying true through the air,[39] it has to be acknowledged that the end of *L'Homme révolté* presents us with myth and lyricism rather than formal analysis or the advocacy of a concrete political system. Camus is optimistic without any real, identifiable reason. As in *Le Mythe de Sisyphe*, he is interested less in the proposing of a system, with all the connotations of exclusion that it would bring with it, than in the presenting of a positive vision. Roger Quilliot and Germaine Brée have both suggested that the ending of *L'Homme révolté* is not based on logic,[40] and John Cruickshank has drawn attention to the notable change in style: 'After 350 pages of admirably clear and direct prose Camus allows himself a series of lyrical flights'.[41] We may wonder whether Camus appreciated the impasse that his criticism of political systems had produced and attempted to remedy its pessimism with a vague optimism, or whether his effort was a spontaneous product of a less conscious sentiment, the result of years of self-indoctrination. But however that may be, it can be argued that the real significance of Camus's work is that 'To a generation which saw no reason for hope it offered hope without reason'.[42] He is still trying to offer himself and his work as an example of 'grandeur', struggling to serve his public: 'L'effort que j'ai fait, inlassablement, pour rejoindre les autres dans les valeurs communes, pour établir mon propre équilibre n'est pas entièrement vain. Ce que j'ai dit ou trouvé peut servir, doit servir à d'autres.'[43]

This notebook entry from 1957 shows Camus reflecting on his achievement and his aims five years after the publication of *L'Homme révolté* and the polemic it engendered. Yet his literary output in the subsequent, final phase of his career does not correspond to the same ideals as the works of the Revolt phase. Neither *La Chute* nor *L'Exil et le Royaume* was part of the planned oeuvre recorded in his notebooks. In fact, in many respects the two books may be seen as examples of the freer creation that Camus had dreamed of. After years of suffering a writing block, he found himself unable to stem the flow of cynicism and irony that forms the content of *La Chute* and it outgrew its place as just one more story in *L'Exil et le Royaume* to become a work in its own right.

The significance of these two final works, then, lies in their position outside Camus's self-imposed programme of works: they show the writer freeing himself from the constraints to which he had previously submitted. After the controversy surrounding *L'Homme révolté*, it seems that Camus began to move away from his conception of his work as an example and started to allow himself to express fully his personal bitterness, using Jean-Baptiste Clamence as his mouthpiece. Hence when Clamence expresses his love of heights, his indifference to human affairs, and his commitment to noble causes, he is essentially being used by Camus to confess his own desire for greatness, his indifference and his guilt. Of course, Clamence is not Camus: Clamence is merely that part of Camus which he had kept hidden from a public more used to seeing him as Rieux, Tarrou or Rambert, a public for whom he would forever be the prophet of the Absurd and the editor of *Combat*. In Clamence, Camus was finally giving public expression to a side of his character that can be discovered in his private notebooks and letters. Clamence illustrates his self-doubt, the bitterness he felt towards Sartre, his desire to escape the punishing demands that his conception of greatness made upon him, just as the characters of *La Peste* express his post-Liberation idealism. These were all aspects of a complex personality, and, in the same way, Jonas would embody his reaction to fame and success, Janine his search for transcendence, and d'Arrast his dream of solidarity and mutual comprehension. Camus's comment on the writer in *L'Homme révolté* was thus a penetrating self-analysis: 'Un personnage n'est jamais le romancier qui l'a créé. Il y a des chances, cependant, pour que le romancier soit tous ses personnages à la fois.'[44]

Beginning to free himself from the constraints he had placed upon himself while writing the constituent parts of his Revolt cycle, Camus was able to express the more negative aspects of his personality in *La Chute* and *L'Exil et le Royaume*. The latter does finish on a note of optimism, but prior to reaching that point we are shown failure, alienation and despair. Janine is given a glimpse of the kingdom, only to return to an insensitive husband; the renegade will betray his God and die, his mouth stuffed with salt; Yvars is unable to show his sympathy for his boss and realises that age has narrowed his horizons; Daru becomes an exile in the land he loves; and Jonas will suffer from his fame, losing sight of his guiding star. In these stories Camus not only allowed himself to give freer expression to the darker side of his personality, but also returned in many respects to a tone present in the book that he described as the source of his 'oeuvre': *L'Envers et l'Endroit*. Both books describe examples of men and women lost in a beautiful but Godless, empty universe. For example, Yvars in 'Les Muets' suffers the same sensation of impotence as the old man and woman in 'Ironie'; they are simply older, and consequently more alone and alienated. And there is a hopelessness present in the earlier work that also exists in Daru's inability to save himself from a situation that overwhelms him. Both books offer a vivid analysis of the absurd futility of life, and only d'Arrast succeeds in overcoming the obstacles in his path. Yet it is uncertain to what extent Camus's last two fictional works are evidence of a deepening pessimism on his part and to what extent the result of the change in his conception of his public role. He probably saw them as stages on the way to the work in which he would demonstrate his coming to terms with his art and obligations, the masterpiece that he felt would confirm his talent and place him amongst his literary heroes. But that work, *Le Premier Homme*, was destined to remain unfinished.

A notebook entry three months prior to Camus's death seems to confirm that he had come to terms with the obsessions that motivated him, attaining a peace of mind that had previously eluded him: 'L'effort le plus épuisant de ma vie a été de juguler ma propre nature pour la faire servir à mes plus grands desseins. De loin en loin, de loin en loin seulement, j'y réussissais.'[45] We have seen that exemplarity did not come easily to Camus, and had to be won through interminable efforts towards self-correction. His letters and, above all, his notebooks document the effort of will involved, but Camus also acknowledged the struggle in one of the last interviews that he gave, on being described by the interviewer as an 'étranger': 'Par nature je suis certainement cela. Mais par volonté et réflexion, j'ai essayé de ne pas me séparer de mon temps.'[46] Yet, to the extent that he shared some of his fictional characters' pessimism, nihilism or cynicism, he had concealed the fact, being intent on producing a relatively optimistic body of journalism and literature that fitted in with his conception of personal greatness and exemplarity. An early comment on Nietzsche can in many ways be seen as equally appropriate to Camus himself:

> Pour beaucoup Nietzsche est, en effet, un optimiste. Mais pour exprimer une opinion personnelle, nous dirons qu'à la lecture de ses livres, on peut se demander si sous ces appels si beaux, si poétiques à la douleur rédemptrice, il ne se cachait pas une âme foncièrement pessimiste mais qui refusait à l'être. Il y a, en effet, quelque chose de forcené dans son optimisme entêté. C'est une sorte de perpétuelle lutte contre le découragement, et c'est ce que nous avons trouvé de plus attirant dans cette figure déjà si étranger.[47]

Certainly, Camus refrained from making public both his personal battle against a writing block and his pessimism over post-Liberation France and the Algerian crisis. His sense of duty to the fragile possibilities that he was always at pains to highlight forbade him public expression of any such despair, regardless of his personal feelings. It was this crushing responsibility that prompted him to reflect in the 'Avant-Propos' to *Actuelles III* in 1958 that 'on attend trop d'un écrivain'.[48] When he offers a vision of the artist of tomorrow, we are not sure that he is not giving his opinion of his own position:

> Le vrai créateur, demain, s'il se trouvait solitaire, connaîtrait une profondeur de solitude dont aucune époque n'a jamais eu l'idée. Il serait seul à concevoir et à servir une civilisation qui ne peut naître sans le concours de tous. Il aurait le soupçon que cette civilisation court sa dernière chance et qu'il est un des derniers à le savoir.[49]

But, in any case, whilst it is possible to argue that Camus's commitment to a politically optimistic literature stifled some of his natural talents, it made much of his published work 'un excellent antidote contre le désespoir total'.[50]

NOTES

1   *L'Eté*, Paris, Gallimard, 1954; reprinted in R. Quilliot and L. Faucon (eds), *Albert Camus. Essais*, Paris, Gallimard ('Bibliothèque de la Pléiade'), 1965 (hereafter *Essais*); p. 864.

2   J. Lévi-Valensi and A. Abbou, *Fragments d'un combat*, Paris, Gallimard ('Cahiers Albert Camus', 3), 1978, p. 630.

3   E. Parker, *Albert Camus - The Artist in the Arena*, Wisconsin, University of Wisconsin Press, 1965, p. 54. Camus's 'Lettre à un désespéré' is in his *Carnets I*, Paris, Gallimard, 1962; p. 181.

4   *Correspondance Albert Camus-Jean Grenier, 1932-1960*, Paris Gallimard, 1981, p. 222.

5   *Essais*, p. 972.

6   *Carnets I*, p. 240.

7   *Carnets II*, Paris, Gallimard, 1964, p. 285.

8   Ibid., p. 292.

9   *Carnets I*, p. 35.

10   Ibid., pp. 40, 47. The six projects were: 'Essai sur les ruines, Mort dans l'âme, Maison devant le monde, Roman, Essai sur Malraux, Thèse'.

11   Ibid., p. 87.

12   *Carnets II*, p. 262; cf. p. 328.

13   Ibid., p. 313.

14   *Carnets III*, Paris, Gallimard, 1989, p. 99.

15   *Essais*, p. 99.

16   Ibid., p. 102; cf. p. 113.

17   *Carnets II*, p. 261.

18   *Carnets III*, p. 240.

19   *Essais*, p. 11.

20   *Carnets III*, p. 220.

21   Camus-Grenier correspondence, op. cit., p. 231.

22   Jean Grenier, *Souvenirs*, Paris, Gallimard, 1968, p. 84.

23   *Carnets III*, p. 11.

24   Ibid., p. 148.

25   Ibid., p. 191.

26   Camus-Grenier correspondence, op. cit., p. 229.

27   Ibid., p. 287. Camus was also to note that women 'n'ont pas comme nous l'obligation de la grandeur' (p. 322)!

28   *Carnets III*, p. 19.

29   Ibid., p. 105.

30   *Carnets II*, p. 92.

31   This play, an 'essai de création collective', was written early in 1936 by Camus and three of his colleagues in the Théâtre du Travail of Algiers. The play presented sympathetically the plight of striking miners in Spain in 1934.

32   *Essais*, pp. 213-43.

33   Ibid., p. 222.

34   Camus-Grenier correspondence, op. cit., p. 96.

35   *Essais*, p. 1704.

36   *Carnets II*, p. 109.

37   Ibid.

38   *Carnets II*, p. 265.

39   *Essais*, p. 709.

40   Ibid., p. 1610; and Germaine Brée, *Camus and Sartre*, London, Calder and Boyars, 1972, p. 133.

41   *Albert Camus and the Literature of Revolt*, Oxford, Oxford University Press, 1960, p. 116.

42   Conor Cruise O'Brien, *Camus*, London, Fontana/Collins ('Fontana Modern Masters'), 1970, p. 32.

43   *Carnets III*, p. 215.

44   *Essais*, p. 448.

45   *Carnets III*, p. 273.

46   *Essais*, p. 1925.

47   *Albert Camus 2: Langue et Langage*, Paris, Minard ('Archives des Lettres Modernes'), 1969, p. 158.

48   *Essais*, p. 900.

49   *Carnets III*, p. 187.

50   Roger Quilliot, *La Mer et les prisons*, Paris, Gallimard, 1956, p. 264.

The Sovereignty of Solitude and the Gift of Writing in Violette Leduc's *La Folie en tête*

MICHAEL SHERINGHAM

Early on in *La Folie en tête*, the second volume of her autobiographical trilogy,[1] Violette Leduc recounts a recent incident. She had been sitting next to Simone de Beauvoir in the Café de Flore, when her attention became transfixed by a perfectly ordinary comb in Beauvoir's hair. For a week the image of the comb had haunted her; as she sought to account for this, she remembered something that had happened when, as a child, she had been out cutting flowers with her beloved grandmother Fidéline. Clinging to her grandmother's legs the child had implored her to sit down, observing that, in the evening light, the misty plain below them resembled the sea:

> - C'est comme si nous étions à la mer, dis-je à Fidéline. Je lui donnais le bras, je tapotais le dessus de sa main, je voulais qu'elle me regarde quand je lui parlais et quand je ne lui parlais pas. Je voulais qu'elle me regarde toujours.
> - Pourquoi dis-tu ça, me demanda Fidéline, tu ne la connais pas.
> Je n'osais pas lui expliquer: la nappe de rosée sur laquelle nous sommes assises, la mer... Le soir immense, la mer... Le son du clairon perdu dans la plaine, la mer...
> - Regarde, dis-je à Fidéline, regarde!

This last exhortation is not prompted by the vista, however, but by a dirty fragment of comb lying on the ground beside the flowers:

- Tu veux le voir?
- C'est sale. Jette ça ...
- Ce n'est pas sale. Tu ne veux pas le voir?[2]

In the face of her grandmother's refusal to show interest in the comb, the child bursts into tears. No further comment is made, but the reader is invited to reflect on the possible connections between the childhood memory and the week-long fixation on Beauvoir's comb. In two respects the passage is untypical of *La Folie en tête* where, unlike *La Bâtarde*, Leduc's childhood is rarely focused on in detail and where, again unlike *La Bâtarde*, explicit references to the period when Leduc is writing are scarce. In other ways, however, the scene brings together, emblematically, a number of important themes and preoccupations. The obsessive relationship with Beauvoir is a central thread in *La Folie en tête*,[3] but the implied identification between Beauvoir and Leduc's grandmother is also characteristic of a tendency for the major figures in Leduc's life to be involved in a network of parallels and substitutions. Then, there is the tension between the desire to be *watched* - to be enveloped in a comprehending look - and the desire to *show*, to displace the look from oneself on to the object of a perception which is *offered* to the other. This in a context where the gift may, as here, be declined, and where refusal is in some measure inevitable, since the need for fusion with the other is generally combined with a contradictory impulse towards separation, independence and sovereignty. In addition, the fact that an ordinary object is at the centre of the two incidents points to the way in which, in Leduc's text, the phenomenal world is constantly involved in a struggle between absorption and repulsion, animism and fetichism, sensual joy and dark phobia, illumination and delusion.

The aim of the reading of *La Folie en tête* which follows is to explore links between the areas already touched on in connection with the comb scene, and to relate them to the unfolding of Leduc's autobiographical project. A preliminary word needs to be said about the relation between *La Folie en tête* and Leduc's previous volume of autobiography. Diegetically, *La Bâtarde* ends with the initial composition (but not publication) of *L'Asphyxie*, Leduc's first novel, and thus with her (re)birth as a writer. For Violette as protagonist, this is no more than another event, albeit one which may herald a new beginning if the faith of her mentor, Maurice Sachs, proves to be justified. But the very prominent extradiegetic narrator, writing twenty years later, acts as a constant reminder that the composition of *L'Asphyxie* was indeed a new start, that Leduc did become a writer and, what is more, that writing has given her a new identity. The constant narratorial intrusions in *La Bâtarde* are therefore proleptic in that they anticipate developments which fall outside the diegetic framework of the text. Leduc's subsequent history is in fact doubly inscribed here: firstly, in her manner of writing which testifies to the mature author she has turned into;

secondly, through allusions to writing which, particularly towards the end of the book, relate specifically to the act and process of writing at particular places and times. In some respects, then, *La Bâtarde* conforms to what could be termed a 'synechdochal' model of autobiography where a part of the narrator's life in fact substantially represents the whole (other examples would be Stendhal's *Vie de Henri Brulard* or Sartre's *Les Mots*, where a wider life-history is explored through the analysis of childhood experience). But, in its redemptive dimension, *La Bâtarde* skirts round the years of struggle, subsequently narrated in *La Folie en tête* and *La Chasse à l'amour*, and puts forward a view of writing, and a portrait of the writer, which belong to a later period.

La Folie en tête, which covers the decade following the writing of *L'Asphyxie* and the more or less total critical and commercial failure of her first three books, differs from *La Bâtarde* in that the gap between the past protagonist and the present writer, instead of being underlined, is played down in favour of a constant interactive process where the past is represented only as it is reconstructed and transformed in the writing present.[4] *La Folie en tête* is purgatorial rather than redemptive, and lacks a clear end-point. Had Leduc completed what would have been a tetralogy, and covered the writing of *La Bâtarde*, and the belated fame and recognition it brought, her overall autobiographical project would have represented, at the level of diegesis, what is already adumbrated in *La Bâtarde*. Ironically, Leduc wrote *La Folie en tête* in the years 1965-1970 when she was enjoying the success and notoriety *La Bâtarde* had brought her, and was living it up in fashionable places and circles. No reference is made to this in the text: the only 'present' we are made aware of is that of the act and process of writing.

Leduc's presentation of the main personal relationships she was involved in during the period covered by *La Folie en tête* - the infatuation with Beauvoir, the edgy dealings with her remarried mother, the disastrous 'engouement' for Jean Genet, and the obsessive passion for the rich homosexual Jacques Guérin which takes her to the brink of madness - involve the excavation of distant memories and the reconstruction of past events.[5] However, the clearest sign that the patterns established in past experiences stem from the present act of 'mise en forme' is the way these individuals are constantly compared with one another (and with figures in her earlier life, familiar from *La Bâtarde*, such as her unknown father, her past lovers - Isabelle, Hermine and Gabriel - and her mentor Maurice Sachs). In fact, as *La Folie en tête* progresses, the main protagonists in Leduc's saga are drawn into a network of substitutions and superimpositions. Simone de Beauvoir, for example, is presented in a number of guises. She is an ideal *alter ego* and role-model, the incarnation of the writer Leduc would like to become. But she is also the very source of Leduc's identity since Leduc only writes *for* Beauvoir.[6] She is both a mother-figure and the object of various kinds of love, from erotic passion to mystical devotion. Violette quickly regretted writing Beauvoir a passionate declaration of love, since this 'lettre de collégienne' casts her heroine in the role of another Isabelle, with whom Violette had an erotic relationship at boarding school.[7] In her maternal role, Beauvoir sometimes occupies the position of Violette's real mother, Berthe, and makes her feel like a naughty child,[8] and at other times is likened to an ideal mother. When Violette takes her real mother to gawp at Beauvoir in the Café de Flore, Berthe takes on the role of sister, a fellow 'collégienne', while Violette imagines that the bells of the church at Saint-Germain-des-Prés are tolling for the burial of the young girl and her mother, leaving the way open for a new maternal bond.[9] Beauvoir is placed in further triangles involving Genet and Jacques. Violette feels guilty at cheating Beauvoir of the love she feels for Genet,[10] and of deceiving her in not revealing the truth about her feelings for Jacques. Beauvoir and Jacques are contrasted in so far as Violette does tell Jacques all about Beauvoir, but they are also equated because ultimately they both reject Violette by remaining distant and aloof.[11]

Leduc's account of her short-lived friendship with Jean Genet makes painful reading.[12] As *protégés* of the literary establishment and as social outcasts they have much in common. Leduc observes wryly at one point that she and Genet are guinea-pigs for the existentialists, 'cobayes pour leur psychologie',[13] and when she and Genet play parts in a home movie shot at Jacques's country house (Genet in the role of a baby, and Violette as his mother!) she observes that three of the people involved are illegitimate.[14] Genet is parallelled with Maurice Sachs, as another homosexual writer who is bound to reflect Violette's passion: 'Un homosexuel de génie, quel programme de sacrifices inouis, quelles suaves immolations en perspective!'.[15] But he is also parallelled with Leduc's mother: 'Genet ressemblait à ma mère. Ils ne pardonnent pas leur enfance aux autres.'[16] Like Berthe, Genet cannot show affection, and thus his physical violence towards her is seen as in some sense natural and predictable.[17]

It is Genet who introduces Leduc to Jacques Guérin, a rich homosexual industrialist and literary patron, and thus gives her access to the social world she associates with her unknown father, the rich 'fils de famille' who got her mother pregnant and then repudiated her. To enjoy the luxury of Jacques's hospitality is to overturn her destiny, and this prompts more specific associations between Jacques and Violette's father. At one point, for example, Leduc wonders if Jacques's 'gestes précieux' resemble those of her father,[18] and later, when Jacques is about to come round to dinner to meet Berthe, Leduc realises that her mother is expecting Jacques to look like the lost father who still haunts them: 'Mon père: des osselets dans un caveau'.[19] Jacques, however, is said to feel drawn to Berthe as to a mother,[20] and Leduc hints that Jacques too is a bastard like her. This parallel between herself and Jacques is underlined when Leduc observes that, unlike most men (and unlike women) Jacques has never been 'cured' of his childhood.[21] But, another strand in this fabric of relationships involves casting Jacques in the role of 'petit garçon' and Violette in the role of father[22] or mother.[23] To become a 'father' is to achieve a double victory over her heredity since it inscribes her in the father-offspring relationship she had been denied, and at the same time extricates her from dependence on her mother. To become a mother is to supply a need which she imputes to Jacques, and thus to circumvent the awkward fact of his lack of desire for her on account of his homosexuality. Other fantasies involving Jacques include a passage where Fidéline (the grandmother) is urged to join Violette and Berthe as a trio of 'fiancées' for him;[24] there are also parallels between Jacques and Hermine, between Violette and Jacques's dog, Blitz, between Jacques and Flavien, a young reader Violette attempts to seduce, and between Jacques and Maurice Sachs.

By insistently emphasising parallels and contrasts between the main figures in her life, Leduc recasts her experience as a claustrophobic, closed circle in which the same unproductive emotional dynamisms are repeated *ad infinitum*. Beauvoir and Genet, Berthe and Jacques, Isabelle and Hermine, Sachs and Gabriel all come to embody, in different but endlessly comparable ways, a fairly limited series of emotional dead-ends, sexual cul-de-sacs, existential impasses.[25] Even the positive aspect of the relationship with Beauvoir is seen to be negative in origin, since it is by patiently tolerating Violette's histrionics, yet always keeping her at a distance, refusing any real bond of affection but constantly encouraging her to write - and to ignore apparent failure - that Beauvoir serves to validate the persona as a writer which, retrospectively at least, will be Leduc's foil against adversity in human relationships. As she writes the past in *La Folie en tête*, Leduc creates an intersubjective network where she is at once central and peripheral. Ultimately, the point of all the parallels, substitutions and superimpositions is that Leduc has no real place in the network of her own past relationships, all of which involve her exclusion, rejection, or marginalisation. Yet this is by no means the whole picture, and what must now be examined is the way, by virtue of a process resembling the Sartrean 'Qui perd gagne', Leduc's very marginality and exclusion are represented as vital constituents in her positive image of herself as a 'solitaire' and, ultimately, as a writer.

A number of key scenes, in the middle sections of *La Folie en tête*, establish links between desire, exclusion and solitude which will be central to the subject position Leduc sees herself occupying as a writer. The treatment of these scenes, which involve social occasions - dinner parties - turns a feeling of being 'out of place' from a relative to a more radical and absolute state of being. On her first visit to Jacques's luxurious house near the Parc Monceau, in autumn 1947, Leduc is conscious of a reversal of social roles, and the identification of Jacques with her father intensifies the effects of his refined formality and politeness, and contributes to a feeling of unreality exacerbated by the rich furnishings. The presence of Genet, in boorish mood, completes the triangle, adding an acute awareness of her femininity to Leduc's self-consciousness: 'J'aurais voulu couper mes jambes, j'étais empêtrée dans ma féminité'.[26] Excluded by the male conversation, Leduc goes through agonies trying to dispose of a piece of meat she cannot swallow, identifies with one of Jacques's paintings - a Soutine representing a rabbit on a butcher's hook - and occupies herself by thoughts of the Spontex dish-cloths she had left to macerate in her garret. Increasingly she feels as if she is invisible: 'Vivre, c'était donc disparaître?',[27] 'je n'existais pour personne. Est-ce que j'existais pour moi-même?'[28] Her journey home, through the empty corridors of the metro, dwarfed by hoardings advertising Lysis bras, is rendered as the lonely Odyssey of 'cette grande écorchée, cette grande esseulée',[29] an old hag muttering oaths and railing against men in glasses (one of her obsessions is the way Jacques fiddles with his horn-rims). In seeking a further invitation, by telephoning Jacques at his factory, Leduc acknowledges her disturbing predilection for self-annihilation: 'Je n'existe plus aussitôt que s'ébauche en moi le projet de revenir chez lui'.[30] In the event, Jacques is absent on this occasion, and just when Violette acknowledges that she is in love with him she is forced to encounter another obstacle to her desires in the shape of his partner Denis, who acts as host on this occasion.

The second major dinner-scene[31] involves Jacques's visit to Violette's new two-room apartment (in the same building as the tiny 'réduit' where she had lived for years with Gabriel) while her mother is staying with her. Jacques and Berthe 's'entendaient à bureaux fermés'[32] - a telling phrase in the circumstances - while Leduc represents herself as a kind of disembodied, immaterial, angelic presence:

> Assise dans mon ciel et mon royaume de nuages blancs, assise dans mon fauteuil de duvets de colombes, je les regardais, je les écoutais. Jacques était de son avis: J'aurais plus d'air, plus de lumière, plus de soleil, de lumière? Elle a ses barreaux radieux, son écuelle étincelante, son astre pour prison ... Violette? Découpée dans un livre d'images, suspendue au-dessus d'eux par un fil retenu au plafond. Elle ne voulait pas s'en aller de là, monsieur, vous ne savez pas comme elle est têtue, vous ne savez pas comme elle est entêtée, elle s'abîmait les yeux, je lui disais.[33]

While Jacques and Berthe natter on about one kind of displacement - from the dark 'réduit' to the sunny 'deux pièces' - Violette experiences other kinds: displacement from the space of social exchange to that of self-enclosed solitude where, as she indicates, the ghosts of the past still linger; and displacement from the framework of 'normal' human relationships into the abstracted world of 'l'amour'- amorous obsession: 'j'aime, je suis en partance, je suis déclassée'.[34] To love Jacques is to be deprived of identity: 'Il sait tout, je ne sais rien, il me sépare de moi-même. Je suis une motte d'amour quand je suis près de lui. Je suis un pauvre lièvre traqué: d'où je loge je suis toujours délogée.'[35] In writing this scene Leduc replaces the original 'soundtrack' with a voice-over monologue which fuses past and present perspectives, and she progressively allows links to emerge between the displacement of solitude and love and the act or process of writing. Jacques offers her a generous advance for a private edition of *L'Affamée* and, to her mother's embarrassment, Leduc goes round to collect the money in cash from Jacques's factory three days later. For Leduc, this is 'justified' not only because it makes some amends for her social victimisation as a rich man's 'bâtarde', Jacques in this case representing her father,[36] but also because the 'work' of unreciprocated love deserves remuneration

> Si l'amour est nécessaire, l'argent est indispensable. Aimer est un travail considérable. Nous ignorons si nous n'y laisserons pas notre peau. Il faut distraire l'amour, l'abriter et le réchauffer. Qu'y a-t-il de dégradant à ce que l'être que vous aimez et qui ne vous aime pas soit bon et généreux avec vous? Plus je vieillis, moins je me crois coupable d'avoir aimé des êtres qui ne m'aimaient pas.[37]

In fact, of course, the money is for love that has already become writing: it is for *L'Affamée*, where Leduc's passion for Beauvoir is turned into literature. To repay Jacques for his generosity, Leduc will steal something back from Beauvoir and dedicate the book to him.[38]

The third dinner scene occurs in the next chapter, when Genet is invited round with his partner Lucien, and Gérard Magestry. Despite the best efforts of the other parties, Leduc's compulsive tendency to coddle and fuss over Genet, to treat him like a star and a genius, irritates him beyond measure, and shortly after the pudding is served,[39] unable to stand it any longer, Genet yanks the table-cloth, sending wine and crockery flying, and hot-foots it out of Leduc's flat in the company of Lucien. In her masochistic way, Leduc has no difficulty in comprehending the negative image of her - as a 'littéraire', as a woman - she imputes to Genet, and if his behaviour constituted 'le plus grand affront de ma vie',[40] she nevertheless finds that her impulse to go immediately round to find him at his hotel leads not to remonstration, or reproachfulness, but to further, and unequivocal, self-abasement. Finding Genet recumbent, she kneels beside him and kisses his chest, asking forgiveness for the injury he had done to her.[41]

If the chapter ended there, we would recognise a psychological mechanism with which Leduc had made us familiar. But a coda, the aftermath of the dinner, takes us in another direction. The scene, right in the middle of *La Folie en tête*,[42] is of central importance and constitutes one of the most impressive passages in Leduc's writing. It describes her return to the empty 'deux pièces', now stinking of spilt wine, and then evokes, with careful attention to rhythm (conveyed by sentence length and spacing), the contents of Violette's mind as she lies down and masturbates without undressing on the cold pine floor. While details about clothing, and short lyrical sentences, chart the progression towards pleasure ('l'avalanche irréelle. Le grand soleil de l'absence'),[43] the experience is portrayed both as one of distance and self-dissociation, and as the achievement of a radiant sovereignty in solitude:

> j'aime Jacques et ne finirai pas de l'aimer. *Miserere, miserere.*
> Tu prends tes aises sur les siècles, ma tristesse. Comme barbouillée, comme vaguement barbouillée du désir de moi-même. Ne me séduis pas, ne me tente pas, Violette. Pas, ici, pas maintenant, pas sur le marbre et le plancher. Tu peux recourir à cela à toute heure du jour et de la nuit donc tu n'es pas abandonnée. Oui, je n'ai que moi. Je me trouble à cette idée; un avant-coureur, mon trouble. Je cède à ce projet ...
> Je m'ouvre.[44]

As she anticipates the slide away from self, and procures in herself the sensual joy which her obsessional love for Genet and Jacques denies her, Leduc conveys, through images of clouds and stars ('Mon doigt. Mon frotteur d'étoiles')[45] a sense of having broken through to an inter-stellar vacancy and silence. Here she is totally alone - 'Je désire, je ne peux désirer que moi'[46] - but, at the same time, strangely liberated from herself, strangely double:

> Je serai brisée je serai bénie. Je serai un couple séparé. Un délire là où rien ne parle. Je serai une aurore et de la charcuterie. Je suis absente, mon âme a pris la clé des champs. Moi sur moi. Moi avec moi. Submergée, naufragée, je dirige mon naufrage. Je baigne mon doigt dans mon ciel.[47]

Here, auto-eroticism is both confrontation with self and deliverance from self, thralldom to others (since it is directed against them) and deliverance from others. Leduc's narrator expresses solidarity with her former self at this point, defiantly affirming the continuing recourse, by the sexagenarian woman, to this 'monotonie vertigineuse' and the all-consuming fire it substitutes for sentiment: 'Pas une plage de tendresse pour se reposer après, comme après l'acte d'amour à deux. Le feu a tout brûlé.'[48] 'Plaisir solitaire' takes on the character of a chosen solitude, a vantage-point giving access to a different apprehension of self. Although it occurs in the aftermath of humiliation and self-abasement with Genet, Leduc's solitary pleasure is neither defeat nor defiance but a strategic move into another dimension, an alternative space. Ultimately, *La Folie en tête* will show how this space finds its full embodiment when encompassed within the field created by the act and process of writing. Writing is portrayed as the ultimate locus of an identity, a sense of existence, where solitude and community, sanity and madness are, ideally, reconciled. But nothing could be more precarious or evanescent than the balance required for writing to manifest its positive aspects. Before looking at it directly, therefore, it is best to approach the space of writing in Leduc more obliquely via some of the areas it adjoins and encompasses.

An obsession with being seen, watched, witnessed is repeatedly found in *La Folie en tête*. The word 'témoin' is recurrent: it applies to the male figure who stares out from each banknote, as Leduc works the Black Market during the Occupation; to birds in the countryside; to her own painted fingernails: 'mes dix témoins'.[49] *Esse est percipi*: the feeling of existence for Leduc is first and foremost existence for others, including the type-setter for her first contribution to *Les Temps Modernes*, a fly on the back of her neck, the postman she imagines regaling with a famous name when she sends a letter to Beauvoir.[50] Clearly, to imagine beneficent looks is to ward off the hostile look one fears, the look which, in Leduc's case, will confirm her original rejection or the taint of her ugliness. To clamour for the Other's look, to advertise one's availability to it, is a prophylactic against the injurious effects of the unsolicited stare. The dynamic of looking and being looked at pervades the entire field in which Leduc's selfhood is constructed. At one end of the spectrum it is prominent in the downward spiral of delusion and paranoia, described in the last third of *La Folie en tête*, where Leduc convinces herself that she is constantly being spied on through a hole in the ceiling of her room,[51] and on one painful occasion goes out into the streets with a dog's name pinned to the back of her coat as in a party game.[52] Looking is also at the heart of Leduc's imaginary self-image and practice as a writer. To write *L'Affamée*, surrounded by photographs of Beauvoir, whom she constantly invoked but did not name, 'c'était me jeter sur ses yeux comme je me serais jetée sur des phares d'auto la nuit'.[53] Having collected copies of her first book, *L'Asphyxie*, from Gallimard Leduc sits on a bus vainly willing the person opposite to notice her, to enquire about the book.[54] Having frightened the woman off, Leduc then switches places, and contemplates the vacant seat. *L'Asphyxie* sells few copies but when Leduc receives fan letters from a couple of provincial youths she loses no time in tracking them down, involving herself in amusing and grotesque efforts at seduction which necessitate an obsessive concern with her physical appearance.

The scenes with Patrice[55] and Flavien[56] involve an especially high turn-over of those one-word or one-line definitions Leduc constantly applies to herself, which constitute another area where looking and writing interact. Like captions beneath a cartoon, these labels pin meaning to appearances, usually articulating the view of herself Leduc ascribes to others in a given situation. Not surprisingly, a majority of the hundred or so instances in *La Folie en tête* are negative. Some relate to her physical appearance: 'potiron', 'laideronne', 'épouvantail', 'citrouille sur le déclin', 'Gros Nez'.[57] Many allude to her sense of being an outcast or social reject: 'la parente pauvre', 'moi soupe populaire', 'clocharde';[58] more masochistically: 'ombre fautive', 'prisonnière et souffre-douleur des rues', 'ressaseuse', 'Cendrillon éperdue'.[59] Some refer to her eccentricity: 'cinglée', 'maniaque',[60] and some to her sexuality: 'dévote exaltée de l'homosexualité', 'jument en chaleur'.[61] In one brilliant passage Leduc describes herself as 'un lad autour de son cheval'[62] when she recalls caressing the Tyrolean shorts worn by Jean Marais in *L'Aigle à deux têtes* during a stay in the actor's bedroom at Cocteau's house in Milly. Several labels relate to her image as a would-be seductress: 'drageuse maniérée', 'dévergondée sur le qui-vive', 'vieille évaporée'.[63]

Yet the negativity which pervades these names is mitigated by a prevailing sense of irony and black humour. One set of labels reflects Leduc's sense of her geographical origins (she was from Valenciennes): she is a 'Femme du Nord', a 'Flamande' from the 'pays des lourds nuages'.[64] This atavistic 'northenness' can be allied with certain other descriptions which, in context at least, seem more positive: 'courageuse', 'femme seule', 'petit poucet', 'lapin disparu dans un haut-de-forme'.[65] And the exhibitionism to which the activity of self-designation testifies, while not necessarily a trait Leduc is entirely happy with, often seems to take on a jubilant, even triumphal air: 'Je suis baroque, ne m'en veuillez pas, c'est malgré moi'.[66] While they may originate in the imagined look of the Other, these images are processed and appropriated so that, when they are featured in Leduc's text, they bear her stamp, they are her labels. Furthermore, by their very multiplicity, these descriptions (which are usually in apposition to the personal pronoun and therefore involve disjunction) tend to break up and offset the imposition of a monolithic identity. Leduc is both 'une adolescente indécente' and 'une grand-mère';[67] the roles she plays in her psychodramas are varied: mutual consistency or plausibility are not required. We can make a comparison here with another of Leduc's stylistic idiosyncracies, the frequent enumerations of properties each preceded by a possessive adjective, as in

> mes gestes, mes tics, mes mouvements, mes détresses, mes élans, mes crises, mes émerveillements, mes trésors, mes déchets, mes chutes, mes bonds, mes déséquilibres, mes redressements, mes extases, mes agonies, mes affaissements, mes guérisons, mes abjections, mes erreurs, mes humiliations, mes écroulements, mes ascensions ... [68]

Or: 'mes microbes, mes miasmes, mes adverbes, mes relents, mes exagérations'.[69] In such enumerations, the insistent use of plural nouns further underlines the immensely varied psychological landscape they evoke. The 'mes' here do not really indicate possession, as if stable traits and attributes were being pinned down, but suggests the infinite 'properties' which the movement of

Leduc's writing tends to identify and to engender.

The concern with being seen, and with the way she is seen, is not purely an obsessive, one-way traffic. In the activity of writing Leduc to some extent controls the image-making process and attenuates the spell-binding fixity of her self-images. In many respects Leduc's writing, where theatricalisation fosters irony, has affinities with the Bakhtinian Carnivalesque. Moreover, in being staged and worked through, a pathological danger-area is potentially transformed into a therapeutic playground. With its escape-hatches and hidden corridors, its endlessly shifting scenery and temporal freedom, writing provides avenues of escape, scope for disappearance as well as performance. In *La Folie en tête* the field of seeing and being seen becomes the site for a struggle between presence and absence, incarnation and transcendence, embodiment and disembodiment.

A second field which connects with the space of writing is that of objects. A prominent feature of Leduc's style involves a kind of animistic, anthropomorphic projection which endows inert objects and other phenomena with an independent life. For example, in the early pages of *La Folie en tête*, the orange folder Leduc purchases for the manuscript of *L'Asphyxie* takes on numerous guises as she carts it about with her from appointment to appointment. In one passage, when she is walking along the *quais*, the focus shifts from the 'chemise orange' to some blue cagebirds, and these are then conscripted into the whimsical vein of fantasy which predominates at this point:

> Un tissu d'amour, un canevas d'amour, ce sont les barreaux. Vous pleuriez, vous embellissiez le ciel. La tentation de jeter la chemise orange dans la Seine, d'acheter ces deux bleutés, de m'enfermer avec eux dans la cage. Leur calme sur leur perchoir me grise. Paris a été libéré, Paris renaît, moi je vais le long des quais pour ce qui s'étiole, pour ce qui meurt de soif et se flétrit.[70]

The passage is generated by a contrast between liberated Paris on the one hand and Leduc on the other, still wedded to a past she cannot expunge ('Février 1945. Paris a été libéré, moi je m'enchaîne').[71] Anthropomorphism links with self-pity, but also with what Leduc calls 'mimétisme et ... anonymat', a capacity to lose her identity and merge with her surroundings which is seen both as a sign of social alienation and as a mark of creative power: 'Souvent je crée à l'intérieur des choses qu'on a créées sans m'attendre'.[72] Inherently unstable and vulnerable, this stance exposes Leduc to the threat of psychological invasion when her defences are down, and it is not surprising that her descent into paranoia, her brush with madness, should have as one of its prime symptoms a tendency for objects - cigarette packets, dog mess, bottle labels - to become the carriers of hostile and destructive meanings. The practice of divination is central here, and it is interesting that, in the midst of her psychic distress, driven to deny the plain fact that her relationship with Jacques has no future, Leduc consults a number of fortune-tellers. In one brilliant scene Leduc, who has previously tried a tarot-specialist, goes to see another 'voyante'. The sight of a piano in the waiting room stirs up the familiar ghosts: 'Tu te crevais pour mes leçons de piano, chère maman ... Résultat, chère mère, ta clocharde, ta propre à rien tend la main chez les voyantes.'[73] Mme Lamballe administers a kind of Rorschach test:

> - Jetez de l'encre sur cette feuille, je vous prie.
> Quel ton. Je veux bien, je veux tout.
> Je lançai son encre avec une force de lutteur. Enfin des pâtés à
> la place des mots ratés et de toutes ces étendues d'adjectifs
> stériles. La plume crache. Je crache et je me fâche, cruelle. Ne te
> plains pas, des vraies aigrettes d'encre. Je t'en ai donné hier
> après-midi, page blanche. Avare, tu ne donnais rien.[74]

The trails and splodges of dark ink briefly promise an alternative to, and deliverance from, the futility of writing. But as Mme Lamballe invites Leduc to visualise the chaotic marks as representations of her 'complications inimaginables', and to see herself as the spider caught in this dark web, pumping her all the while for the information which, more than ink-blots, will provide the material for the fortune-teller's wisdom, Leduc progressively recognises that the only 'revelation' on offer is common sense and that Mme Lamballe can only tell her what she already knows: 'Ça n'ira pas plus loin que l'amitié'.[75] Having initially been idealised, the ink-blots take on a negative and threatening objectivity, as they fail to live up to their promise, but then change again and become manifestations of a truth which, however unpalatable, is given all the more weight (given Leduc's respectful attitude to money) for costing 1,000 francs - especially since Mme Lamballe's fee includes the right to take away the blotted paper.

Animism, divination, the relationship with objects thus oscillate between positive and negative poles, madness and well-being. If the obsessional object can be a symptom of psychic disarray then, equally, a capacity to focus intently on, and to capture, the phenomenal world in its mysterious objectivity, its 'thereness', is often represented as a trait in Leduc which comes to her rescue, extricating her from abstraction and 'engloutissement' in her mental world. One passage, among many that could be cited, concerns a feature of the Paris streets:

> Je me promenais, de Faidherbe-Chaligny à la Nation, tout
> m'épatait. Jusqu'au bourrelet de loques ficelées près des égouts,
> sur la grille au pied de l'arbre. A quoi sert-il? Il n'est jamais

entre des mains. Toujours mouillé, toujours noirâtre, toujours repoussant. Dérision d'un tapis roulé. Une pauvre chose, comme nous disons un pauvre type. Quelle est son utilité? Mystère. C'est presque de la vie, ce bourrelet dans une rue, la vie l'emporte sur les idées.[76]

Most *habitués* of Paris will recognise these dark bundles of rolled-up rags, and may have wondered like Leduc what they are doing there. In fact they have an important practical purpose, serving to regulate the flow of water along the gutters. Since she does not know this, Leduc views the mysterious object in a non-utilitarian way, as a pure thing, a radiant phenomenon like the pair of shoes painted by Van Gogh (whose letters Leduc refers to) or the knife-rest contemplated in Beckett's *Molloy* (a novel which thrills Leduc when it appears in 1951),[77] an object which fascinates Molloy precisely to the extent that he cannot fathom what its function is. For Leduc there is something 'life-like' ('C'est presque de la vie') about the 'bourrelet', a quality that is antithetical to ideas. This derisory 'non-carpet' asks nothing of Leduc, it does not look at her. Rather, it requires her attention, her look, if it is to find any sort of recognition. What Leduc can provide is the gift of her look, and the vehicle of this provision is her writing.

As in *La Bâtarde*, but more insistently, *La Folie en tête* comprises regular bulletins concerning the act of writing. *La Folie en tête* covers the period when *L'Affamée* and much of *Ravages* (especially the section which was initially censored by Gallimard, and then published separately, in modified form, as *Thérèse et Isabelle*) were written, and when she evokes the composition of these works Leduc tends to put forward generalisations about the process of writing which also encompass the writing of *La Folie en tête* itself. The first extensive passage of this kind[78] occurs at the point where Simone de Beauvoir has read and expressed enthusiasm about the manuscript of *L'Asphyxie*, but suggested certain changes. Violette re-reads her work in the light of Beauvoir's gaze, recognising that these pages now encapsulate a desired identity - 'ta réalité, ce sont ces feuillets'[79] - not only by virtue of their content, but more importantly by virtue of their style. This leads into a meditation on writing which emphasises the notion of craft and hard work; indeed, the whole passage is built around an opposition between inspiration and application. Not for Leduc the 'orages de la création',[80] the trance of the initiate. Writing is more like furniture-polishing or shoe-mending, even when it consists in a passionate search for the only word which will do, the 'mot définitif', the adjective which will release ('débloquer') the sensation to be rendered.[81] Writing, however, does not make things present, in fact it underlines their absence: 'Qualifier, c'est prendre dans ses bras un absent. Tout ce que nous écrirons sera absent.'[82] Addressing the 'tendres nuances' of the sky, over towards Nation, Leduc writes: 'laissez-vous prendre, je vais vous détruire, puisque je vais vous trahir ...'.[83] Yet if it engenders absence, betrayal and even destruction, writing nevertheless brings about a marriage: 'Je marierais du matin au soir les adjectifs avec les sons, les couleurs et les parfums'.[84] Words may betray things, but they capture qualities and sensations - an order of realities which lies between subjectivity and objectivity, the concrete and the mental.

The same themes, images and attitudes recur in subsequent passages concerning writing.[85] Thus, the unglamorous housecoat ('blouse de ménagère') Leduc puts on as part of the 'grand cérémonial de l'écriture'[86] becomes the emblem of the writer as an artisan, a humble 'employée' or a 'paysan'.[87] Rather than creation *ex nihilo*, writing involves supreme perseverance and concentration: 'un vertige d'exactitude', 'une plongée pour une nuance'.[88] Patience is rewarded by sudden 'strikes': 'Ecrire ... c'est être une abeille féroce', 'ma plume, soudain, gobait l'image comme le chien gobe la mouche'.[89] In one passage Leduc gives a brilliant evocation of the attempt to recapture accurately the intensity of erotic sensation she had experienced with Isabelle: 'Le sexe. Combien je voudrais notre viande nue sur la feuille de cahier ... Je vendrais tout pour une plus grande exactitude.'[90] Yet even here there are doubts, and the notion that writing is mendacious or destructive is never far away. If writing is often equated with giving (a connection which will be further explored presently), then the 'don' may be that of the 'donneuse' Leduc had once been when, in a tight corner, she had betrayed some of her Black Market suppliers.[91] Leduc hesitates between seeing her writing as an act of reparation for her treachery, and as a perpetuation of it. In similar fashion, when Leduc writes 'Ecrire c'est indiquer'[92] she plays on two meanings of the verb 'indiquer': to point out, and to grass or betray. If writing may simply betray or - another recurrent and ambiguous word - *exploit* phenomena, it may have the same limitations with regard to the writer. 'Ecrire, c'est se délivrer. C'est faux. Ecrire, c'est ne rien changer.'[93] Leduc is well aware of the constant contradiction between writing as an instrument of change and transformation, and writing as an agent of fixity and perpetuation, between writing as the espousal of the real, and writing as dissolution and cancellation of reality. The ambivalence of writing is the same as that which applies to solitude: 'J'annule l'endroit ou je reviens au solitaire'.[94] And equally: 'Ecrire ... c'est détruire en se détruisant'.[95] At one point Leduc, having asserted that 'J'existe quand j'écris',[96] tries to pin down the nature of this existence-in-writing:

> Qu'est-ce que je suis quand j'écris? Une délivrance, mais je suis absente. Toujours moi dans ce que j'écris. Toujours. Mais je donne sans compter à ce terrible papier. Qu'est-ce-que-je-suis-quand-j'écris, cette fois je te serre à la gorge, copiste. Qu'est-ce que je suis quand j'écris ... un paysan, il cède à l'angélus, la page est vaste à remplir.[97]

The whole gamut of Leduc's ambivalent feelings about writing are here. Writing falsifies and betrays phenomena; writing promises deliverance from self, but in fact perpetuates selfhood in the mode of a certain kind of absence. And yet, despite this emphasis on negativity, there is the persistent affirmation that to write is to give, and to give unstintingly ('donner sans compter') and the insistence that writing is above all else a gift.

What remains, finally, to be explored is the logic of the gift in *La Folie en tête*, where the verb 'donner' and its cognates occur very frequently. Perhaps the best starting-point is this sentence, 'Celui qui donne ne devient pas fou',[98] because it hints at what is at stake in the idea of giving for Leduc, and at how far the real beneficiary of the gift may be the giver rather than the recipient.[99] The sentence is part of Leduc's explanation of her reaction to being insulted by Genet, when she had kissed his chest and asked his forgiveness. Giving is here a way of denying the affront, wiping it out and supplanting it with another narrative. The selfless gift of herself, of her generosity, to Genet protects Leduc against full acknowledgement of what had happened. By a kind of magic, tinged with fraudulence, Leduc's gift annihilates Genet's act.

It is Simone de Beauvoir, however, who is at the centre of the network of giving and receiving in *La Folie en tête*. Leduc writes, above all, for Beauvoir.[100] Yet Beauvoir demands nothing of Leduc, and indeed the economy of the gift is quite different in Beauvoir's case: 'Ce qu'elle donne, elle le donne une fois pour toutes. Ce qu'elle ne donne pas, elle ne le donnera jamais. Je l'ai compris.'[101] From Beauvoir to Leduc, the limits of giving are clearly defined and finite. But the essence of Beauvoir's gift is to provide an imaginary demand which Leduc can fulfil by giving unconditionally and infinitely; 'je lui donnerai ce soir le poids de l'oiseau quand il se joue des branches, je lui donnerai le regard d'un sous-bois ... je lui donnerai la lueur au bout du sentier'.[102] It is the absolute lack of reciprocity in their relationship which makes Leduc's art of giving absolute and infinite: 'Elle n'avait rien à me donner, je n'avais rien à lui donner. Mais entre le début et la fin de mes phrases, quel amour impossible j'apportais!'[103] To give to Simone de Beauvoir is to give gratuitously. At the heart of the myth of writing established in *La Folie en tête* is the notion of writing as gratuitous gift, a gift which is understood to extricate Leduc from her 'complications inimaginables', to exonerate her from the charge of betrayal on the personal front. Conscious that she may have deceived Beauvoir and Jaques, Leduc writes:

> Tout peut m'être pardonné: personne ne m'aime, personne ne m'aimera. Est-ce que je les trompe quand je leur donne, en recopiant mon travail un 15 août 1967 à onze heures trente-sept:
> Le chatoiement des oliviers dans les hautes herbes, celui des

> feuilles, la lumière verte, la lumière châtiée du cyprès, le bleu
> inconsistant, le bleu glacé, le glacis d'un ciel parfait
> d'indifférence
> l'haleine saccadée de la brise, sa timidité, ses caprices les
> collines au loin noyées dans leurs pleurs bleutés?
> Je ne les trompe pas. Je vois et je regarde pour eux.[104]

With its precise reference to a date and time in the context of the work's composition, the 'moment de l'écriture', this is the sole example of a kind of passage to be found quite regularly in the latter part of *La Bâtarde*.[105] In that work, such passages, addressed to the reader in general, declared unequivocally the equation of writing and giving, and the achievement on Leduc's part of a new-found identity as a writer. The gift of writing, writing as giving, was presented unequivocally as a triumph over the negativity of the past Leduc was seeking to exorcise.

By contrast, *La Folie en tête* demonstrates a more complex and ambiguous attitude to the gift of writing, and above all an awareness of the needs which may underlie the strategy of giving. In the passage just quoted, Leduc's willingness to exercise her craft, to hunt for the exact words to render the nuances of the landscape, is represented as a way out of tainted human relations based on deception. Yet the notion that she does this on behalf of others is questionable. In fact, through the gratuitous gift of her writing, Leduc places herself outside the structure of exchange; she does not create a new community, she extricates herself from community and underlines her solitude. The ability to give may be part of Leduc's idea of genius - Cocteau is one example[106] - but she also indicates in various ways her awareness that gratuitous giving (the repeated phrase is 'donner sans compter') may be a form of control, a kind of transaction which is not all that different from the less glorious, indeed often somewhat sordid instances of giving we find in both *La Bâtarde* and *La Folie en tête*.[107] Envious of her neighbour's 'salle à manger Henri II' Leduc gets Jacques to buy her the same: 'Il me la doit. Pourquoi me la doit-il? Je ne sais pas. Il me la doit, il me la doit.'[108] The massive, artificial, reproduction furniture[109] is a grotesque parody both of the opulence she was denied by her father's treachery, and of the emotions Jacques does not feel for her. The extorted gift is a reification, a substitute for affective relationships which cannot exist. Ideally, the gift of writing, in its gratuitousness, is a way out of the tainted world of extortion and recrimination, into a sphere of pure giving, beyond reciprocity. This is a realm of sacrifice: 'Ecrire, c'est donner sa chaleur'[110] and Leduc is willing to pose as a martyr on behalf of the pure appearances she would like to celebrate and to show. But Leduc knows this is not the whole story, that the benefits of writing are achieved at high cost.

Ultimately, in its presentation of the logic of giving, *La Folie en tête* points to the inevitable failure of writing to provide a way out of the labyrinth of solitude. The space of writing may appear to transcend the tribulations of everyday desire, to offer a haven outside or beyond experience, and to delineate a new identity. But writing cannot turn solitude into community, and the obligation under which Leduc places her readers by her giving, while it calls for real gratitude, simply perpetuates the endless struggle for love and recognition which writing could channel but never finally resolve.

NOTES

1 References are to the original Gallimard edition of *La Folie en tête*, published in 1970 (abbreviated to FT). The other volumes are *La Bâtarde* (Gallimard, 1964) and the posthumous *La Chasse à l'amour* (Gallimard, 1973), edited by Simone de Beauvoir.

2 FT, pp. 53-54.

3 Beauvoir's approval for the manuscript of *L'Asphyxie* and her decision to recommend its publication are presented as a major turning point in Leduc's life in the early chapters of FT.

4 Isabelle de Courtivron observes that, in FT, 'the temporal levels conflate so thoroughly with one another that no distinction remains between living and writing about living' (*Violette Leduc*, Boston, Twayne, 1985, p. 66).

5 On several occasions Leduc draws attention to the interaction of past and present in her writing; e.g. FT, pp. 28, 116, 140, 168, 172, 344, 364.

6 FT, p. 55. Just as *La Bâtarde* gave a new version of events previously covered in fiction, so FT provides an alternative to the fictionalised account of Leduc's passion for Beauvoir in *L'Affamée* (1948).

7 FT, p. 66.

8 FT, p. 310.

9 FT, p. 174.

10 FT, p. 131.

11 On triangular relationships see Courtivron, op. cit., p. 85, and my *French Autobiography: Devices and Desires*, Oxford, Clarendon Press, 1993, pp. 215-16. On relationships in Leduc's fiction see Alex Hughes, *Violette Leduc: Mothers, Lovers and Language*, MHRA (forthcoming).

12 For a brief account of this relationship see V. Marin La Meslée, 'Genet, Leduc: admiration et jalousie' in *Magazine littéraire*, no. 313, September 1993, pp. 37-38, and also Sheringham, op. cit., pp. 210-19.

13 FT, p. 119.

14 FT, p. 349.

15 FT, p. 125.

16   FT, p. 145.
17   FT, p. 163.
18   FT, p. 144.
19   FT, p. 179.
20   FT, p. 180.
21   FT, p. 183.
22   FT, p. 170.
23   FT, p. 369.
24   FT, p. 182.
25   For an extremely illuminating discussion of this topic in *La Bâtarde* see Alex Hughes, 'Desire and its Discontents: Violette Leduc's *La Bâtarde* and the Failure of Love' in A. Hughes and K. Ince (eds), *Desiring Writing*, Berg (forthcoming).
26   FT, p. 142.
27   FT, p. 141.
28   FT, p. 145.
29   FT, p. 148.
30   FT, p. 156.
31   FT, pp. 178-90.
32   FT, p. 181.
33   FT, p. 181.
34   FT, p. 179.
35   FT, p. 182.
36   FT, p. 185.
37   FT, p. 189.
38   FT, p. 220.
39   FT, p. 204.
40   FT, p. 205.
41   FT, p. 207.
42   FT, pp. 208-12.
43   FT, p. 211.
44   FT, p. 209.
45   FT, p. 209.
46   FT, p. 210.
47   FT, p. 210
48   FT, p. 211.
49   FT, pp. 16, 25, 32.
50   FT, pp. 56, 121, 131.
51   FT, p. 319.
52   FT, p. 401.
53   FT, p. 130.

54   FT, pp. 107-08.
55   FT, pp. 253-62.
56   FT, pp. 263-77. For a discussion of this aspect of FT see Sheringham, op. cit., pp. 153-56.
57   FT, pp. 182, 300, 218, 255, 238.
58   FT, pp. 244, 247, 339.
59   FT, pp. 313, 334, 365, 403.
60   FT, pp. 103, 149.
61   FT, pp. 127, 302.
62   FT, p. 218.
63   FT, pp. 242, 253, 350.
64   FT, pp. 68, 360, 112.
65   FT, pp. 106, 361, 132, 132.
66   FT, p. 360. On self-designation in *La Bâtarde* see Sheringham, op. cit., p. 219.
67   FT, pp. 310, 272.
68   FT, p. 51.
69   FT, p. 236.
70   FT, p. 25.
71   FT, p. 24.
72   FT, p. 25.
73   FT, p. 339.
74   FT, p. 339.
75   FT, p. 342.
76   FT, p. 241.
77   FT, pp. 53 and 214 for the references to Van Gogh; and FT, p. 311 for *Molloy*.
78   FT, pp. 51-53.
79   FT, p. 51.
80   FT, p. 52.
81   FT, p. 52.
82   FT, p. 52.
83   FT, p. 52.
84   FT, p. 53.
85   FT, pp. 87-88, 114-17, 254, 295-98, 410-11.
86   FT, p. 114.
87   FT, pp. 88, 130, 254.
88   FT, pp. 116, 114.
89   FT, pp. 114, 116.
90   FT, p. 298.
91   FT, p. 87. On this see M. Broc-Lapeyre, 'Du trafic à la littérature',

Critique, no. 282, November 1970, pp. 935-43.

92   FT, p. 410.

93   FT, p. 115.

94   FT, p. 228.

95   FT, p. 105.

96   FT, p. 254.

97   FT, p. 254.

98   FT, p. 207.

99   The dialectic of giving in *La Folie en tête* has many affinities with the reflections on 'le don' to be found in the recent work of Jacques Derrida. See J. Derrida, *Donner le temps, Vol. 1. La fausse monnaie*, Paris, Galilée, 1991, and G. Bennington / J. Derrida, *Jacques Derrida*, Paris, Editions du Seuil, 1991, pp. 176-89.

100   FT, p. 55.

101   FT, p. 66.

102   FT, p. 68.

103   FT, p. 110. It is possible to identify the construction of a self-image as giver well before the writing of her autobiography in Leduc's letters to Beauvoir in the late 1940s and early 1950s where the word 'donner' is recurrent. See 'Lettres à Simone de Beauvoir', *Les Temps Modernes*, no. 495, October 1987, pp. 1-41.

104   FT, p. 181.

105   On this see Sheringham, op. cit., p. 152.

106   FT, p. 240.

107   In *La Bâtarde* cf. Hermine's gift of the 'tailleur anguille' discussed in the article by Hughes (see note 25).

108   FT, p. 302.

109   FT, p. 314.

110   FT, p. 411.

Antecedents for Genet's Persona

DAVID WALKER

The bulk of Genet's early prose work is autobiographical in character: for convenience we will be focusing on *Notre-Dame des fleurs, Miracle de la Rose* and *Journal du Voleur*, in which this is clearly the case, but *Querelle de Brest* and *Pompes funèbres* have many of the same characteristics.[1] However, the existential self is something Genet is bent on repudiating. A dominant theme in Genet's work is that of the transfiguration of existence into essence through the intervention of writing. Though present in the earlier texts, it appears at its most highly-developed in *Journal du Voleur*. Referring to the possibility of simply enumerating the incidents in his life, he writes:

> Puis-je dire que c'était le passé - ou que c'était le futur? Tout est déjà pris, jusqu'à ma mort, dans une banquise de *étant* ... car je refuse de vivre pour une autre fin que celle même que je trouvais contenir le premier malheur: que ma vie doit être légende c'est-à-dire lisible et sa lecture donner naissance à quelque émotion nouvelle que je nomme poésie. Je ne suis plus rien, qu'un prétexte.[2]

Many of the terms used in this passage are key leitmotifs throughout the works. For the moment it will suffice to underline how time, space, existence, all are to be subsumed by what Genet calls the 'poésie' of his 'légende'.

The problematics of autobiography are not ignored in this perspective, but they are subordinated to the aesthetic adventure:

> Avec des mots si j'essaie de recomposer mon attitude d'alors, le lecteur ne sera pas dupe plus que moi. Nous savons que notre langage est incapable de rappeler même le reflet de ces états défunts, étrangers. Il en serait de même pour tout ce journal s'il devait être la notation de qui je fus. Je

préciserai donc qu'il doit renseigner sur qui je suis, aujourd'hui que je l'écris. Il n'est pas une recherche du temps passé, mais une oeuvre d'art dont la matière-prétexte est ma vie d'autrefois. Il sera un présent fixé à l'aide du passé, non l'inverse. Qu'on sache donc que les faits furent ce que je les dis, mais l'interprétation que j'en tire c'est ce que je suis - devenu.[3]

Attempts to revive or record the past with any accuracy are defeated by the nature of language and the estranging effect of time. The past can only serve as the pretext for the creation of a work of art intended to stabilise a version of the present self: but the ambiguous temporal nature of the project is nicely caught in Genet's deliberate hesitation between the present auxiliary and the past participle of 'ce que je suis devenu'. Chronology is an effect of perspective generated in the present. Rather like the painted backdrop for a stage performance, the past is an aesthetic dependency of the present. By the same token the past is always present, continuously impinging on the current self: so that the view Genet tends to reproduce annuls the developmental passage of time, construing the past as contemporaneous with the present.[4] Ultimately, the text hovers out of time, between an insubstantial, ungraspable past and a present problematised by the incursions of its antecedents.[5] The movement of oscillation thus produced is announced at the outset as a source, for Genet, of 'émoi', the concomitant of poetry.[6]

The challenging qualities of *Journal du Voleur* are underlined by the confrontational mode Genet is adopting: 'ce que j'ai recherché surtout c'est d'être la conscience du vol dont j'écris le poème, c'est-à-dire: refusant d'énumérer mes exploits, je montre ce que je leur dois dans l'ordre moral, ce qu'à partir d'eux je construis'.[7] On the one hand he is not simply writing a narrative to boast about his crimes - 'refusant d'énumérer mes exploits': on the other, he claims his thieving provided him with a moral basis for the construction of his sense of self, which is, all the same, a way of challenging the morality of the respectable world. Moreover, if we are to believe him he carried out each burglary as if it were an 'acte rituel' with 'une unicité terminale',[8] so that the real defiance of the respectable world, 'embellissant ce que vous méprisez',[9] consists in giving morality (or immorality) second place to 'le poème'.

Part of this might be attributable to the influence of Sartre, with whom Genet became acquainted in 1944, and in whose company he spent a great deal of time in the years when he ruminated on and began writing *Journal du Voleur*.[10] It is interesting to note that *Journal du Voleur* alludes only briefly to that pre-Sartrean part of Genet's life which is manifest in *Notre-Dame des fleurs* and *Miracle de la Rose*. Its text arches over these to connect, broadly, his spells in Eastern Europe and Spain - his 'séjours dans la mendicité et dans la prostitution' between 1930 and 1940[11] - directly to the explicitly post-War,[12] post-Cocteau[13] individual he had become when this book was written and published. The analytical edge to much of this text, the symptomatic emphasis it places on 'conscience',[14] perhaps also betray the context out of which it arose. Even Genet's essentialist definition of poetry seems coloured by specifically phenomenological conceptualising:

> Le mot voleur détermine celui dont l'activité principale est le vol. Le précise en éliminant - pendant qu'il est ainsi nommé - tout ce qu'il est autre que voleur. Le simplifie. La poésie consiste dans sa plus grande conscience de sa qualité de voleur. Il se peut que la conscience de toute autre qualité capable de devenir essentielle au point de vous nommer est également la poésie.[15]

This is not to suggest that Genet espoused this other intellectual world to the exclusion of his previous concerns: on the contrary, the consistency of his thematics is as striking as the extent to which they proved capable of appropriation to fit the Sartrean agenda. But *Journal du Voleur* does mark a kind of turning point, and it does have features - notably a dimension of theorising - that the earlier works do not. An elementary but far-reaching detail which has a bearing on the distinction is the status of Genet vis-à-vis 'la Relégation perpétuelle' in the three works we are considering. At the time of *Notre-Dame des fleurs* and *Miracle de la Rose* Genet had the threat of a life sentence hanging over him, the 'condamnation à la Relègue' having a 'goût funèbre', evoking 'l'office des morts' and plunging him into a despair from which he sought refuge in his imagination.[16] It is in fact a condition of the 'sainteté' to which he aspires.[17] In *Notre-Dame des fleurs* he explains that following the recent abolition of transportation people in his position are condemned to virtual entombment in a prison cell: 'Personne ne peut dire si je sortirais d'ici ... Les Relégués demeurent jusqu'à la fin de leurs jours dans les massives Centrales ... j'y commence une existence de vrai mort ... J'accepte d'y vivre comme j'accepterais, mort, de vivre dans un cimetière.'[18] Genet insisted in later life that he began writing because he did not know whether he would ever get out of prison.[19] Here then, his writing is a post mortem exercise, his references to the construction of his 'légende' having a Mallarméen ring - 'Tel qu'en lui-même enfin l'éternité le change'. The theme of death and transfiguration remains in *Journal du Voleur*, but in this later text there is a forward-looking impetus almost completely missing from the earlier works. Significantly, it is in this text that he remarks on the condemnation to 'la relégation' of his old croney Rasseneur - a prominent figure in *Miracle de la Rose* - in precisely the same week that 'une pétition d'écrivains demandait, pour la même peine, ma grâce au Président de la République'.[20] In other words, Genet is contemplating freedom as he writes *Journal du Voleur*. Thus, rather than simply consigning his past life to a *Légende dorée* to rival that of Christ, as was the aim in *Miracle de la Rose*,[21] he here looks to his autobiography as a basis for future transfigurations. This further refines the temporal complexities evoked above.

But is this an autobiography? The title *Journal* seems to offer something else, a record of the existential present, as it were, rather than a recapitulation of the past. And this special quality calls for further comment. The fact is that although the book does not comprise the dated entries we expect of a diary, the present of a discursive situation is very much in evidence, as we have already noted. Genet appears to be using the chronicle of his antecedents as a means of constructing his self in the present. He is doing explicitly what most autobiographers do implicitly. But he is doing it in a way that is nonetheless peculiar to him, because he appears to be attempting to construct himself as an essence, rather than as an existent, in the present of writing. This is in keeping with Genet's assertion that he is already dead, a motif elaborated on notably by Sartre.[22] What we have here, therefore, is a diary charting the assertion of the present self through the assemblage of its past exploits.[23]

> Ce journal que j'écris n'est pas un délassement littéraire. A mesure que j'y progresse, ordonnant ce que ma vie passée me propose, à mesure que je m'obstine dans la rigueur de la composition des chapitres, des phrases, du livre lui-même, je me sens m'affermir dans la volonté d'utiliser, à des fins de vertus, mes misères d'autrefois. J'en éprouve le pouvoir.[24]

The process moves in the direction of making future writing unnecessary. Repeatedly in the course of *Journal du Voleur* Genet refers to his diminishing need to continue as his persona is constituted in the writing: 'Ainsi ne veux-je plus écrire, je meurs à la Lettre',[25] he declares in a telling pun.

Elsewhere, in a revealing passage, he has this to say: 'A moins que ne survienne, d'une telle gravité, un événement qu'en face de lui mon art littéraire soit imbécile et qu'il me faille pour dompter ce nouveau malheur un nouveau langage, ce livre est le dernier'.[26] Writing is therefore a means of mastering misfortune - in particular, Genet says, of drawing from it a lesson for future conduct:

> Par l'écriture j'ai obtenu ce que je cherchais. Ce qui, m'étant un enseignement, me guidera, ce n'est pas ce que j'ai vécu mais le ton sur lequel je le rapporte. Non les anecdotes mais l'oeuvre d'art. Non ma vie mais son interprétation. C'est ce que m'offre le langage pour l'évoquer, pour parler d'elle, la traduire. Réussir ma légende.[27]

We come back to where we started from - 'la légende'. Again, the past - 'ce que j'ai vécu' - is not the key to this autobiographical bricolage, but its being present

- its present being - in the writing. We note too the system of equivalences Genet establishes through the opposition between life, lived experience, anecdote on the one hand, and what language permits: tone, interpretation, and art on the other.

In actual fact the references to art are slightly out of place, because the drift of Genet's argument, in *Journal du Voleur*, tends to downplay art in favour of 'poésie', which, put crudely, might be said to consist in the shudder provoked in the reader by the encounter with Genet's self-made persona. In this perspective his 'légende' is a very specific, one might say almost practical strategy:

> Par légende je n'entendais pas l'idée plus ou moins décorative que le public connaissant mon nom se fera de moi, mais l'identité de ma vie future avec l'idée la plus audacieuse que moi-même et les autres, après ce récit, s'en puissent former.[28]

While therefore Genet is planning for his text to have a particular impact on his reader, this will in part be via the impact he intends it also to have on himself - specifically on the way he lives his life in the future.

It is in this way that Genet arrives at his own version of the dialectical (or overlapping) relationship between life and writing, between autobiography and existence. On the one hand, in the words of a key phrase from *Le Balcon*: 'Mon histoire fut vécue afin qu'une page glorieuse soit écrite, puis lue. Ce qui compte, c'est la lecture.'[29] On the other hand, to adapt Gide to the particular chronological perspective we have in *Journal du Voleur*, the writer 'doit, non pas raconter sa vie telle qu'il l'a vécue, mais la vivre telle qu'il *l'aura racontée*'.[30] Or again, as Genet puts it in *Le Funambule*: 'Ressembler plus tard à cette image de lui qu'il s'invente aujourd'hui'.[31] This is what Malgorn calls Genet's 'devenir-figuré'.[32]

The final pages of the *Journal* pick up the motifs we have considered and assemble them in a form of 'envoi' seeking to define what Genet has attempted in this book. Here it is notable that Genet repudiates the notion of art, which for him will always be the realm of the absent, the abstract, the emblem, in favour of a kind of confrontation with life, perhaps inspired by Sartrean notions of freedom and responsibility, but inflected by Genet's own preoccupations:

> Ce livre ne veut pas être, poursuivant dans le ciel son trajet solitaire, une oeuvre d'art, objet détaché d'un auteur et du monde. Ma vie passée je pouvais la dire sur un autre ton, avec d'autres mots. Je l'ai héroïsée parce que j'avais en moi ce qu'il faut pour le faire, le lyrisme. Mon souci de la cohérence me fait un devoir de poursuivre mon aventure à partir du *ton* de mon livre. Il aura servi à préciser les indications que me *présente le passé*.[33]

Genet has established a persona - embodied in a *tone* of perverse lyricism - for himself in the present through his work on elements from his past. This in turn carries with it the obligation to adhere faithfully to lines the exercise has laid down for his future, 'sans chercher à escamoter les fatigues, les horreurs de la démarche'. On the one hand he seeks the 'joies' of 'la pauvreté et le crime' which he labels metaphorically as 'le bagne ... cet endroit du monde et de l'esprit'. On the other hand, although these latter are what he prizes above all that normal society (addressed as 'vous') can offer, he simultaneously needs and must seek out 'votre reconnaissance, votre sacre', to validate his legend.[34] Ultimately his autobiography becomes his 'Genèse', the story of how the rest of the foreordained story began and arose from it. The book

> contient - doit contenir - les commandements que je ne saurais transgresser: si j'en suis digne il me réservera la gloire infâme dont il est le grand maître ... ne serait-ce logique que ce livre entraînât mon corps et m'attirât en prison ... par une fatalité qu'il contient, que j'y ai mise, et qui, comme je l'ai voulue, me garde comme témoin, champ d'expérience, preuve par 9 de sa vertu et de ma responsabilité.[35]

Genet thus seeks to assert himself as the *fons et origo* of his own essence, the manufacturer of his own existence and the programmer of his own future, the book he writes having established his destiny as the product of his own will. The reader too, it is implied, will have little choice but to condemn him to prison for what he has written. Genet began in life, as he says, by seizing the initiative from those who first accused him: 'A chaque accusation portée contre moi, fût-elle injuste, du fond du coeur je répondrai oui'.[36] By this stage he would appear to be planning to usurp the prerogative of the putative Creator himself, attaining 'une solitude me conférant la souveraineté'.[37] This again is a special characteristic of Genet's autobiography. Rather than writing a retrospective summary and conclusion on his life, Genet is actually writing his future. The past is made present, the present is in effect an anticipation of a future. And the self, far from being a narcissistic construct, is an element in a 'pacte autobiographique' that involves attacks on the reader's assumed morality. 'Cette autobiographie répond aux lois du genre et les dépasse', as Arnaud Malgorn puts it.[38] In this sense, then, Genet uses his antecedents to take possession of his future - because he appears to have one. He also has a particular kind of past that facilitates the writing of this autobiographical work. At the time of his earlier texts, as he indicates in *Journal du Voleur*, 'l'ennui de mes journées de prison me fit me réfugier dans ma vie d'autrefois',[39] but the 'autrefois' of these earlier works is of a different character, and is used in different ways, from what is the case in *Journal du Voleur*. At the time of writing this latter work, he could recount his own past in the certainty that, thanks to the efforts of Cocteau, Sartre, Marc Barbezat and others, this past had already acquired an aura of notoriety - or 'gloire infâme'. He had a myth on which to embroider his legend, the relationship with a public that this presupposes being an essential ingredient in that aggressive, subversive, disorienting dialogue with the reader that animates so much of his text.

In *Notre-Dame des fleurs* and *Miracle de la Rose* he does not have the same kind of past of his own which has been thus determined by a public reputation. As a result the construction of antecedents, simultaneously determining a relationship with the public and underlining his challenge to moral values, can be seen at work in particularly interesting ways. At this stage in Genet's career, autobiography is bound up inextricably with meditations on representations of criminals, on 'la gloire qu'ils secrètent et que j'utilise à des fins moins pures', as he will put it in *Journal du Voleur*.[40] With this in mind we may now focus on several interrelated topics that emerge from a reading of these earlier books.

Philippe Lejeune remarks: 'Une histoire de l'autobiographie aujourd'hui devrait être l'histoire des résistances aux modèles de récit (et de vies) qu'imposent à la fois la tradition littéraire et scolaire et le jeu des médias'.[41] In Genet's case resistance to models has a particular acuity, given his delinquent posture; and his concern with notions of notoriety - aspects of the 'légende' - gives the impact of the media (the press, for the era in question) a particular significance.

Genet confronts models of behaviour and representations of the self simultaneously. As a vagabond with a criminal record he fell foul of the ruling concerning the 'carnet anthropométrique', a document containing details of his 'état civil', physical characteristics and general description, which he was required to present to the authorities at regular intervals. He recounts how he first learned about it on returning from Spain to France, in the course of a brutal interview with local gendarmes: 'J'apprenais l'existence de l'humiliant carnet anthropométrique. On le délivre à tous les vagabonds. A chaque gendarmerie on le vise. On m'emprisonna.'[42] Albert Dichy and Pascal Fouché record that Genet was 'inculpé de défaut de carnet anthropométrique' in June 1939,[43] but he had been living with aspects of this phenomenon from an early age, having been subject to the state's inquisitorial attentions since childhood.[44] *Miracle de la Rose* comments on it: 'Tous les gars qui passent par Fontevrault doivent laisser leur signalement anthropométrique aux archives de la Centrale. On me fit donc sortir de la salle vers 2h pour monter au greffe, afin d'être mesuré (les pieds, les mains, les doigts, le front, le nez) et photographié.'[45]

Michel Foucault points out the importance in the development of penal systems of the rise of this kind of apparatus: 'Le châtiment légal porte sur un acte; la technique punitive sur une vie', he writes; and he continues: 'L'introduction du "biographique" est importante dans l'histoire de la pénalité.

Parce qu'il fait exister le "criminel" avant le crime et, à la limite, en dehors de lui.'[46] The prisoner, therefore, becoming aware of the 'criminal biography' in his encounters with the penal system, is at pains to construct his self and life, the 'autobiographical', as a form of resistance to this officially-sanctioned identity. He refers thus to the process - signalling in passing how it flies in the face of popular received opinion about a criminal's moral or intellectual capacities, something else to commend it in his eyes:

> Construire sa vie minute par minute en assistant à sa construction, qui est aussi destruction à mesure, il vous paraît impossible que je l'ose prêter à un voleur sans envergure. On ne voit capable de cela qu'un esprit sévèrement entraîné. Mais Harcamone était un ancien colon de Mettray, qui avait là-bas bâti sa vie minute par minute.[47]

This self-construction resists the institutional version, as often as not by appropriating and subverting it. Legal records show that time and again Genet falsified his own identity, and his criminal career consisted substantially of trafficking in forged identity papers.[48]

Moreover, for the writer he aimed to be, the possibility of a criminal autobiography 'avant le crime et à la limite en dehors de lui' is not without interest. Thus Genet can write of the prison warders and officials and the 'formative' discipline they imposed: 'Ils écrivaient mon histoire. Ils étaient mes personnages. Ils ne comprenaient rien à Mettray. Ils étaient idiots.'[49] Similarly, he takes to task more than once the campaigning journalists who wrote reports on prison conditions, expressing wonderment at 'ce qui provoquait l'indignation d'un Albert Londres, d'un Alexis Danan'.[50] The culmination of this latter stance will occur in L'enfant criminel, in which he more or less tells would-be reformers to mind their own business and leave the delinquent children to see to it that reformatories carry on performing their proper function, i.e. producing criminal youngsters.[51] All these efforts on the part of the 'Ideological State Apparatuses', or of the Benthamite 'Panopticon' analysed by Foucault, can be commandeered by the resolute creations of the criminal himself.

Genet creates the criminal heroes of his books with systematic reference to the standard procedures of forensic documentation. In so doing he creates an image of himself, of course: his aim in Notre-Dame des fleurs, for example, is to 'refaire à ma guise ... l'histoire de Divine que je connus si peu, l'histoire de Notre-Dame des fleurs, et n'en doutez pas, ma propre histoire'. Significantly, his starting point is as follows: 'Signalement de Notre-Dame des fleurs: taille 1m. 71, poids 71kg., visage ovale, cheveux blonds, yeux bleus, teint mat, dents parfaites, nez rectiligne'.[52] The description has been lifted - stolen, as it were - straight from the prison records. Elsewhere, Genet will refer to his own 'photographies de l'identité judiciaire' in Journal du Voleur, commenting on them to revive the experience and the character behind, and belying, 'la fixité que m'imposait le photographe officiel'.[53] He tells how he fell in love with the newspaper photograph of Marc Aubert, executed for treason and referred to at the start of *Notre-Dame des fleurs*, saying that he still carries it around with him.[54] In both *Notre-Dame des fleurs* and *Miracle de la Rose*, he enthuses about the beauty and compelling charm of Maurice Pilorge as evidenced in a mug-shot reproduced in, and cut out lovingly from, the popular crime magazine *Détective*.[55]

A related exploitation of mock-forensic methods can be seen in the way the autobiographical element in Genet's texts mimics the movement of testimony under interrogation or the inquisitorial gaze of the tribunal - which it invites, or rather provokes. The tribunal constitutes one of the schemas of Genet's spiritual existence: in *Journal du Voleur* God is defined as 'mon tribunal intime', and sainthood as the moment 'quand va cesser le tribunal, c'est-à-dire que le juge et le jugé seront confondus'.[56] The narrative of *Notre-Dame des fleurs* reaches its climax in the trial of the hero, and is intercut with allusions to the narrator's own appearances before the examining magistrate, confrontations during which, in his own words, he practises 'la ruse des aveux partiels. Spontanément, j'avoue un peu, afin de mieux celer le plus grave.'[57] He then reflects on the complex strategies by which he and the magistrate attempt to outwit each other: mirroring the text's own labyrinthine anticipations of the reader's scrutiny. Notre Dame in court, required to recount to the jury what he has already retailed numerous times to the police and the examining magistrate, 'décida de raconter autre chose. Pourtant, dans le même temps, il racontait exactement cette histoire qu'il avait dite avec les mêmes mots aux policiers, au juge, à l'avocat, aux psychiatres ... Il relisait son crime comme une chronique se relit, mais ce n'était plus vraiment du crime qu'il parlait.'[58] Repetition produces a different narrative, in effect (as does Borges's Pierre Ménard, recopying *Don Quixote*). This further problematises the autobiographical project, along lines that Arnaud Malgorn sees operating consistently in Genet's writing as he repeats and rewrites texts - and even rumours and anecdotes he himself put into circulation in the first place: 'L'autobiographie chez Genet n'est pas tant une oeuvre de faussaire que le palimpseste d'autres textes, sans cesse effacés et réécrits'.[59] However one looks at it, this is a strategy to unsettle the gaze of the inquisitor and reassert the peculiar integrity of the prisoner's evasive confession. 'Les prisons sont pleines de bouches qui mentent', Genet warns. 'Chacun raconte de fausses aventures où il a le rôle de héros.'[60] But the fuller implications of the topos are restated in *Miracle de la Rose* when he tells how the prison governor seeks to get to the bottom of Harcamone's murder of a warder. Genet reports through rumour and hearsay a story at the heart of which is the defeat of the officer's probing (the use of the word 'traître' to describe the process is worthy of note):

> La scène du prétoire, qui précéda les interrogatoires de la Police Judiciare et du juge, me fut connue grâce à des recoupements traîtres, faits dans la conversation silencieuse des gâfes. Harcamone comparut devant un directeur affolé d'être en face d'un mystère aussi absurde que celui que propose une rose dans tout son éclat. Il voulait savoir ce que signifiait ce meurtre ... mais il se heurtait à l'ignorance d'Harcamone, et il ne pouvait non plus compter sur une explication mensongère car l'assassin était plus fort.[61]

The enigma presented by the criminal constitutes the core of the text, as the allusion to the rose, linking it with the book's title, indicates. It is the essence of Genet's counter-biographies and of his own autobiographical enterprise. The criminals' beauty is a 'beauté en creux' inaccessible to the respectable reader.[62] 'Les crimes d'Harcamone ... apparaîtront des actes idiots', Genet writes.[63] But they are not supposed to make sense - they are intended to unmake it. Like certain words which 'sont un danger pour la compréhension pratique du discours', these acts 'font surgir la poésie'.[64] It is perhaps an obvious thing to say, but Genet is not confessing so that we may condemn or understand him. The crux of the matter is highlighted in the narrator's references to his lover Bulkaen. He actually started writing *Miracle de la Rose* 'pour jouir par les mots du souvenir de Bulkaen'.[65] However, when the two went through a phase of exchanging secret notes (a furtive correspondence 'où nous parlions de nous', Genet says - indicating its autobiographical qualities), Bulkaen signed himself 'Illisible' and Genet in turn addressed him as 'Mon Illisible'. Quite apart from the further subversive parody of official records contained in these allusions, Genet makes the point that 'Pierre Bulkaen restera pour moi l'indéchiffrable'.[66] The text concludes with a reprise of this theme, underlining the impenetrability of what it is seeking to glorify: the book will transmit his heroes' reputation, Genet says, but so far as knowing who they are is concerned, there can be no explanation. 'Si je quitte ce livre, je quitte ce qui peut se raconter. Le reste est indicible.'[67] The hero's biography - the narrator's autobiography - is the aura around an ungraspable truth. Put another way, the attainment of being 'lisible', having a 'légende', is conditional upon the preservation of the existential self as 'illisible'.

The informing source of such criminal auras - as it is of the photographs whose function has already been pointed out - is the *fait divers*. It furnishes an important pretext for Genet's biographical and autobiographical recreations, and one which bulks extremely large in his work. *Notre-Dame des fleurs* starts with several *faits divers*, and the reverie of which the book is entirely made up arises from a series of newspaper clippings and photographs stuck on the narrator's cell wall. *Miracle de la Rose* alludes repeatedly to items from the 'chronique' and in its closing lines Genet confesses a compulsion to 'fouiller les vieux journaux' and speaks of an article on the death of Maurice Pilorge (which we know inspired his first poem, 'Le condamné à mort'). Indeed, he refers elsewhere to the production of a 'héros déjà idéalisé puisque mort et réduit à l'état de prétexte à l'un de ces poèmes brefs que sont les faits divers':[68] a statement which confirms that this phenomenon precisely exemplifies Genet's own aesthetic.

It will clarify our argument to define more closely the place of the *fait divers* in the mechanisms which Genet's work brings into play. The murder by Notre-Dame des fleurs of an old man appears in the newspapers as just such an item. His name thereby becomes known 'de la France entière', we are told. Certain kinds of readers merely pass over it, but Genet's preferred readers, 'les écoliers et les petites vieilles ... ceux qui vont tout au fond des articles, flairant l'insolite et l'y dépistant à tout coup',[69] tremble with delight - and envy - as they read. Their reaction, Genet stresses, is that of the 'voyageur taciturne et fébrile' who on arriving in a new town, heads for the 'bouges, quartiers réservés, bordels', guided by 'des mots de passe échangés par les subconscients et qu'il suit de confiance'. Murder, theft, rape, armed attacks - these, says Genet, are the '"Barrios Chinos" des journaux'.[70] Now, the Barrio Chino, as he points out in *Journal du Voleur*, is that 'quartier réservé' of Barcelona, inhabited by an extraordinary rabble of disreputable and dangerous low-life characters, where Genet himself elected to live and whose lifestyle he chose to espouse in the early 1930s.[71] It is in fact an essential part of his autobiographical landscape: 'Mon aventure si, géographiquement elle s'arrêtait à Barcelone s'y devait poursuivre profondément, de plus en plus profondément, dans les régions de moi-même les plus reculées'.[72] So when he connects it with the *fait divers*, he is putting in place a significant series of correspondences which underlines his own identity as a denizen of the *fait divers* while highlighting the collusion of certain kinds of readers in the creation of his autobiographical space. 'Pour me comprendre une complicité du lecteur sera nécessaire', as he puts it.[73]

The nature of this complicity hinges not infrequently on a mutual familiarity with the *fait divers*. It is worth remembering that the thirties saw a tremendous vogue for the *fait divers*, not just among the mass public but also among intellectuals, from Gide and the surrealists onwards. It can be argued that we cannot truly understand the initial impact of Genet's work without taking account of the way it played on its first readers' fascination for *faits divers*. Cocteau and Sartre, for example, were both afficionados of *Détective*.[74] Genet's writing presupposes in the reader an extensive prior knowledge of this disreputable domain. Certain aspects of Genet's work stem from his having come to understand and colonise or assert his place in the world - on the margins of society - by exploiting the arm's-length but fascinated collusion with it that society adopted as a posture, and which he could see exemplified in the role it accorded to *faits divers*. This is the domain where society's repressed impulses are contained and observed, where 'l'immonde' ferments to sustain 'le monde'. 'Il est impossible que les grands courants sociaux ... prennent prétexte dans des raisons avouables au grand jour', he asserts. 'Il faut rêver longtemps pour agir avec grandeur et le rêve se cultive dans les ténèbres.'[75]

The *fait divers* therefore provided Genet with a particularly appropriate - because insidious - means of penetrating the society that excluded him. His writing entered through the back door as it were, via the ill-acknowledged and inadequately policed collective subconscious. At the same time, however, the *fait divers* rubric also provided him with role models, the stuff from which to create a persona.[76] Both these aspects, and several of their implications, can be seen immediately in the opening lines of *Notre-Dame des fleurs*:

> Weidmann vous apparut dans une édition de cinq heures, la tête emmaillotée de bandelettes blanches, religieuse et encore aviateur blessé, tombé dans les seigles, un jour de septembre pareil à celui où fut connu le nom de Notre-Dame des Fleurs.

The whole book is summed up here. The climax of Notre Dame's notoriety as hero of the *fait divers* is prefigured and exemplified in the serial murderer: the allusion is to a famous photograph of his appearance before the examining magistrate after having sustained head wounds during his arrest (in December 1937, in fact). But equally important, as Genet steals furtively into the lives of 'bourgeois attristés', the voice that he finds to articulate his presence is at its very origin a challenge to the hypocrisy of these readers whose 'vie quotidienne est frôlée d'assassins enchanteurs, élevés sournoisement jusqu'à leur sommeil qu'ils vont traverser, par quelque escalier d'office qui, complice pour eux, n'a pas grincé'.[77] Genet affirms his identity only indirectly as the one who unveils that complicity linking the first two characters to feature in the text: Weidmann and 'vous'.

In a sense this is in keeping with the stance of a writer who has no identity, imprisoned and exiled as he is, and who is reduced thereby to being a spectator of what he chronicles. He will trace his presence obliquely, and will speak of himself to his reader through the intermediary of his heroes. Thus the text continues:

> Un peu plus tôt, le nègre Ange Soleil avait tué sa maîtresse. Un peu plus tard, le soldat Maurice Pilorge assassinait son amant ... vous vous le rappelez ... Enfin, un enseigne de vaisseau, encore enfant, trahissait pour trahir: on le fusilla.

The infamy of these criminals is invidiously constructed by the reader's own recognition of their names or acknowledgement of the celebrity presupposed by the exophoric article.[78] It is only after listing them thus that Genet declares his hand: 'Et c'est en l'honneur de leurs crimes que j'écris mon livre'. He places himself at the bottom of a systematically arranged hierarchy descending from the most notorious to the unknown: the implication is that he proposes to ascend it.[79] He catalogues the sources from which he culled clippings and photographs of these criminal exploits and stuck them to the cell wall; he then integrates their notoriety into his autobiography, as he announces his intention to 'écrire une histoire ... ma propre histoire' of which they and he will be the heroes, and which will be 'une parcelle de ma vie intérieure'.[80] Indeed, it is probably not by chance that he gives the date of Weidmann's first appearance in the papers, erroneously, as September: that was the date when he himself first featured in the *fait divers* rubric of *Le Petit Parisien* on receiving his first prison sentence.[81] Nor would it have escaped his notice that Weidmann was executed on the same day as Genet was jailed in Châlon-sur-Saône.[82]

Genet's is a spiritual autobiography modelled on the lives of the criminals who have inspired him. 'J'envie ta gloire', he says in *Notre-Dame des fleurs*, apostrophising Pilorge. 'J'irais bien facilement à la guillotine, puisque d'autres y sont allés, et surtout Pilorge, Weidmann, Ange Soleil, Soclay ... ces créations forment tout mon concert spirituel passé.'[83] Elsewhere he refers to himself as 'moi qui recrée ces hommes, Weidmann, Pilorge, Soclay, dans mon désir d'être eux-mêmes'.[84]

Here we rejoin once again the 'légende' from which we started. As Sartre puts it, Genet's dream is to 'venir à soi comme un autre, sous l'aspect légendaire d'un criminel'.[85] It is in the nature of the denizens of the *fait divers* that their renown circulates as rumour and gossip as much as in printed form. While press cuttings as such play an important role in Genet's texts, it is also notable that his heroes' reputations precede them via other channels. The source material for *Notre-Dame des fleurs* came to his attention via lawyers' chat and prisoners' conversations as well as news items.[86] The 'forçats' passing through Fontevrault on their way to Saint-Martin-de-Ré speak, in a casual way that leaves Genet and the other inmates stunned, 'de tous les princes du crime à qui les journaux firent un nom immense ... je fus émerveillé comme on devait l'être lorsqu'on pouvait entendre Murat tutoyer Napoléon'.[87] The children in Mettray trade stories of notorious villains:

> Chacune de leurs histoires ... ne nous était pas connue avec une exacte précision mais, soit parce que son auteur en avait parlé à mots couverts, soit que lui-même arrivât, escorté et précédé d'une réputation qui s'était accumulée ... ces histoires avaient fini par se savoir, mais dans une forme assez vague, imprécise ... Donc chaque histoire était connue sous une forme légendaire.[88]

This is the stuff legends are made of: the *fait divers*, 'ces poèmes brefs', transmit precisely that lyrical distillation of a life that circulates independently of author, text and pretext, and which Genet seeks to achieve through his written (and oral) versions of his biography.

Significantly, he seeks to achieve this effect at the expense of the reader, who as we have seen is drawn into the louche celebration willy-nilly, from the very beginning. Genet forces the voyeuristic complicity of the bourgeois who is invited to acknowledge that s/he reads the 'chronique' for the gory bits too: 'Vous savez par *Paris-Soir* qu'il fut tué, lors de la révolte à Cayenne',[89] he says of the murderer Clément Village, and in connection with his brutal crime he alludes to 'cette histoire, que vous lûtes dans les journaux'.[90]

In this connection, however, Genet reveals that he himself did *not* read the story - much to Village's dismay when the two met in prison. 'Il fut chagrin que je ne me souvinsse pas de cette histoire, que vous lûtes dans les journaux'.[91] Wrong-footing the reader, Genet indicates that he is less immersed in the *fait divers* than the latter. This is an important point, as emerges from a passage of *Miracle de la Rose* that brings out the underlying thrust of the autobiographical in these early texts:

> Si j'écrivais un roman, j'aurais quelque intérêt à m'étendre sur mes gestes d'alors, mais je n'ai voulu par ce livre que montrer l'expérience menée de ma libération d'un état de pénible torpeur, de vie honteuse et basse ... soumise au prestige, subjuguée par les charmes du monde criminel. Je me libérais par et pour une attitude plus fière.[92]

The 'sujet de l'énonciation', being distinct from the 'sujet de l'énoncé', does not share the foibles of the narrated self. In *Notre-Dame des fleurs*, too, at the same moment as he speaks of recreating his criminal heroes from a desire to emulate them, Genet adds that 'fidélité à ses personnages' is not his strong point, since 'je me suis depuis longtemps résigné à être moi-même'.[93]

While subjecting the reader to the prestige and charms of the criminal world, Genet himself speaks as one who has, he says, broken the spell they cast on him. The mechanism enabling him to do this is autobiographical writing, the aesthetico-therapeutic discipline that we have seen him discuss explicitly in *Journal du Voleur*.

As he moves beyond murder to foreground betrayal as his theme, Genet continues to draw his inspiration from news clippings featuring notorious traitors. But by the time of *Journal du Voleur* the systematic nature of the exercise has come to the fore. Of collaborators during the Occupation he writes: 'Ce qui m'avait fait détacher et conserver ce morceau de journal où sont leurs photographies, c'est le désir d'en tirer nourriture pour une argumentation en faveur de la trahison'.[94] He returns to Pilorge, saying 'J'acceptais qu'il me fût non un exemple, mais une aide pour parcourir une route jusqu'à un ciel où j'espère le joindre (je n'écris pas le rejoindre)'.[95] Ultimately, he views his autobiography as a poor substitute for those lives - and deaths - he refers to, and dismisses as an illusion the hope that he might achieve their kind of notoriety, however much his alleged acquaintance with some of them might seem to give his life a certain significance:

> Soclay, Pilorge, Weidmann, Serge de Lenz, Messieurs de la Police, indicateurs sournois, vous m'apparaissez quelquefois parés comme de toilettes funèbres et de jais, de si beaux crimes que j'envie, aux uns la peur mythologique qu'ils inspirent, aux autres leurs supplices, à tous l'infamie où finalement ils se confondent. Si je regarde en arrière je n'aperçois qu'une suite d'actions piteuses. Mes livres les racontent ... J'eus tant de mal pour réussir si mal ce que font si vite mes héros.[96]

If he retains 'peut-être'[97] a cult for Pilorge and his ilk, it is one from which the sentimental attachments of former times have been filtered out, one that is now sustained by a much more analytical stance, concerned critically with the nature of the criminal's image in society. Notoriety, after all, is merely a further form of subjection to society's gaze; throwing the criminal image back in the face of the bourgeoisie does not in itself achieve control over the relationship between judge and accused.[98]

The very title of *Journal du Voleur* announces that the work is engaging with this question. We have seen that the text itself does not conform to the standard generic expectations it at first seems to prompt: it does not consist of dated entries. In fact, the genre it really plays on is the criminal's memoirs from prison, a form much prized by writers and readers of the *fait divers*. The criminal's own testimony, direct and unmediated, commands a special kind of attention because it speaks from beyond those bounds that even the judicial system exists to confirm: the more so since, as in the case of Landru, the criminal's intimate record of his misdeeds might constitute the principal evidence that condemns him. Thus, the cover of *Détective* for 27 September and 4 October 1934 vaunted *Le Journal de Violette Nozières* - 'un document formidable' - while she awaited trial for poisoning her mother and father.[99] The magazine's extensive coverage of Weidmann's life in prison focused with regret on his failure to 'livrer par écrit les secrets de son étrange nature' despite the facilities made available to him to do so.[100] In the same number, however, the headline 'Le carnet d'un assassin' introduced extracts from the diary of one Louis Philippe, referred to as 'Le Weidmann Lyonnais'. Born in 1910, the same year as Genet, he was sent to the reformatory at Mettray in 1926, the same year that Genet was sent there, after being found guilty of inflicting grievous bodily harm on his mother. He left Mettray in the same way that Genet did, by enlisting for military service, and thereafter committed a series of murders beginning with that of the second officer of the ship on which he was serving.[101] Genet may well have encountered this criminal with whom he had so much in common and who achieved precisely that parallel with Weidmann that Genet's writing was to pursue. All of which gives extra point to the fact that Philippe's writings are ironised and become the butt of that self-righteous censoriousness that seems to typify crime reports of the time. A more sophisticated commentator, Colette, in all probability discussing the issue of *Détective* in which Weidmann and Philippe featured together, indicates that Weidmann remains 'pour notre esprit, hors de portée' and refers tellingly to the function of writing in these cases:

> Ecrire est la plus grande tentation du prisonnier, qui débute dans la rédaction par le mensonge littéraire, mais glisse peu à peu vers la tentante, vers l'incroyable vérité. Un carnet, un crayon, et Philippe, émule ambitieux de Weidmann, se perd.[102]

Genet's writing can be seen as a response to the implicit challenge here: how can the former inmate of Mettray offer his own testimony and attain the notoriety of a Weidmann without playing into the hands of his judges? The point emerges in *Journal du Voleur* when he returns, significantly, to the photograph of Weidmann alluded to at the start of his first book and analyses the qualities that ensure that Weidmann does not fall foul of the image-appropriating machinery of the media. Second-rate villains whose photos he compares this with look unimpressive, and not just because of the nature of the print, the angle of the photograph: 'Contre eux ils avaient la mauvaise qualité du papier, du tirage, d'avoir été saisis aux instants pénibles. Ils avaient la mine de gens pris au piège, mais à celui qu'ils se sont tendu, au piège intérieur.' Weidmann is a different case altogether: 'Sur la très belle photo qui le montre dans ses bandes Velpeau Weidmann blessé par le flic qui l'arrêta, c'est aussi une bête prise au piège, mais à celui des hommes. Contre lui, sa propre vérité ne se retourne pas pour enlaidir sa gueule.'[103]

By the time he writes *Journal du Voleur*, Genet too is seeking ways of manifesting his truth without compromising it, without making it available for misinterpretation or misappropriation.[104] This represents a return to 'l'illisible' - what he here calls 'l'impossible nullité':[105] it is perhaps 'la transparence'[106] he might achieve if he were able to 'bondir au coeur de l'image'[107] and suppress the existential self altogether. The idea of it will continue to haunt his work, especially his theatre, where it will find perhaps its most authentic expression in Said of *Les Paravents*, who disappears at his moment of triumph, leaving behind him simply a suggestion of a 'chanson': an insubstantial poetic aura.[108]

NOTES

1 I am grateful to the British Academy for financial support to facilitate the research on which part of this paper is based. Page references using the abbreviations ND (*Notre-Dame des fleurs*), and MR (*Miracle de la Rose*) are to: Jean Genet, *Oeuvres complètes*, vol. 2, Paris, Gallimard, 1951; and those using JV to *Journal du Voleur*, Paris, Gallimard, 1949.

2 JV, pp. 125-26.

3 JV, pp. 75-76.

4 There is of course a great deal of Proustian influence to be discerned in Genet's treatment of the past. See Richard Coe, *The Vision of Jean Genet*, London, Peter Owen, 1968, pp. 73-74; Jean-Bernard Moraly, *Jean Genet: La vie écrite*, Paris, La Différence, 1988, pp. 69-83; Arnaud Malgorn, *Jean Genet qui êtes-vous?*, Lyon, La Manufacture, 1988, p. 70.

5 For a subtle and brilliant exposition of the mechanisms this brings into play - 'how a past which can only be apprehended through the distortions of the present might relate to a present which can only be understood in terms of the past that produced it' - see Michael Sheringham, 'Narration and experience in Genet's *Journal du Voleur*', *Studies in French Fiction: a Festschrift for Vivienne Milne*, ed. Robert Gibson, London, Grant and Cutler, 1988, pp. 289-306.

6 JV, p. 9.

7 JV, p. 100.

8 JV, pp. 31-32.

9 JV, p. 116.

10 See Harry E. Stewart and Rob Roy McGregor, *Jean Genet: a biography of deceit 1910-1941*, New York, Peter Lang, 1989, pp. 143-57 and passim.

11 JV, pp. 76, 153.

12 JV, p. 116.

13 JV, p. 47.

14 See, for example, JV, p. 118.

15 JV, pp. 258-59.

16 MR, pp. 322-23; cf. 395.

17 MR, p. 215.

18 ND, pp. 12, 95, 97.

19 See for example the interviews reproduced in Malgorn, pp. 163, 172. The extent to which this was true is still difficult to ascertain, despite the work of Stewart, McGregor, Moraly, and Albert Dichy and Pascal Fouché, *Jean Genet, essai de chronologie 1910-1944*, Paris, Bibliothèque de littérature

française contemporaine, 1988. But certainly the possibility arose repeatedly between 1939 and 1942 (Dichy and Fouché, pp. 175-93), casting its shadow over the writing of *Notre-Dame des fleurs* and *Miracle de la Rose*. Indeed it appears that it was only via inadvertence or deliberate leniency that Genet escaped it in November 1943 (Stewart and McGregor, pp. 131-34); a circumstance he perhaps alludes to in an interview with Robert Poulet in 1956: 'Par chance, j'ai rencontré un juge d'instruction qui, dans un mouvement de générosité, m'a épargné la relégation, en déchirant subrepticement dans mon dossier la copie de mon casier judiciaire' (in Malgorn, p. 161).

20   JV, pp. 53-54.

21   MR, pp. 256-57.

22   *Saint Genet, comédien et martyr*, Paris, Gallimard, 1952, pp. 9-22, 25-26.

23   A severe appraisal of the mendacity involved in the process can be found in Stewart and McGregor, op. cit., pp. 54 ff.

24   JV, p. 65.

25   JV, p. 116.

26   JV, p. 217.

27   JV, pp. 217-18.

28   JV, p. 218.

29   See *Le Balcon*, ed. David H. Walker, London, Methuen, 1982, pp. 133, 118 and note on p. 191.

30   See André Gide, *Journal 1889-1939*, Paris, Gallimard ('Bibliothèque de la Pléiade'), 1951, p. 29; my italics, indicating modified text.

31   'Le Funambule', in *Oeuvres complètes*, vol. V, Paris, Gallimard, 1979, p. 15.

32   Op. cit., p. 17.

33   JV, pp. 284-85.

34   Ibid.

35   Ibid.

36   JV, p. 186.

37   JV, p. 184. Sartre calls this 'sauter en arrière de lui-même pour se placer à l'origine de sa propre nature', op. cit., p. 497.

38   Op. cit., p. 56.

39   JV, p. 115.

40   JV, p. 117.

41   'Les projets autobiographiques de Georges Perec', in *Parcours Perec*, textes réunis par Mireille Ribière, Lyon, Presses Universitaires de Lyon, 1990, p. 68.

42   JV, 97.

43   Op. cit., p. 173.

44   Edmund White underlines the important role played by such official scrutiny in shaping the writer's life and work: see *Genet*, London, Chatto and Windus, 1993, especially pp. 47-48, 60, 67, 182. Two critics in particular explore the juridical dimension of Genet's theatrical rhetoric, which arguably stems from the same source: Jeannette Savona, 'Théâtre et univers carcéral: Jean Genet et Michel Foucault', *French Forum*, 10, no. 2 (1985), pp. 201-13, and *Jean Genet*, Basingstoke, Macmillan, 1983; and Maria Paganini, 'L'inscription juridique dans *Les Bonnes* de Jean Genet', *Romanic Review*, 80, no. 3 (1989), pp. 462-82.

45   MR, p. 313.

46   Michel Foucault, *Surveiller et Punir*, Paris, Gallimard, 1975, p. 255.

47   MR, pp. 224-25.

48   See the documents reproduced by Dichy and Fouché, and Stewart and McGregor, op. cit.

49   MR, p. 264.

50   MR, pp. 264, 308.

51   See 'L'enfant criminel' in *Oeuvres complètes*, vol. V, pp. 377-93.

52   ND, p. 12.

53   JV, pp. 90-92.

54   JV, p. 77.

55   ND, pp. 53-55; MR, p. 327. It is interesting to note the important role played by photographs in Genet's texts. They are clear instances of an item 'que présente le passé', through which the past remains strikingly present. The problematic relationship of language to the past it seeks to retrieve is overlaid by a different interaction, between the visual and the linguistic, when Genet constructs his antecedents in this way. The overlap between the public and the private is another issue they raise. It would be productive to compare Genet's case with the photographs Gide writes of in *Si le grain ne meurt*, or with the example of Barthes in *Barthes par Barthes* and *La Chambre claire*. *Le Balcon* goes further, depicting photographers who specialise in creating 'une image vraie, née d'un spectacle faux', and explicitly linking 'la lecture' with 'l'image' (op. cit., pp. 115-18). This reminds us that in *Notre-Dame des fleurs*, too, the referential value of photographs is dubious since the narrator is not prepared to guarantee that they depict the individuals he chooses to see in them (ND, p. 10). As so often in Genet's work we find ourselves dealing with effects of secondary signification arising from the evacuation of a reliable referent.

56   JV, p. 261.

57   ND, pp. 103-04.

58   ND, p. 156.

59   Op. cit., pp. 28-29.

60   MR, p. 217.

61   MR, p. 309.

62   JV, p. 117.

63   MR, p. 216.

64   MR, p. 217.

65   MR, p. 214.

66   MR, p. 232.

67   MR, p. 395.

68   MR, p. 225.

69   ND, p. 148.

70   ND, p. 149.

71   JV, p. 26.

72   JV, p. 33.

73   JV, p. 17.

74   See my article 'Cultivating the *fait divers*: *Détective*', in *Nottingham French Studies*, 31, no. 2 (1992), pp. 71-83.

75   MR, pp. 210-11.

76   Harry E. Stewart has done much to clarify the inspiration Genet drew from such sources. See for example his 'Jean Genet's favourite murderers', *The French Review*, 60, no. 5 (1987), pp. 635-43; 'Louis Ménesclou, assassin and source of the "Lilac Murder" in Genet's *Haute Surveillance*', *Romance Notes*, 26, no. 3 (1986), pp. 204-08. See also Stewart and McGregor, op. cit.

77   ND, p. 9. The 'escalier' could legitimately be seen as an image of the way the *fait divers* works.

78   Use of the article for exophoric reference corresponds to cases where 'what is being referred to is well known or visible for the interlocutor'. See Anne Judge and F. G. Healey, *A Reference Grammar of Modern French*, London, Edward Arnold, 1985, p. 28.

79   There is a clear link here with *Haute Surveillance*, whose original title was *Préséances*, and whose plot turns on the hierarchy among criminals.

80   ND, p. 12.

81   *Le Petit Parisien*, no. 22120, 22 septembre 1937, p. 5: 'Parmi 20 larcins différents, un déserteur avait dérobé des autographes de Charles I et de François 1er'. The full text is reproduced in Dichy and Fouché, op. cit., pp. 159-60.

82   See Stewart and McGregor, op. cit., pp. 93-94. By the time Genet came to write *Notre-Dame des fleurs* the vicarious parallels with Weidmann might be said to have developed to the extent that he was facing a life sentence in the form of the 'relégation perpétuelle'. A not-dissimilar set of connections with Weidmann's career is developed by Abel Tiffauges in Tournier's *Le Roi des Aulnes*.

83   ND, p. 54.

84   ND, p. 141. It should be underlined that the self-projection does not respect the facts of his heroes' lives: Stewart and McGregor point out that whatever Genet knew of Pilorge he had read in the newspapers, since, contrary to his numerous assertions, there is no evidence of an actual acquaintance of any kind. Moreover, Pilorge was not a homosexual and the man he killed was not his lover. 'Pure invention' is the judgement these researchers pass on Genet's version of events, although certain details of Notre Dame's trial do echo reports of that of Pilorge. Similarly, despite what Genet says, neither Ange Soleil nor Soclay were guillotined. See op. cit., pp. 86-88, 99 n. 21; and 'Genet's favourite murderers', loc. cit., pp. 639-40.

85   Op. cit., p. 480.

86   ND, p. 9.

87   MR, p. 319.

88   MR, pp. 316-17.

89   ND, p. 90.

90   ND, p. 84.

91   ND, p. 84.

92   MR, p. 206.

93   ND, p. 141.

94   JV, p. 159.

95   JV, p. 159.

96   JV, pp. 117-18.

97   JV, p. 159.

98   This problem will be the central element of *Les Nègres*.

99   *Détective*, no. 309, pp. 7, 8, 9; no. 310, pp. 4, 5.

100   *Détective*, no. 541, 9 mars 1939, p. 4.

101   *Détective*, no.541, 9 mars 1939, pp. 6-10. It is noteworthy that Philippe's biography develops that nautical dimension of the Mettray experience, evoked at length in *Miracle de Rose* (e.g. MR, pp. 226, 237, 243-44), to which *Querelle de Brest* also owes much; this latter novel may well echo the story of Philippe.

102   *Oeuvres complètes de Colette*, vol. III, Paris, Flammarion, 1950, p. 438. Colette covered the Weidmann trial for *Paris-Soir*. See my article, 'Cultivating the *fait divers*: *Détective*', loc. cit.

103   JV, pp. 159-60.

104   Cf. Sheringham, loc. cit., p. 295: 'Genet's quest is not so much for a new image of himself, a new hypostasis as the Thief, or the Poet, but for a flight or at least a distancing from all images'.

105   JV, p. 100.

106   JV, p. 229.

107   JV, p. 229.

108   Barthes offers a meditation on the problem, using some of the same terminology as Genet, in 'L'Image', *Le bruissement de la langue*, Paris, Seuil, 1984, pp. 389-97.

Hervé Guibert: Autobiographical Film-Writing Pushed to its Limits?

JEAN-PIERRE BOULÉ

> J'ai été très frappé par l'introduction des
> *Essais* de Montaigne qui disait: 'J'ai
> voulu me peindre nu', ça a fait tilt, je me
> suis dit que c'était quelque chose que je
> pourrais mettre en exergue à tout ce que
> j'ai fait '[1]

Hervé Guibert came to the attention of the general public with *A l'ami qui ne m'a pas sauvé la vie* and *Le protocole compassionnel*.[2] In these two books he set down on paper his struggle with AIDS. In one he described 'la prise de conscience de la maladie et son travail sur le corps et l'âme', in the other 'l'étonnement et la douleur, la rage et la tristesse d'un homme de trente-cinq ans dans lequel s'est greffé le corps d'un vieillard'.[3] *Le protocole compassionnel* ended with him saying: 'J'ai commencé à tourner un film. Mon premier film.'[4] Guibert died on Friday 27 December 1991; on Thursday 30 January 1992 TF1 broadcast Guibert's film *La Pudeur ou l'Impudeur*, a film he had made himself with a camcorder between June 1990 and March 1991. Our purpose here is to study *La Pudeur ou l'Impudeur*, firstly by placing this film in the context of the other art forms used by Guibert, then by tracing the background to the film project, so that the meaning of this development in Guibert's work can be analysed, before its content is examined. The commitment evident in the film leads us to believe that Guibert has pushed autobiographical film-writing to its ultimate frontiers.

Guibert used a variety of art forms: writing, photography, drawing, painting and film-scripts.[5] In charge of the 'Photos' section of *Le Monde* from 1977 to

1985, then at *L'Autre Journal* in 1986, Guibert wrote in *L'Image fantôme*, in connection with a photograph he was unable to take because he did not have his camera with him:

> je n'ai d'abord mis en train [l'écriture] que pour me défaire de mon regret photographique. Il me semble maintenant que ce travail de l'écriture a dépassé et enrichi la transcription photographique immédiate ... car la photographie est une pratique englobeuse et oublieuse, tandis que l'écriture ... est une pratique mélancolique.[6]

Writing thus seems to take precedence for Guibert over photography. Following his death, Antoine de Gaudemar wrote:

> Dire la vérité tout en appelant son récit roman ... quand je disparaîtrais [remarquait-il ... en 1988] j'aurais tout dit, je me serais acharné à réduire cette distance entre les vérités de l'expérience et de l'écriture. Jamais sans doute parmi les écrivains d'aujourd'hui, projet littéraire n'a en effet été lié à un tel souci de réduire au minimum la marge entre ces deux vérités.[7]

In *Le protocole compassionnel* Guibert writes:

> C'est mon âme que je dissèque à chaque nouveau jour de labeur qui m'est offert ... Sur elle je fais toute sorte d'examens, des clichés en coupe, des investigations par résonance magnétique, des endoscopies, des radiographies et des scanners dont je vous livre les clichés, afin que vous les déchiffriez sur la plaque lumineuse de votre sensibilité.[8]

Guibert's work could even be described as 'photographic writing'. This is, moreover, the title of a chapter in *L'Image fantôme* in which he notes in connection with Goethe's *Journey to Italy* that Goethe re-created his journey from his diary and the letters he sent from Italy. Guibert comments:

> L'écriture de la lettre et l'écriture du journal sont les deux écritures les plus proches ... ce sont les deux écritures d'une même texture, d'une même immédiateté photographique ... Le paysage du journal est ... une carte postale. Le paysage du roman ... est presque un tableau.[9]

Taking up this idea, Hector Bianciotti draws a parallel with writing: 'D'où vient que son esthétique, voire son éthique d'écrivain, ait consisté pour le principal, à mettre la vie au net au fur et à mesure qu'il vivait ou qu'elle se déroulait devant lui, par une sorte de transcription immédiate et continue'.[10] Bianciotti locates the foundations of Guibert's literary project in *L'Image fantôme*. Similarly,

Michel Braudeau claims that *A l'ami qui ne m'a pas sauvé la vie* was the project 'd'écrire avec son sang'.[11] In fact, all Guibert's work springs from his private diary, from which he sometimes transferred passages to his books.[12] In *Le protocole compassionnel* he says: 'C'est quand ce que j'écris prend la forme d'un journal que j'ai la plus grande impression de fiction'.[13]

This form of writing, however, is not always satisfactory. There are events which *refuse* to be described in writing. During the 'Ex-Libris' programme,[14] Guibert tells the interviewer, M. Poivre d'Arvor, that he was unable to transcribe Michel Foucault's bursts of laughter in his book: 'on peut les réécrire dix fois, les déchirer, les refaire, c'est en dessous'. In *Cytomégalovirus*, his hospital diary, the entry for the night before his operation (a pneumothorax), dated 24 September 1991, records: 'Rien écrit ce soir. Trop choqué. J'essaierai demain.'.[15] In *Le protocole compassionnel*, following a fibroscope examination, he writes: 'Chez moi, j'ouvris mon journal, et j'y écrivis: "Fibroscopie". Rien d'autre, rien de plus ... J'étais devenu incapable de raconter mon expérience.'[16] Similarly, in *L'Homme au chapeau rouge*, he explains how he is unable to recreate in writing his sittings with the artist Yannis:

> J'avais un vrai mystère à raconter, donc quelque chose d'insaisissable: la fuite de la chair dans la peinture, la saignée progressive de l'âme sur la toile ... Fallait-il ... révisionner l'instant pour le reconstituer dans un maximum de détails?[17]

This would seem to be an allusion to video. Similarly, in *Mes Parents* he stops writing poems and instead writes cinematographic sequences: 'C'est cela que je vois et que j'ai envie de composer: des mouvements de caméra'.[18] In *L'Image fantôme* he explains how Peter Handke's diary corresponds closely to the workings of a video recorder:

> Il met son quotidien en écriture au fur et à mesure qu'il le vit: la retranscription est presque immédiate mais elle est aussi continue, plus que des photos on pourrait imaginer un appareil vidéo qui double sa vue et sa conscience d'une longue bande ininterrompue.[19]

Having written with his blood, Guibert also decided to write with his body in the film *La Pudeur ou l'Impudeur*, the development of which we may now trace.

Since the drug AZT had been unsuccessful in halting the progress of the disease, Guibert was in a very weak condition and could no longer write. Mme Pascale Breugnot, a television producer who had read *A l'ami qui ne m'a pas sauvé la vie*, wrote to him:

> Puisque vous prétendez ne plus écrire, et bien sûr cela ne regarde que vous, il ne tient qu'à vous de recommencer ou de renoncer à recommencer, mais pour l'instant, je vous propose d'occuper cette zone intermédiaire en réalisant un film dont vous seriez à la fois l'auteur et le sujet.[20]

Guibert comments: 'La formule n'était pas mal choisie: à la limite je n'avais jamais fait que cela',[21] stressing that directing a film had been one of his childhood dreams. This project did not meet with the unanimous approval of those close to Guibert. His best friend and former lover, Jules, thought the proposal was 'degrading'.[22] Guibert himself speaks of Mme Breugnot as a 'bestial' producer,[23] and even as a 'vulture'.[24] His enthusiasm for the film was naturally influenced by his own physical and mental condition:

> Hier ... j'avais même envie du film, j'ai rappelé la productrice de télé ... je voulais profiter de la fibro du jeudi matin pour la filmer, un seul gros plan sur mon visage avec le tuyau qui rentre dans la gorge. Aujourd'hui cette idée m'écoeure.[25]

It is worth recalling that he was unable to capture the first fibroscope examination in writing.[26] At certain times he does not take the camcorder with him when he goes to see Claudette Dumouchel, his doctor, explaining: 'je n'avais pas envie de mettre ce machin entre nous. C'est encore trop tôt, il faut laisser la relation se bâtir toute seule sur les regards';[27] on another occasion he writes: 'Ma soeur a refusé que je la filme, j'en suis presque soulagé'.[28] At other times he insists to his doctor: 'Vous ne pouvez tout de même pas m'empêcher de me filmer, c'est mon corps, ce n'est pas le vôtre'.[29] When she asks him his reasons for filming such a private examination, he replies: 'il me semble suffisamment rare pour mériter qu'on en laisse une trace'.[30] Describing one of the sessions which is filmed with the masseur, Guibert begins to voice his own doubts: 'je filme cette nudité décharnée, touchante et effrayante à la fois, pour quoi faire?',[31] but when the session is over, he says to his masseur: 'Je crois que nous venons de filmer un des documentaires les plus bizarres qui soient'.[32] It is worth noting that Guibert began making his film by filming the masseur: 'il a fait cinq cassettes du masseur'.[33] Similarly, in *L'Homme au chapeau rouge* he relates how he had to negotiate with the surgeon before he was able to film the operation on him for the ablation of a ganglion, which was supposedly either lymphomatic or tuberculous.[34]

In any case, the film was completed, and edited by Maureen Mazureck from twelve hours of pictures into a programme lasting 58 minutes;[35] it was shown on television in the French-speaking part of Switzerland in October 1991. In France nobody wanted the film: 'La Sept, Canal+ et la Cinq l'ont refusé'.[36] It was finally scheduled to be shown on TF1 on the night of Sunday 19 to Monday 20 January 1992, but it was cancelled at the last minute following a letter of protest from the National AIDS Council (CNS). M. Etienne Mougeotte, Vice-President of TF1, offered the members of the CNS the chance to view the film and 'de diffuser un commentaire préalable à la diffusion du film de manière à avertir de son contenu les personnes sensibles'.[37] The film was re-scheduled and was shown on TF1 on Thursday 30 January 1992 at 11.15 pm.

Why did Guibert agree to this 'filmed writing' of his body? On 'Ex-Libris' he explained to Poivre d'Arvor why he photographed one of his great-aunts, Suzanne, in such a way that - although she was still alive - she looked like a corpse. He took these photos to free himself 'of the anguish of photographing her corpse'. In the same programme he explained that he had refused to allow his photograph to be taken for three years because of his skeletal appearance (indeed, he had lost 18 kilos in one year),[38] but that filming was not the same: 'le film, à la limite ... c'est vivant'.[39] He also accepted the idea of being photographed naked by Jules; he thought of suggesting to the painter Barcelo in *Le protocole compassionnel* that he should pose nude, having already thought of the title of the series: 'Nude AIDS Victim';[40] and he gave his agreement to Hector to appear on stage naked during a performance in Avignon.[41] Art makes it possible to fight decay: 'Et Hector avait bien saisi le sens de cette prestation, d'aller au bout d'un dévoilement ... Etait-ce un moyen de me soulager d'une hantise, un exorcisme de cette maigreur désespérante?'[42] At the same time, he tells Jérôme Garcin that he is writing the sequel to *Le protocole compassionnel* which is 'une tentative, par le récit, d'évacuer le sida, de m'en débarrasser'.[43] Similarly, in *Cytomégalovirus* he writes: 'Faire de la torture mentale (la situation dans laquelle je me trouve, par exemple) un sujet d'étude, pour ne pas dire une oeuvre, rend la torture un peu plus supportable'.[44] In this way 'l'oeuvre est l'exorcisme de l'impuissance',[45] as Guibert himself writes. Once the work has been written and has expelled from the consciousness 'la maladie inéluctable ... le comble de l'impuissance',[46] it is never again to re-enter his consciousness. Guibert says he never viewed any of the 'vingt-trois cassettes de quarante cinq minutes, soit plus de dix heures de film' that he recorded.[47] Once *La Pudeur ou l'Impudeur* had been completed, he had no desire to see the film;[48] nor did he insist that the film be broadcast in his lifetime.[49] This was by no means a new attitude on his part, and the concept of exorcism is the key to an understanding of his work. Guibert never re-read his books, as he revealed to Poivre d'Arvor, whether it be *Les Chiens*,[50] *A l'ami qui ne m'a pas sauvé la vie* ('Je n'ai pas eu le courage de le relire'), or *Le protocole compassionnel* ('Je n'ai pas eu le courage de le relire parce que c'est le sida'). With regard to the fifty pages he mislaid on his trip to Africa, he explained that he did not want to rewrite them 'parce qu'une fois que les choses sont écrites elles sont pour moi comme effacées'.[51] Similarly, concerning his last wishes (to be buried on the isle of Elba), he said to Poivre d'Arvor: 'A partir du moment où je l'ai écrit, je m'en fiche'. Literature is, as it were, an outlet, a release.

Having established this fact, it is worth noting, however, that Guibert made one exception to the rule he had set himself: he wanted to view the operation he had filmed (the ablation of a ganglion) and to film himself while viewing it. He can thus be seen in *La Pudeur ou l'Impudeur* sitting in his armchair watching the operation. Switching off his video, this is what he feels: 'Quand j'arrêtai la bande, ma douleur avait redoublé, et je me mis à écrire quelque chose de tout à fait inattendu ... j'écrivis un texte sur le peintre Yannis ... toute la nuit ... me relevant du lit pour le compléter'.[52] This creative writing bulimia was provoked by seeing the operation and the flashback to the past which he would never normally have permitted himself. Discussing this episode, Raymond Bellour analyses the process of artistic creation in Guibert's work as follows: 'On voit ici le circuit qui s'agence ... entre le corps, tous les régimes et degrés de l'image, peinture - photo - vidéo - (cinéma), et l'écriture qui en ressort, en ressort'.[53] Furthermore, we shall discover by examining the contents of *La Pudeur ou l'Impudeur* that the source of the film's commentary may be found in Guibert's private diary, which was also used for the books already published, thus confirming Raymond Bellour's comment.

In Guibert's youthful writings, published in 1977, a prescient book that already gives an idea of the contents of *La Pudeur ou l'Impudeur*, are to be found the following extraordinary words:

> Mon corps ... sous l'effet de la douleur, est mis dans un état de théâtralité, de paroxysme, qu'il me plairait de reproduire, de quelque façon que ce soit: photo, film, bande-son.
>
> ... mettre en marche un mécanisme de retranscription: éructations, déjections ... M'ingénier à les photographier, à les enregistrer. Laisser parler ce corps convulsé, haché, hurlant.
>
> Mon corps est un laboratoire que j'offre en exhibition, l'unique acteur.[54]

The film itself, which is a veritable chronicle of a death foretold, makes us share, thanks to the camcorder, all the aspects of daily life for an AIDS patient: we follow Guibert as he visits the doctor, the masseur, as he does his exercises, on holiday and at home, in bed and sitting in his armchair, and - something that might have been shocking - we even follow him into the bathroom to see him washing his private parts and into the toilet to watch him defecating. Franck Nouchi considers that this constitutes a 'description clinique et poétique de ce qu'Hervé Guibert appelle "le processus de détérioration amorcé dans mon sang par le sida" ... Guibert, photographe, connaît trop le sens de l'image pour en marteler la signification. Il laisse l'image parler, même si cela peut parfois choquer.'[55] Guibert's commentary is very often limited to re-reading passages that we can identify as being passages from his books, either directly,[56] or indirectly.[57] It is a fair assumption that these passages first appeared in Guibert's private diary, the primary source of his writing. This hypothesis is confirmed by Maureen Mazureck, the film's editor, according to whom Guibert did not initially want to have any words accompanying the film (apart from the interviews with his great-aunts), then 'finalement, il a lu son journal qu'il a enregistré sur cassette'.[58] As for the crudest images in the film, they are not really shocking, since, as Franck Nouchi rightly understood, they form part of the everyday reality of AIDS, as is confirmed by the film's editor: 'Le voir aux toilettes, par exemple, aurait pu devenir gênant, dans un autre contexte. Mais là, on sent que cela fait partie de sa lutte pour la vie.'[59] Guibert himself shot the entire film, without technical assistance. Most of the time he positioned the camcorder then moved into the field of view; the shot is therefore often fixed. At other times, as for example when he was filming the beach and the sea, the trembling of his arm is apparent in the picture. But, as Antoine de Gaudemar writes: 'Paradoxalement, cette apparente grossièreté ne tire pas le film dans le sens du document-vérité, mais plutôt dans celui d'une chronique aléatoire et fragile',[60] just like the trembling hand of the writer.

We have now reached the film's climax, but before considering it from this angle it seems appropriate to look back briefly, since film writing is so closely linked to the writing of books and to photography. The diagnosis of AIDS made Guibert write: 'Soudain à cause de l'annonce de ma mort, m'avait saisi l'envie d'écrire tous les livres possibles, tous ceux que je n'avais pas encore écrits'.[61] This book-writing bulimia was constantly threatened by the other solution: 'je choisirais entre le suicide et l'écriture d'un nouveau livre'.[62] The possibility of suicide keeps re-appearing,[63] either because the pain is unbearable (thus, after the first fibroscope examination, Guibert writes: 'la violence de cet examen fait immédiatement surgir la nécessité du suicide'),[64] or because he knows there is no hope ('En vérité, j'avais émis le dessein, sans en parler à personne, même pas à Jules ... d'aller me suicider, si l'hypothèse lymphome était confirmée').[65] Advised by a doctor friend, Guibert inquired about the dosage of digitalin he would need to take his life.[66] He then succeeded in obtaining the two fatal doses in Italy,[67] thus having at his disposal the means of killing himself,[68] and he took them with him on all his travels. He even put into words the possibility of killing himself in this way: 'J'étais désespéré, prostré au fond du fauteuil rouge, prêt à renoncer à Vincent, certain que je ne tiendrais jamais jusqu'au DDI, que la Digitaline me soulagerait avant'.[69]

In the meantime, he put into effect the project of interviewing for the film, on the subject of AIDS, his two great-aunts, Suzanne who was 95 and Louise who was 85.[70] This is, we feel, perhaps the only moment in the film in which it leans more toward the second element of the title, *La Pudeur ou l'Impudeur*,. since he wants to know what his two great-aunts would think if he killed himself! He begins the conversation on the subject of AIDS, then goes on to talk about suffering, before asking Suzanne: 'Est-ce que tu penses qu'il faut se suicider quand on a très mal?' (Suzanne, disabled, is confined to a chair, a home-help tries to feed her with porridge and she groans continually because of the pain in her back.)[71] When he questions Louise, he asks her - having again prepared the ground - 'Est-ce qu'il faut se suicider quand on est comme moi?' The climax is reached when he inquires: 'Si par exemple un jour t'apprenais que je me suicide, qu'est-ce que tu en penserais? ... Tu m'en voudrais?' Louise replies that she would be very sad: 'je t'aime, figure-toi!'.[72] Guibert comments: 'Elle ne me l'a jamais dit, mais l'intercession de la caméra qui tourne lui permet de le dire, c'est incroyable'.[73]

An eerily prescient passage on suicide is to be found in *La Mort propagande*, the youthful writings published in 1977:

> la mort ... Moi je veux lui laisser élever sa voix puissante et qu'elle chante, diva, à travers mon corps ... Ne pas laisser perdre cette source de spectaculaire immédiat, viscéral. Me donner la mort sur une scène, devant des caméras. Donner ce spectacle extrême, excessif de mon corps, dans ma mort. En choisir les termes, le déroulement, les accessoires.
>
> Le public sera pris de convulsions, contractions, répulsions ... Son corps général, à son tour, se mettra à parler ... Qui voudra bien produire mon suicide, ce best-seller? Filmer la piqûre qui donne la mort la plus lente ...?[74]

This text actually corresponds to the script of *La Pudeur ou l'Impudeur* such as it is described in *A l'ami qui ne m'a pas sauvé la vie*. In fact, a part of this book is repeated in the film's commentary: 'je me verserais dans un verre d'eau ces soixante-dix gouttes, je l'avalerais, et puis qu'est-ce que je ferais? Je m'étendrais ... combien de temps ça prendrait pour que mon coeur cesse de battre?'[75]

In a remarkable 'mise en abîme' in *La Pudeur ou l'Impudeur* we witness a live game of Russian roulette: Guibert pours a lethal dose of digitalin into a glass of water, then, closing his eyes, he moves this glass of water around on the table together with another glass of water, before drinking one of them; he stretches himself out on an armchair, waiting either to wake up or to die. When he wakes up, the film's commentary is as follows: 'Je suis sorti épuisé de cette expérience, comme modifié. Je crois que filmer ça a changé mon rapport à l'idée du suicide.' Maureen Mazureck, the film's editor, confirms: 'il a vraiment mis les gouttes dans l'un des deux verres ... il est allé jusqu'à se glisser un bas sur la tête pour respirer moins bien.'[76] At the end of the film, we see Guibert typing the following words: 'La vidéo ... peut aussi faire le lien entre photo, écriture et cinéma. Avec la vidéo, on s'approche d'un autre instant, de l'instant nouveau avec, comme en superposition, dans un fondu enchaîné purement mental, le souvenir du premier instant.' Everyone knows that on the day before his 36th birthday, 13 December 1991, Guibert attempted suicide by taking a massive dose of digitalin. He was admitted to the Antoine Béclère de Clamart Hospital, where he died 14 days later, on 27 December 1991. Perhaps he thought he had tamed death itself.

In any case, Guibert had already announced his death. In *Cytomégalovirus*, his hospital diary, which he risked blindness to write while the cytomegalovirus was attacking his eyes ('Je risque de devenir aveugle, on m'a crevé un poumon lors d'une opération en me faisant un pneumothorax, j'ai eu une hémorragie, je suis resté deux jours couché complètement immobile en réanimation'),[77] are to be found his last published words, written on 8 October 1991, two months before his suicide attempt:

> Ecrire dans le noir?
> Ecrire jusqu'au bout?
> En finir pour ne pas arriver à la peur de la mort?[78]

This death was already familiar to him - 'j'étais passé à un autre stade de la mort, comme imprégné par elle au plus profond je n'avais plus besoin de son décorum mais d'une intimité plus grande avec elle, je continuais inlassablement de quérir son sentiment ... sa peur et sa convoitise'[79] - so that Guibert was in a sense the director of his own death. *La Pudeur ou l'Impudeur* will remain a high point, 'une véritable oeuvre cinématographique' in which 'l'impudeur de ce "corps de vieillard" ... ne sert qu'à masquer la pudeur des sentiments, l'amour d'une vie qui s'échappe'.[80] Guibert wrote right to the end, both in his autobiographical books which he wrote with his blood, photographically, and in this autobiographical film, which he wrote with his body and with film. Antoine de Gaudemar situates *La Pudeur ou l'Impudeur* midway between Guibert's *writing* in which he 'disait ne connaître aucun "frein", aucun "scrupule"',[81] and his *photography*, which he practised 'd'une façon rétive, prudente, soupçonneuse'.[82] Arnaud Marty-Lavauzelle, chairman of Aides (an association providing support for AIDS sufferers), stated with regard to *La Pudeur ou l'Impudeur*: 'Chez Guibert, la création ... sert d'accélérateur, de visualisation de tous les effets de la mort. C'est non seulement l'action du virus mais sa volonté qui le conduit à la mort. Et finalement, de quoi est-il mort? De son suicide. Du virus? De sa création?'[83]

The question that must remain open at the end of our analysis is whether Guibert has reached the very limits of autobiographical (film-)writing with *La Pudeur ou l'Impudeur*. In any case, he has perhaps invented a new autobiographical genre: existential thanatography.[84] He himself liked to quote Marguerite Duras's expression, 'J'écrirai, même après ma mort',[85] which he described as a 'formule géniale'.[86] It may point to the ultimate autobiographical genre, one still to be invented.

NOTES

1 Hervé Guibert, interviewed by Christophe Donner, *La Règle du jeu*, 3, No. 7 (May 1992), p. 145.

2 *A l'ami qui ne m'a pas sauvé la vie* (ASV), Paris, Gallimard, 1990; *Le protocole compassionnel* (PC), Paris, Gallimard, 1991.

3 PC, back cover (text signed 'H.G.').

4 PC, p. 227.

5 He is the co-author with Patrick Chéreau of the film-script *L'homme blessé*, Paris, Editions de Minuit, 1983.

6 *L'Image fantôme*, Paris, Editions de Minuit, 1981, p. 24. In the interview with Christophe Donner (op. cit., pp. 155-56), Guibert compares the camcorder with the Rollei 35, the camera with which he took his photos, and praises the camcorder.

7 Antoine de Gaudemar, 'Hervé Guibert, la mort propagande', *Libération*, 28 and 29 December 1991, p. 26. Guibert's quoted words are taken from the following interview: 'Les aveux permanents d'Hervé Guibert', *Libération*, October 1988, p. 12.

8 PC, pp. 80-81.

9 *L'Image fantôme*, pp. 74-75.

10 Hector Bianciotti, 'Jusqu'au bout de la nuit', *Le Monde*, 29-30 December 1991, p. 10.

11 Michel Braudeau, 'Le beau diable', *Le Monde*, 24 January 1992, p. 24.

12 *Mes Parents*, Paris, Gallimard, 1986, p. 93. In an interview he gave in 1988, he explained: 'J'ai commencé à tenir un journal en 1978 ... Ce journal est le principal de ce que je fais, c'est ma colonne vertébrale. Chaque livre est une excroissance, une ramification.' In 'Les aveux permanents d'Hervé Guibert', op. cit.

13 PC, p. 87.

14 Broadcast on 28 February 1991. We would like to thank M. Poivre d'Arvor for providing us with a cassette of the programme.

15 *Cytomégalovirus*, Paris, Editions du Seuil, 1992, p. 59.

16 PC, p. 60.

17 *L'Homme au chapeau rouge* (HCR), Paris, Gallimard, 1992, p. 108.

18 *Mes Parents*, p. 82.

19 *L'Image fantôme*, p. 77.

20   PC, p. 174.
21   Ibid.
22   PC, p. 35.
23   PC, p. 65.
24   PC, p. 174.
25   PC, p. 103.
26   PC, p. 60.
27   PC, p. 103.
28   PC, p. 102.
29   PC, p. 225.
30   Ibid.
31   PC, p. 99.
32   PC, p. 100.
33   'Maureen Mazureck: "Sa façon de regarder un lézard!"', quoted by Annick Peigné-Giuly, *Libération*, Saturday 18 and Sunday 19 January, 1992, p. 23.
34   HCR, p. 39.
35   Patrick Kéchichian, 'TF1 décide le report de la diffusion du film d'Hervé Guibert', *Le Monde*, 19-20 January 1992, p. 20. In a certain sense, Maureen Mazureck is more the *author* of the film than Guibert. See, however, the flattering things he says about her in the interview with Christophe Donner (op. cit.), pp. 150-51.
36   Michel Braudeau, op. cit., p. 24.
37   Franck Nouchi, 'Le film d'Hervé Guibert devrait être diffusé jeudi 30 janvier sur TF1', *Le Monde*, 22 January 1992, p. 10. See also J.-P. Boulé, 'The postponing of *La pudeur ou l'Impudeur*: Modesty or Hypocrisy on the part of French television', *French Cultural Studies*, no. 3 (October 1992), pp. 299-305.
38   PC, p. 27.
39   See note 15.
40   PC, p. 25.
41   Ibid.
42   PC, pp. 25-26.
43   'Hervé Guibert son dernier entretien', interview with Jérôme Garcin, *L'événement du Jeudi*, October 1990. Reprinted in the issue of 2-8 January 1992, p. 108.
44   *Cytomégalovirus*, p. 54.
45   ASV, p. 248.
46   Ibid.
47   HCR, pp. 39-40.
48   Op. cit., p. 109.

49   Annick Peigné-Giuly, 'Du caméscope à l'écran', *Libération*, 18 and 19 January 1992, p. 22.

50   *Les Chiens*, Paris, Editions de Minuit, 1982.

51   HCR, p. 154.

52   HCR, pp. 42-43.

53   Raymond Bellour, 'Vérités et mensonges', *Le Magazine littéraire*, No. 296 (February 1992), p. 70.

54   *La Mort propagande*, Paris, Régine Desforges, 1977; reprinted 1991, p. 183.

55   Franck Nouchi, 'La mort annoncée', *Le Monde*, 22 January 1992, p. 10.

56   Passages quoted from *A l'ami qui ne m'a pas sauvé la vie*, by order of appearance: pp. 13-14, 15, 218. From *Le protocole compassionnel*, by order of appearance: pp. 17, 102, 9-11, 15, 99-100, 149.

57   Similar passages in *Le protocole compassionnel*, pp. 14, 48-49, 102, 149, 131, 224-25. In *L'Homme au chapeau rouge*, pp. 41-42.

58   'Maureen Mazureck: "Sa façon de regarder un lézard!"', quoted by Annick Peigné-Giuly, op. cit., p. 23.

59   Ibid.

60   Antoine de Gaudemar, 'Guibert, sa mort, son oeuvre', *Libération*, 18 and 19 January 1992, p. 24. The problematic question of truth and sincerity has to be considered if we take into account these words of Guibert's: 'C'est vrai que ce jeu de la vérité et de la sincérité, poussé un peu dans des excès, m'amène à ce qui doit être, j'imagine, comme une très grande impudeur, mais en fait je crois être très pudique ... je suis quelqu'un qui, depuis que je suis enfant, se cache, qui cache son corps, qui cache au point qu'on a pu me dire hypocrite, je cache, je ne me déshabille pas, je ne sais pas combien de fois j'ai baisé dans ma vie, peut-être plus d'une centaine de fois, je ne saurais pas dire, mais peut-être je me suis déshabillé au maximum cinq fois. Je suis très très très pudique. J'ai peur' (Hervé Guibert, interviewed by Christophe Donner, op. cit., p. 146).

61   ASV, p. 70.

62   ASV, p. 56.

63   ASV, pp. 201-02.

64   PC, p. 56 and p. 57.

65   HCR, p. 16.

66   ASV, p. 202.

67   ASV, pp. 243-44 and p. 250.

68   PC, p. 11.

69   PC, p. 143; see also p. 30.

70   PC, pp. 100-02 and pp. 224-25.

71   PC, pp. 224-25.

72   PC, p. 102.

73   Ibid.

74   *La Mort propagande*, pp. 184-85.

75   ASV, pp. 218-19.

76   'Maureen Mazureck: "Sa façon de regarder un lézard!"', quoted by Annick Peigné-Giuly, op. cit., p. 23.

77   *Cytomégalovirus*, p. 80.

78   Ibid., p. 93.

79   ASV, p. 150.

80   Franck Nouchi, op. cit.

81   Antoine de Gaudemar, op. cit., p. 24.

82   Ibid. On this subject read Hervé Guibert's preface to his book of photographs: *Le seul visage*, Paris, Editions de Minuit, 1984, pp. 5-7.

83   Quoted by Eric Favereau, 'Un "crudity show" aux vertus ambigües', *Libération*, 18 and 19 January 1992, p. 22.

84   It was Serge Doubrovsky who gave us the idea for this category during a conversation regarding the genre he has created: 'autofiction'.

85   Op. cit., p. 108.

86   Ibid.

Conclusion

TERRY KEEFE

The chapters in this volume were not written to a tight or narrow brief. They reflect a common interest in, firstly, the autobiographical process and, secondly, writers who are part of, or have some kind of link with, the French existentialist current of thought of the 1940s. But they also display certain differences in emphasis and methodology. The studies were not brought together with the explicit intention of advancing autobiographical theory as such. Nor was the expectation that they could make progress towards solving the complex philosophical problems of the self. Yet, in treating as case-studies a number of interrelated French authors from the last fifty-five years or so - the primary texts examined here were all written in the period 1938-1991 - the essays make, collectively, a contribution of substance to the investigation of a number of major issues concerning the broad autobiographical project.

In a recent book of his own, one of the contributors, Michael Sheringham, has examined the personal relationships between some of the authors treated here, and reflected usefully on the concept of 'existentialist autobiography'.[1] It is perhaps in relation to this category, therefore, that we should first attempt to place the analyses in this volume. Of the writers discussed here, three are not among those considered by Sheringham under the rubric of 'existentialist autobiography'. However, two of them - Nizan and Camus - might well have been, in so far as both were part of the network of relations that encompasses all of the others, and their views were not sufficiently far from the core of existentialism to exclude them on ideological grounds. (Hervé Guibert, born in 1955, was not known to our other authors and stands in a different kind of relationship to existentialism.) The factor that dictates the exclusion of Nizan and Camus is presumably that they did not publish autobiographies in the formal sense, for these constitute the central concern of Sheringham's book, as they do of most studies of autobiography.[2] Although, thanks to critics such as

Philippe Lejeune, there has been a growing interest in other autobiographical forms, theorists of autobiography have, understandably, concentrated primarily on the literary genre; that is, on books published *as* autobiographies. Furthermore, only secondarily, if at all, have they focused specifically on existentialist autobiography. By contrast, the present volume starts from a particular engagement with individual writers in some way linked to French existentialism, does not argue for one particular theory of autobiography, and casts its net over a much wider range of phenomena than formal autobiographies.

The extent to which the volume reaches beyond the autobiographical genre as it is normally understood may be one of the first features to strike many readers, since attention is paid here, in differing degrees, to: private letters, diaries, journals and notebooks, prefaces, published or broadcast interviews, films, photographs, video-films, and so on (as well as to novels and plays). In some cases these forms are brought into play - even made the main object of focus - *because* the author has written no autobiography as such, but in others *in spite of* the fact that he/she has also published formal autobiographical works. In any case, the assumptions made - though perhaps left unformulated - are that such sources can indeed offer 'autobiographical' information, and that they thereby provide real or potential material for the writing of autobiographies proper. This also opens up, of course, the possibility of comparing and contrasting the evidence from these other sources with statements made and views expressed in formal autobiographies. The procedures involved in such comparisons are in some ways similar to, but in others quite distinct from, the well-established practice - also represented here - of looking at the content of novels or plays in relation to what we learn about the author's life from autobiographical sources, or as themselves in some sense autobiographical.

None of these processes, however, is tantamount to either devaluing the autobiographical genre in its narrower sense, or ignoring recent insights into its nature. The chapters by Edmund Smyth and Michael Sheringham offer very close and subtle readings of autobiographies by Sartre and Violette Leduc - readings that would not have been possible before the advances in the theory of autobiography highlighted in the Introduction. And there is an obvious awareness on the part of the authors of this volume that, as a genre, autobiography cannot possibly consist in a mere mechanical, 'objective' registering or transcription of what has happened to the writer in the past; an awareness that autobiography is - albeit sometimes in an extended sense of the term - *writing*, with all the elements of textual construction that we now know this to involve. On the other hand, no contributor here appears to have any particular inclination to revert to the extreme point to which this insight was taken by earlier literary theorists, and to accept the 'death of the author' or the 'death of the subject'. In all instances the working assumption appears to be that autobiographical texts, whether they take the standard form or that of more intimate, less formal writings, are produced by identifiable individuals, whose lives, at one level of accuracy or another, are describable. There is no reluctance to consider Sartre to be the author of *Les Mots*, Leduc the writer of *La Folie en tête*, etc.

Now, it is in implicitly building upon this position that one may come to have a use for the idea of an 'existential self', for - depending upon the context and the purposes of the discourse - the development involved may be a small and unproblematic one. The existential self of the individual writer will in some sense correspond to, or perhaps even be identical with, the potentially describable life. It can be invoked not in order to make specific ontological or metaphysical claims about selfhood, but primarily to draw a *contrast*. Its main function is to indicate and highlight two points: that the 'official' self of at least certain types of writing is *constructed*; and that it may be possible to compare or contrast this self with another, 'existential' self, or at the very least with evidence from the same source showing that the official self *is*, indeed, constructed.

It is clear that in a strictly philosophical context, a much more precise definition of 'existential self' would be required, and that this would be an extremely controversial matter. Sartre's views on the self - and one of his very first philosophical works was *La Transcendance de l'Ego. Esquisse d'une description phénoménologique*[3] - would clearly be of relevance to an elaborated concept of the existential self, and aspects of these views come directly under consideration in a number of the chapters of this volume. But this takes us back to the point that the volume is not centred on existentialism, or even 'existentialist autobiography' as such. As recent commentaries show, there are many complexities to Sartre's position that would take us very far away indeed from the processes of autobiography.[4] Moreover, the fact that, at least in early Sartrean philosophy, the self is *always* a construct would constitute a significant problem. Yet for present purposes it is probably sufficient to remember that for Sartre the 'pour soi', or consciousness, enjoys a freedom and spontaneity that stands in precisely the same kind of relation to the constructed ego as does (what our contributors understand by) the 'existential self' to the self constructed in writing. Sartre considers that the essential role of the ego may be to hide from consciousness its own spontaneity,[5] and one of the themes dwelt upon by, or even motivating, many of the chapters in this volume is the possibility of modifying, distorting or disguising the existential self by constructing a public or 'official' self. Other chapters show authors anxious to *avoid* such distortion.

It is also vital to recall, however, Sartre's general commitment, throughout his early philosophy, to rejecting the idea of a universal human nature and the associated concept of an inner individual essence.[6] The whole range of specific and detailed implications that this rejection has for the autobiographical process cannot be charted here, but it is clear that any kind of autobiographical writing intended to locate and describe the inner essence or inner self of its author would be, on this view, necessarily misconceived. If, for the early Sartre, it continues to make sense to talk of an individual's 'essence' at all - and it is sometimes forgotten that the assertion that 'l'existence précède l'essence' actually entails that there *is* an essence to be preceded by existence - this can now be explained only in terms of the individual's existence out in the world. Like notions of a fixed inner self, ideas of a transcendental (or 'pure') ego that does not itself belong to, but is *presupposed by*, the world, and of the individual as uninvolved onlooker - such ideas are ones that Sartre repudiates, and they constitute, precisely, another aspect of what emphasis on the 'existential self' is designed to reject. Whatever else it is or is not, the existential self is a subject actively engaged in the world and attempting to exercise some capacity to make choices and impose meanings.[7] On one level, therefore, the construction of a self in autobiography is just one more manifestation of the existential, sense-conferring subject's engagement with the world. But this particular type of construction risks becoming a strange, paradoxical, and deceptive activity, in so far as the writing process itself may make it veer towards the static rather than the dynamic, the necessary rather than the contingent, the unified rather than the fragmentary.

If autobiography in its formal sense is a search for the *unity* of a series of phenomena or experiences, if it is Lejeune's 'histoire d'une personnalité', then the 'existential self', by definition, is not identical with that unity or that 'histoire'. It is even, to one degree or another, in tension with the constructed self. As the raw material for the constructed, autobiographical self, it is, like all raw material, to some extent, *resistant* to the construction process. As Sartre, among other philosophers, has pointed out, the very resistance of the air is indispensable if flying is to take place, the very resistance of the water indispensable if we are to swim.[8] One or two chapters here dwell on the construction process as such, and demonstrate that it is not confined to the autobiographical genre in any narrow sense (Emma Wilson, Steve Robson). Others trace the nature of the resistance involved, and some of these suggest that the resistance was a good deal greater than is apparent from a reading of the autobiography proper (Terry Keefe). The risks involved in a conscious construction of the self, and the nature of the writers' reactions to those risks are what make the autobiographies of Sartre, Genet and Leduc such fascinatingly complex enterprises in the different ways so well brought out by the contributors to this volume.

David Walker emphasises that Genet attempts to repudiate the existential self and deliberately seeks to transfigure existence into essence, by creating a 'légende' for himself through writing. But whereas Michael Scriven's argument that Sartre's *Carnets* are more representative of his existential self than *Les Mots* is based on the view that the latter text is written from a retrospective, totalising vantage-point, Edmund Smyth comes to the conclusion that the main narrative of *Les Mots* is ultimately compatible with the reality of the existential self, since this emerges as a composite of texts, voices and words. Both Genet and Sartre, moreover, are shown, in their distinctive ways, to be using their past and their past personae in order to elaborate a new, present self, thus making the autobiographical process a basis for future transfiguration of the self. And Michael Sheringham demonstrates that much of the significance of *La Folie en tête* lies in the fact that Leduc plays down the gap between past protagonist and present writer by representing the past only as it is reconstructed in the act and process of writing.

To the extent that Leduc writes for what we might call therapeutic reasons, there is also a link with what Benedict O'Donohoe finds in some of Sartre's plays. He suggests that Sartre may have been pursuing the image of his father, in spite of the fact that *Les Mots* hardly implies that this would be likely, and that the plays register 'sentiments that Sartre imagines he might have felt had his father lived'. We may even suppose, then, that Sartre was working something out of his system in the plays, and that doing so enabled him to record things in his autobiography that he would not otherwise have been able to say. (It is interesting to speculate, in a similar vein, that had Beauvoir not 'killed Olga on paper' in *L'Invitée*, she might not have been able to go on to write about the trio in the way that she did in *La Force de l'âge*.) Apart from its intrinsic interest, this type of possibility serves as a clear warning that there are dangers of circularity in using an autobiography as the source of information about an author's life, then looking to see whether the life is illustrated in his/her plays and novels. Rather than exemplifying aspects of the formal autobiography, fiction may have played a crucial role in making the autobiography what it is. One might see Dilthey as arguing the interesting broader point that an important general feature of the autobiographical process is that the subject choosing which aspects of his/her past to relate is a subject *already influenced and formed by* those very factors.[9]

But autobiographers do not write primarily for themselves. In the light of reader-response theory and particularly Lejeune's discussion of the 'pacte autobiographique', it is no surprise that a number of contributors should emphasise the importance of the reader's role in the autobiographical process. What constitutes a somewhat different slant on that role in these essays, however, is the extent to which it is stressed that autobiography can constitute a kind of *act*. Steve Robson's chapter confirms that even the case of Camus illustrates this point in a negative way, in that he never ceased to be conscious of a duty to serve others through his writings, and of his role as an example or a writer of exemplary works, abstaining from autobiography precisely because he was afraid of the way in which it might affect his readers. By contrast, as interpreted by Smyth and Mary Orr respectively, Sartre and Nizan are both seen to set out with the deliberate intention of shaking and disturbing the bourgeois prejudices of theirs. Nizan is said to be consciously revolting against the bourgeois genre of autobiography in his fiction, and revolutionising it by turning the individual self into a universal voice speaking on behalf of others ('autrebiographie'). Genet, too, of course, wishes to challenge the morality of respectable people, but in his special circumstances certain kinds of autobiography can have even more specific purposes. David Walker shows that, just as he makes the self an element in a distinctive pact that involves outwitting the bourgeois reader by forcing his/her voyeuristic complicity and thereby imposing the 'légende' that hides his existential self, so, in penal institutions, Genet constructed a self that resisted the system's own construction of a criminal's life by subverting it.

Yet, whatever their effects, and whatever the intentions behind them, there is no suggestion in this volume that formal autobiographies alone involve the construction of self. Although four of the studies here dwell at length on letters and diaries, journals, or notebooks, no facile assumption is made that private letters and diaries automatically record 'the truth' about the writer's life, or capture his/her 'essence'. Terry Keefe is essentially engaged in an exercise of comparison as such, and shows that, whatever we may think of Beauvoir's letters and diaries, they allow us to scrutinise some of the precise ways in which she constructs her self in *La Force de l'âge*; although he does also imply that the more intimate texts might be said to be *mis*-used in the writing of that text. Emma Wilson is concerned to show that Beauvoir constructs a self in *all* of the different forms of writing, and also stresses that the particular problems of being a woman caught between the roles of subject and object of desire cause Beauvoir to lose some control over her diary, which becomes ambiguous and ambivalent. Michael Scriven prefers Sartre's *Carnets* to *Les Mots*, but broadly on grounds of their greater spontaneity, rather than because they reveal more about Sartre. And Steve Robson shows only that there is one *side* to Camus that comes out in his private but not in his public writings. Furthermore, in his chapter on *Les Mots*, Edmund Smyth begins by attacking, directly and explicitly, the view that letters and diaries are more 'authentic' than formal autobiographies.

Nevertheless, difficult though it is to formulate such a view with any precision, this volume as a whole could be thought to suggest that it is unwise to dismiss *every* version of it out of hand, at least as long as we have fairly standard models of these different forms of writing in mind, and standard sequences. For one thing, it is simply a fact that in many cases authors use their earlier letters and diaries in writing their autobiographies as such. This does not, of course, make the former more 'authentic' than the latter (there are undoubtedly cases where authors themselves repudiate their earlier versions of the past, in order to replace them with different versions). But it does remind us of the normal chronological sequence, and of the particular importance accorded to letters and diaries by many autobiographers themselves. (The case of an author studiously ignoring his/her earlier intimate writings in composing an autobiography would be a delicate one to analyse!) The matter of the timing of composition is, after all, highly significant. That a letter written to describe the previous day's experiences may exhibit a constructing of the past or of the self *to the same degree* as an autobiography written thirty years later may be undeniable, but it is a wholly theoretical point that actually has relatively little application.

While it is perfectly clear that no genre as such can give any *guarantee* of 'authenticity', or even of any greater measure of authenticity than any other genre, in practice - for a whole variety of general reasons to do with distance in time, memory, differences in intention, and changes of perspective - we read diary-entries and letters with the broad expectation that they will be more reliable *in detail* than structured autobiographies, unless special circumstances are known to have prevailed. Or, to put the matter differently, we tend to expect diaries and letters to be more representative of the 'existential self' than autobiographies. For if the claim that they are intrinsically more likely to display 'the truth' or the writer's 'true self' is - like the belief that they constitute a 'natural' form of writing - wholly unjustifiable, perhaps even senseless, the proposition that they usually contain more *truths* is less obviously so. We need not linger over the absurd objection that there are no truths at all in autobiographical writings, but it has to be acknowledged that the 'usually' takes some of the force out of this assertion. Yet rather than disarming it altogether, it throws much of the emphasis back onto the issue of readers and the nature of the expectations that they have of different forms of writing. A definition of the genre of autobiography might have to involve reference to a process tantamount to construction of the self: definitions of letters and diaries would probably not.

Certainly, if the justification for claiming that letters and diaries are *not* more authentic than autobiographies is simply - as sometimes seems to be the case - that *writing* is involved in both cases, then the inference is obviously invalid. It could only be made valid by adopting the premiss that *all* writing (about the self? about the past?) is inauthentic, and there is neither any obvious reason for accepting such an assertion, nor any easy way of ascribing any meaning to it. (Is all *spoken* recollection of the past/construction of the self, too, alleged to be inauthentic?) All texts involve textual construction; perhaps all texts about the self involve construction of the self; and perhaps all constructed selves can potentially be compared with an 'existential self'. However, it does not follow from any of this that all constructions of the self are 'inauthentic'. Similarly, there is the gravest difficulty in giving any content or sense to the not-uncommon assertion that all autobiographical writing is fiction. This is not to deny, of course, that in any given instance it may be possible to demonstrate that a letter or diary-entry is as fanciful, or as inaccurate, or as fictional as the corresponding section of an autobiography written very much later. But the important point is that demonstrating this would involve having some *third* (and reliable) source of information against which to compare the other two. Any generalisation affirming that both forms of writing are equally distant from the facts (that is, are 'fiction'), but simultaneously implying that we have no access

189

to facts in any case is self-defeating, rather in the same way as the assertion that all coins are counterfeit! Almost all of the methods of inquiry upon which the contributions to this volume are based imply, or at the very least are compatible with, the belief that there are autobiographical truths, or that some autobiographical statements are more 'authentic' than others. The broad inclination on the part of many of the contributors to link the existential self, in some kind of general way, more closely with diaries and letters, etc. than with formal autobiographies requires much more careful scrutiny, as does the very concept of the 'existential self'. But the inclination is more defensible than blanket generalisations about the inauthenticity of all forms of writing.

Ultimately, of course, it may not prove especially fruitful to debate whether the possibilities of deception, or self-deception, are in general greater in autobiography than in letters and diaries. But this volume, apart from confirming that we are fully justified in paying attention to the latter as part of the autobiographical process, does demonstrate the need to address questions about intimate writings that are more rarely asked than questions concerning autobiography proper, and yet shed much indirect light upon it. These questions centre, in large part, as already implied, on the conventions that are commonly adopted in the writing of letters or diaries and the assumptions commonly made in reading them. (The parallel questions about novels and plays that arise when one is comparing these with autobiography are, of course, ones that have long been of interest for separate reasons.) The cases of Sartre and Beauvoir, in this respect, are particularly fascinating ones. In a curious, but far from unique, reversal of the normal expectations, Sartre, at least, was writing his letters partly with posterity in mind;[10] and both were deliberately keeping diaries that they intended the other to see and comment on. Among the interesting issues that this raises are ones of number (does the notion of an autobiography written for one single person make complete sense?); genre (how would an autobiography written for one person differ from intimate private letters? and what, if anything, stops a diary from being an autobiography as such?); gender (are the incidents of Beauvoir's war diary essentially narrated for a male reader? how do we know?); and class (if autobiography really is a bourgeois genre, what are the full implications of this, and how does it show by contrast with letters and diaries?). Many of these issues are not new ones, but the individual manifestations of the autobiographical project considered here and the focus on the existential self bring them all into particular prominence.

An examination of Hervé Guibert is an entirely appropriate addition to the study of our other authors, in that, in spite of the significant gap in time (he was born in 1955 and is therefore of a very different generation), and in spite of the fact that there is no reason to regard him as an existentialist thinker, the parallels between Guibert's autobiographical enterprise and those of our earlier writers are specific and significant ones.[11] What makes his case such a suitable *terminal* point to our inquiry is his use of new media and his determination to pursue autobiography as close to the moment of death as possible.

In *La Mort propagande* Guibert noted in 1977 that he had perhaps never stopped re-writing *La Nausée*, and that Sartre's perception adjoined his own.[12] Certainly, Antoine Roquentin's decision, on the first page of *La Nausée*, to 'écrire les événements au jour le jour' could scarcely be a more accurate description of the autobiographical intentions of Guibert himself, whose practice of diary-writing, uses of his own diary in other writings and film, and intense interest in the diaries of others enable many parallels to be drawn with topics treated elsewhere in this volume. And if, having passed from photography to writing, he then passed from writing to film, this was because Guibert eventually came to believe that film - being a more *living* medium - allows even more accurate recording of life itself.[13] Indeed, somewhat paradoxically in view of all of the theoretical arguments deployed since the existentialist period, it could be said that Guibert's belief in the possibility of directly, immediately and continuously *transcribing* life into some artistic form - be it photographs, writing, 'écriture photographique', or film - is a much simpler, firmer and more naive one than in the case of any earlier autobiographer considered here. When writing, for instance, he deliberately sets out to 'réduire cette distance entre les vérités de l'expérience et de l'écriture'. Yet his very use of different media in the context of his general autobiographical project produces stimulating juxtapositions. For one thing, he reminds us that there is a potential reflexivity in the medium of film that parallels that of writing, for in *La Pudeur et l'Impudeur* he films himself viewing the film that he had had made of his own operation! Sometimes, too, possible differences between the media appear to be registered, as when Guibert acknowledges that the very presence of the camera can directly interfere with relationships (not necessarily for the worse: his aunt says that she loves him for the first time because she is being filmed). But then we may begin reconsidering whether, say, the exchange of letters between Sartre and Beauvoir is not also a formative factor in their relationship. In any case, the theoretical issues raised concerning the autobiographical potential of the different media and the interrelationship between them surely deserve much further exploration.

Jean-Pierre Boulé's reflections elsewhere on what is called in French 'le reality show' point to further intriguing areas closely related to autobiography,[14] and, of course, the fact of Guibert's illness and approaching death provokes still other important links and questions. The suggestion that *La Pudeur ou l'Impudeur* may have constituted some kind of exorcism, outlet or release reminds us once more of the possible *therapeutic* value of the autobiographical process in general. Yet the terminal nature of his case adds a great deal to the point. One might fruitfully speculate on the link between Guibert's film and, say, Beauvoir's *Une Mort très douce*, describing the painful last three months of her mother's life, or *La Cérémonie des adieux*, tracing Sartre's illnesses and degeneration during his last ten years, as well as his death.[15] It is for others to pronounce on the matter of influences,[16] but there are clearly strong autobiographical elements to both pieces by Beauvoir, although they each centre on someone dear to her. Interestingly, if there is no difficulty in accepting that a writer may be, in a substantive and substantial way, writing about herself/himself in writing about someone else, there is probably more room for debate about the degree to which a given writer like Guibert is writing about others in writing about himself; and whether, apparently more oddly, he is *filming* others in filming himself. Again, what could be a wholly abstract issue becomes very real by virtue of the desperate nature of Guibert's plight. A few days before *La Pudeur ou l'Impudeur* was originally scheduled to be shown, the French national committee for Aids (CNS) stated that the film 'met en scène un témoignage individuel et n'a aucunement valeur de témoignage d'information ou d'exemple généralisable à toutes les personnes vivant avec le VIH'.[17] In addition to confirming - graphically, even if only by implication - a point that has emerged forcefully from these chapters, that to publish (or film) an autobiography is to perform an *act* of some kind, the statement thereby touched upon, albeit unwittingly and in the gravest of human contexts, some of the most complex and profound problems concerning the nature, reach and value of autobiography - problems about the genre that probably carry it in the opposite direction to those of the existential self. Exactly how, why, and how much does autobiography, whether it concerns the existential or the constructed self, affect and move *others*?

NOTES

1   M. Sheringham, *French Autobiography. Devices and Desires*, Oxford, Clarendon Press, 1993.

2   As they are of another recent work on autobiography: John Sturrock, *The Language of Autobiography. Studies in the First Person Singular*, Cambridge, Cambridge University Press, 1993. Sturrock explicitly defends his decision to consider only canonical autobiographies.

3   *Recherches philosophiques*, No. 6, 1936-37, pp. 85-123. Edited in book form, with an introduction, notes and appendices by Sylvie Le Bon: Paris, Librairie philosophique J. Vrin ('Bibliothèque des textes philosophiques'), 1966.

4   See, for instance, in Christina Howells (ed.), *The Cambridge Companion to Sartre* (Cambridge, Cambridge University Press, 1992): Hazel Barnes, 'Sartre's ontology: the revealing and making of being' (pp. 13-38), and Christina Howells, 'Conclusion: Sartre and the deconstruction of the subject' (pp. 318-52); and in Ronald Aronson and Adrian van den Hoven (eds), *Sartre Alive*, Detroit, Wayne State University Press, 1991: Hazel Barnes, 'The role of the ego in reciprocity' (pp. 151-59), and Kathleen Wider, 'A nothing about which something can be said: Sartre and Wittgenstein on the self' (pp. 324-39).

5   *La Transcendance de l'Ego* (Le Bon edition), p. 81.

6   It hardly needs emphasising that Beauvoir's application of this rejection to the case of women in *Le Deuxième Sexe* was a critical factor in the evolution of modern feminism.

7   This aspect of the development of existentialism out of phenomenology is concisely explained by Robert C. Solomon (ed.), *Phenomenology and Existentialism*, Littlefield Adams Quality Paperbacks, Savage (Maryland), 1972.

8   In *La Transcendance de l'Ego*, Sartre argues that the (constructed) 'Moi' can exercise no control over the basic spontaneity of consciousness, since the instrument of the will is itself an object 'qui se constitue pour et par cette spontanéité'. In cases where I try to *will myself* to go to sleep or to stop thinking of something, 'il est nécessaire *par essence* que la volonté soit maintenue et conservée *par la conscience radicalement opposée à celle qu'elle voulait faire naître*' (Le Bon edition, pp. 79-80).

9   See Sheringham, op. cit., pp. 2-4.

10   This should also serve to remind us that *any* generalisations made about the autobiographical process on the basis of the cases of the authors studied in this volume are somewhat suspect by virtue of the fact that all are, in any case, writers to begin with.

11   In an interesting recent account of the influence of existentialism, Michel Contat has explicitly named Guibert as one of the French writers working 'dans la lignée de l'existentialisme'; 'Une philosophie pour notre temps, entretien avec Michel Contat, propos recueillis par François Ewald', *Magazine littéraire*, no. 320 (April 1994), 18-26, p. 25.

12   *La Mort propagande*, p. 15.

13   Everyone aware of the existence of film must have been tempted at one stage or another by this belief, yet the heavy editing that took place in order to produce *La Pudeur ou l'Impudeur* is just one of many factors to remind us of the inadequacy of this view.

14   'The postponing of *La Pudeur ou l'Impudeur*: modesty or hypocrisy on the part of French television?', *French Cultural Studies*, no. 3 (October 1992), pp. 299-305.

15   Simone de Beauvoir, *Une Mort très douce*, Paris, Gallimard, 1964; *La Cérémonie des adieux*, Paris, Gallimard, 1981.

16   Guibert's *A l'ami qui ne m'a pas sauvé la vie* revealed Foucault's illness to the public in the way that the second of these works by Beauvoir did Sartre's; and there may even be some slight similarity between the dedications to *La Cérémonie des adieux* ('A ceux qui ont aimé Sartre, l'aiment, l'aimeront') and *Le Protocole compassionnel* ('A toutes celles et à tous ceux qui m'ont écrit pour A l'ami qui ne m'a pas sauvé la vie').

17   See Frank Nouchi, 'Le film d'Hervé Guibert devrait être diffusé jeudi 30 janvier sur TF1', *Le Monde*, 22 January 1992, p. 10.

List of Contributors

Jean-Pierre Boulé is Reader in French at Nottingham Trent University. He is the author of *Sartre Médiatique*, and editor of a special edition of *Nottingham French Studies* devoted to Hervé Guibert.

Terry Keefe is Professor of French Studies at Lancaster University. He is the author of *Simone de Beauvoir: A Study of her Writings*, *French Existentialist Fiction*, and a critical study of *Les Belles Images* and *La Femme Rompue*.

Benedict O'Donohoe teaches French at LSU Southampton, and is the editor of a critical edition of *Les Jeux sont faits*. He is currently working on a *File on Sartre*.

Mary Orr teaches French at the University of St Andrews. She is the author of *Claude Simon: The Intertextual Dimension*.

Steve Robson recently completed an M.Phil. on Camus at Keele University.

Michael Scriven is Professor of French at the University of Bath. He is the author of *Sartre's Existential Biographies*, *Paul Nizan*, and, most recently, *Sartre and the Media*.

Michael Sheringham is Professor of French at the University of Kent. He is the author of a critical study of Samuel Beckett's *Molloy*, and *French Autobiography: Devices and Desires*.

Edmund Smyth teaches French at the University of Liverpool. His books include *Postmodernism and Contemporary Fiction*, and his *Aesthetics of the Nouveau Roman* will be published later this year.

David Walker is Professor of French at the University of Keele. He is the author of *André Gide* and critical studies of Camus, Genet and Robbe-Grillet. He is completing a book on the *fait divers*.

Emma Wilson is a Research Fellow of New Hall, Cambridge, and has written on Michel Tournier and Marguerite Duras, as well as Simone de Beauvoir.

Select Bibliography

(The following list brings together the most important primary and secondary items referred to in the preceding chapters and notes, adding some other relevant references on the subject of autobiography.)

B. Alluin and J. Deguy (eds), *Paul Nizan écrivain*, Lille, Presses Universitaires de Lille, 1988.

A. J. Arnold and J.-P. Piriou, *Genèse et critique d'une autobiographie. Les Mots de Jean-Paul Sartre*, Paris, Minard, 1973.

P. Assouline, 'A la recherche des carnets perdus', *Lire*, no. 175, April 1990, pp. 35-44.

D. Bair, *Simone de Beauvoir. A Biography*, London, Jonathan Cape, 1990.

R. Barthes, *Roland Barthes par Roland Barthes*, Paris, Editions du Seuil, 1975.

M. Beaujour, *Miroirs d'encre: Rhétorique de l'autoportrait*, Paris, Editions du Seuil, 1980.

S. de Beauvoir, *L'Invitée*, Paris, Gallimard, 1943.

    Le Deuxième Sexe, Paris, Gallimard, 1949.

    Mémoires d'une jeune fille rangée, Paris, Gallimard, 1958.

    La Force de l'âge, Paris, Gallimard, 1960.

    La Cérémonie des adieux, suivi de Entretiens avec Jean-Paul Sartre, Paris, Gallimard, 1981.

    Journal de guerre, Paris, Gallimard, 1990.

    Lettres à Sartre, édition établie et annotée par Sylvie Le Bon de Beauvoir, Paris, Gallimard, 1990.

P. Bénichou, 'Simone de Beauvoir raconte à Pierre Bénichou l'histoire des *Carnets de la drôle de guerre*', *Le Nouvel Observateur*, 25 March 1983, pp. 56-58.

J.-P. Boulé, 'The postponing of *La pudeur ou l'Impudeur*: Modesty or Hypocrisy on the part of French television', *French Cultural Studies*, no. 3 (October 1992), pp. 299-305.

    Sartre médiatique, Paris, Minard, 1993.

G. Brée, *Camus and Sartre*, London, Calder and Boyars, 1972.

J.-J. Brochier (ed.), *Paul Nizan intellectuel communiste 1926-1940*, Paris, Gallimard, 1967.

M. Broc-Lapeyre, 'Du trafic à la littérature', *Critique*, no. 282, November 1970, pp. 935-43.

E. Bruss, *Autobiographical Acts: The Changing Situation of a Literary Genre*, Baltimore, Johns Hopkins University Press, 1976.

C. Burgelin (ed.), *Lectures de Sartre*, Lyon, Presses Universitaires de Lyon, 1986.

M. Calle-Gruber and A. Rothe (eds), *Autobiographie et biographie*, Paris, Nizet, 1989.

A. Camus, *Essais*, Paris, Gallimard ('Bibliothèque de la Pléiade'), 1954.

    Actuelles III, Paris, Gallimard, 1958.

    Carnets I, Paris, Gallimard, 1962.

    Carnets II, Paris, Gallimard, 1964.

    Carnets III, Paris, Gallimard, 1989.

    Correspondance Albert Camus-Jean Grenier, 1932-1960, Paris, Gallimard, 1981.

R. Coe, *The Vision of Jean Genet*, London, Peter Owen, 1968.

A. Cohen-Solal, *Paul Nizan, communiste impossible*, Paris, Bernard Grasset, 1980.

    Album Sartre, texte de A. Cohen-Solal, Paris, Gallimard ('Bibliothèque de la Pléiade'), 1991.

D. Collins, *Sartre as Biographer*, Cambridge, Mass., Harvard University Press, 1980.

M. Contat, *Explication des 'Séquestrés d'Altona'*, Paris, Minard, 1968.

M. Contat and M. Rybalka (eds), *Les Ecrits de Sartre*, Paris, Gallimard, 1970.

M. Contat and J. Deguy, '*Les Carnets de la drôle de guerre* de Jean-Paul Sartre, effets d'écriture, effets de lecture', *Littérature*, no. 80, December 1990, pp. 17-41.

I. de Courtivron, *Violette Leduc*, Boston, Twayne, 1985.

G. Craig and M. McGowan (eds), *Moy Qui Me Voy*, Oxford, Clarendon Press, 1989.

M. Crosland, *Simone de Beauvoir: The Woman and her Work*, London, Heinemann, 1992.

J. Cruickshank, *Albert Camus and the Literature of Revolt*, Oxford, Oxford University Press, 1960.

H. Davies, *Sartre and 'Les Temps Modernes'*, Cambridge, Cambridge University Press, 1987.

J. Dayan, *Simone de Beauvoir* (un film de Josée Dayan et Malka Ribowska), Paris, Gallimard, 1979.

P. De Meo (ed.), *Perspectives sur Sartre et Beauvoir*, *Dalhousie French Studies*, 1986 (numéro spécial).

A. Dichy and P. Fouché, *Jean Genet, essai de chronologie 1910-1944*, Paris, Bibliothèque de littérature française contemporaine, 1988.

S. Doubrovsky, *Autobiographiques: de Corneille à Sartre*, Paris, P.U.F., 1988.

P. J. Eakin, *Fictions in Autobiography: Studies in the Art of Self-Invention*, Princeton, Princeton University Press, 1985.

M. Evans, *Simone de Beauvoir: A Feminist Mandarin*, London and New York, Tavistock, 1985.

E. Fallaize, *The Novels of Simone de Beauvoir*, London, Routledge, 1988.

P. Forster and I. Sutton (eds), *Daughters of de Beauvoir*, London, The Women's Press, 1989.

M. Foucault, *Surveiller et punir*, Paris, Gallimard, 1975.

D. Fuss (ed.), *Inside/Out: Lesbian Theories, Gay Theories*, London and New York, Routledge, 1991.

J. Garcin, 'Hervé Guibert son dernier entretien', *L'événement du jeudi*, 2-8 January 1992, p. 108.

A. de Gaudemar, 'Guibert, sa mort, son oeuvre', *Libération*, 18/19 January 1992, p. 24.

J. Genet, *Journal du Voleur*, Paris, Gallimard, 1949.

    Oeuvres complètes, Paris, Gallimard, 1951.

R. Gibson (ed.), *Studies in French Fiction: a Festschrift for Vivienne Mylne*, London, Grant and Cutler, 1988.

A. Gide, *Journal 1889-1939*, Paris, Pléiade, 1951.

R. Goldthorpe, *La Nausée*, London, HarperCollins, Unwin Critical Library, 1991.

J. Gratton, '*Roland Barthes par Roland Barthes*: Autobiography and the Notion of Expression', *Romance Studies*, 8, 1986, pp. 57-66.

J. Grenier, *Souvenirs*, Paris, Gallimard, 1968.

H. Guibert, *La Mort propagande* , Paris, Régine Desforges, 1977.

    L'Image fantôme, Paris, Minuit, 1981.

    A l'ami qui ne m'a pas sauvé la vie, Paris, Gallimard, 1990.

    Le Protocole compassionnel, Paris, Gallimard, 1991.

    L'homme au chapeau rouge, Paris, Gallimard, 1992.

    Cytomégalovirus, Paris, Seuil, 1992.

C. Howells, *Sartre. The Necessity of Freedom*, Cambridge, Cambridge University Press, 1988.

    (ed.), *The Cambridge Companion to Sartre*, Cambridge, Cambridge

University Press, 1992.

G. Idt, 'L'Autoparodie dans *Les Mots* de Sartre', *Cahiers du XXème siècle*, no. 6, Klinksieck, 1976.

    '*Les Chemins de la liberté*: les taboggans du romanesque', in *Obliques*, M. Sicard (ed.), 18-19, Paris, Editions Borderie, 1979, pp. 75-94.

G. Idt and J.-F. Louette, 'Sartre et Beauvoir épistoliers en guerre: "Voilà de la lettre ou non?"', *Etudes Sartriennes 5: Itinéraires, Confrontations*, Université Paris X (RITM, 5), 1993.

A. Jardine, 'Death Sentences: Writing Couples and Ideology', *Poetics Today*, vol. 6, nos. 1-2 (1985), pp. 119-31.

A. Jefferson, 'Autobiography as Intertext: Barthes, Sarraute, Robbe-Grillet', in M. Worton and J. Still (eds), *Intertextuality*, Manchester, Manchester University Press, 1990, pp. 108-29.

T. Keefe, *Simone de Beauvoir: A Study of her Writings*, London, Harrap, 1983.

    'Simone de Beauvoir's Second Look at her Life', *Romance Studies*, no. 8 (Summer 1986), pp. 41-55.

E. Kosofsky, *Between Men: English Literature and Male Homosocial Desire*, New York, Columbia University Press, 1985.

J. Lecarme, '*Les Mots* de Sartre: un cas limite de l'autobiographie', *Revue d'Histoire Littéraire de la France*, 75, 1975, pp. 1047-61.

M. Le Doeuff, *L'Etude et le rouet*, Paris, Seuil, 1989.

I. Leduc, *La Bâtarde*, Paris, Gallimard, 1964.

    La Folie en tête, Paris, Gallimard, 1970.

    La Chasse à l'amour, Paris, Gallimard, 1973.

M. Leiris, *L'Age d'homme*, Paris, Gallimard, 1946.

P. Lejeune, *Le Pacte autobiographique*, Paris, Seuil, 1975.

    Je est un autre, Paris, Seuil, 1980.

    Moi aussi, Paris, Seuil, 1986.

J. Lévi-Valensi and A. Abbou, *Fragments d'un combat*, Paris, Gallimard ('Cahiers Albert Camus', 3), 1978.

B.-H. Lévy, *Les Aventures de la liberté*, Paris, Grasset, 1991.

A. Malgorn, *Jean Genet, qui êtes-vous?*, Lyon, La Manufacture, 1988.

P. de Man, *Allegories of Reading*, Yale, Yale University Press, 1979.

    'Autobiography as De-Facement', in *The Rhetoric of Romanticism*, New York, Columbia University Press, 1984, pp. 67-82.

V. Marin La Meslée, 'Genet, Leduc: admiration et jalousie', *Magazine littéraire*, no. 313, September 1993, pp. 37-8.

G. May, *L'Autobiographie*, Paris, P.U.F., 1979.

J. Mehlman, *A Structural Study of Autobiography*, New York, Cornell University Press, 1974.

B. Moraly, *Jean Genet: La vie écrite*, Paris, La Différence, 1968.

P. Nizan, *La Conspiration*, Paris, Gallimard, 1938.

    Chronique de septembre, Paris, Gallimard, 1939.

    Ecrits et Correspondance, 1926-1940, Paris, Maspero, 1970 (two vols).

C. C. O'Brien, *Camus*, London, Fontana/Collins, 1970.

B. O'Donohoe, 'Sartre's theories on death, murder, and suicide', *Philosophy Today*, no. 25, 1981, pp. 334-56.

J. Olnay (ed.), *Autobiography: Essays Theoretical and Critical*, Princeton, Princeton University Press, 1980.

M. Paganini, 'L'inscription juridique dans *Les Bonnes* de Jean Genet', *Romanic Review*, 80, no. 3 (1989), pp. 462-82.

E. Parker, *Albert Camus - The Artist in the Arena*, Wisconsin, University of Wisconsin Press, 1965.

R. Pascal, *Design and Truth in Autobiography*, London, RKP, 1960.

A. Peigné-Giuly, 'Du caméscope à l'écran', *Libération*, 18-19 January 1992, p. 22.

R. Quilliot, *La Mer et les prisons*, Paris, Gallimard, 1956.

H. Rabi, 'Les thèmes majeurs du théâtre de Sartre', *Esprit*, 18, no. 10, October 1950.

M. Ribière (ed.), *Parcours Perec*, Lyon, Presses Universitaires de Lyon, 1990.

J.-P. Sartre, *La Transcendance de l'Ego* (ed. Sylvie Le Bon), Paris, Librairie philosophique J. Vrin ('Bibliothèque des textes philosophiques'), 1966.

    La Nausée, Paris, Gallimard, 1938.

    L'Etre et le Néant, Paris, Gallimard, 1943.

    Théâtre I, Paris, Gallimard, 1947.

    Situations I, Paris, Gallimard, 1947.

    Situations II, Paris, Gallimard, 1948.

    Situations III, Paris, Gallimard, 1948.

    Les Mains sales, Paris, Gallimard, 1948.

    Saint-Genet, comédien et martyr, Paris, Gallimard, 1952.

    Les Mots, Paris, Gallimard, 1964.

    Les Séquestrés d'Altona, Paris, Gallimard, 1960.

    Un Théâtre de situations (eds M. Contat and M. Rybalka), Paris, Gallimard, 1973.

    Situations X, Paris, Gallimard, 1976.

    Oeuvres romanesques, édition établie par M. Contat et M. Rybalka, Paris, Gallimard ('Bibliothèque de la Pléiade'), 1981.

    Les Carnets de la drôle de guerre. Novembre 1939 - Mars 1940, Paris, Gallimard, 1983.

    Lettres au Castor et à quelques autres, Paris, Gallimard, 1983.

J. Savona, *Jean Genet*, Basingstoke, Macmillan, 1983.

    'Théâtre et univers carcéral: Jean Genet et Michel Foucault', *French Forum*, 10, no. 2 (1985), pp. 201-13.

A. Schwarzer (ed.), *Simone de Beauvoir aujourd'hui*, Paris, Mercure de France, 1984.

M. Scriven, *Sartre's Existential Biographies*, London, Macmillan, 1984.
Paul Nizan Communist Novelist, London, Macmillan, 1988.
Sartre and the Media, London, Macmillan, 1993.

M. Sheringham, *French Autobiography. Devices and Desires*, Oxford, Clarendon Press, 1993.
'Narration and experience in Genet's *Journal du Voleur*', *Studies in French Fiction: a Festschrift for Vivienne Milne*, ed. R. Gibson, London, Grant and Cutler, 1988.
Preface to *French Autobiography: Texts, Contexts, Poetics, Romance Studies*, 8 (Summer 1986) and 9 (Winter 1986).

E. J. Smyth (ed.), *Postmodernism and Contemporary Fiction*, London, B.T. Batsford, 1991.

R. C. Solomon (ed.), *Phenomenology and Existentialism*, Littlefield Adams Quality Paperbacks, Savage (Maryland), 1972.

J. Steel, *Paul Nizan, un révolutionaire conformiste?*, Paris, Presses de la fondation nationale des sciences politiques, 1987.

G. Steiner, 'Sartre: The Suspect Witness', *The Times Literary Supplement*, 3 May 1991.

H. E. Stewart, 'Jean Genet's favourite murderers', *The French Review*, 60, no. 5 (1987), pp. 635-43. 'Louis Ménesclou, assassin and source of the "lilac murder" in Genet's *Haute Surveillance*', *Romance Notes*, 26, no. 3 (1986), pp. 204-08.

H. E. Stewart and R. R. McGregor, *Jean Genet: a biography of deceit 1910-1941*, New York, Peter Lang, 1989.

J. Sturrock, *The Language of Autobiography. Studies in the First Person Singular*, Cambridge, Cambridge University Press, 1993.

O. Todd, 'J.-P. Sartre on his Autobiography' (interview), *The Listener*, 6 June 1957, p. 915

P. Verstraeten, *Violence et éthique*, Paris, Gallimard, 1972.

D. Walker, 'Cultivating the *fait divers*: *Détective*', *Nottingham French Studies*, 31, no. 2 (1992), pp. 71-83.

H. Wenzel (ed.), *Simone de Beauvoir: Witness to a Century*, Yale French Studies, no. 72, 1986.

E. White, *Genet*, London, Chatto and Windus, 1993.

Index